King Stephen
and The Anarchy

King Stephen
and The Anarchy

Civil War and Military Tactics in
Twelfth-Century Britain

CHRIS PEERS

Pen & Sword
MILITARY

First published in Great Britain in 2018 by
Pen and Sword Military
an imprint of
Pen and Sword Books Ltd
47 Church Street
Barnsley
South Yorkshire S70 2AS

ISBN 978 147386 367 5

Printed and bound in England
by TJ International Ltd, Padstow, PL28 8RW

Typeset in Times by Chic Graphics

Pen & Sword Books Ltd incorporates the imprints of
Pen & Sword Archaeology, Atlas, Aviation, Battleground, Discovery,
Family History, History, Maritime, Military, Naval, Politics, Railways,
Select, Social History, Transport, True Crime, Claymore Press,
Frontline Books, Leo Cooper, Praetorian Press, Remember When,
Seaforth Publishing and Wharncliffe.

For a complete list of Pen and Sword titles please contact
Pen and Sword Books Limited
47 Church Street, Barnsley, South Yorkshire, S70 2AS, England
E-mail: enquiries@pen-and-sword.co.uk
Website: www.pen-and-sword.co.uk

Contents

List of Plates

List of Maps

Prologue: A Dynasty of Conquerors

It all started – as did so many things in England's history – when a group of tired and sweat-stained horsemen urged their exhausted mounts into one last uphill charge in the fading light of an October evening. Not long before that they had been facing destruction, nervously casting backward glances towards the sea which had brought them there, as the English line still stood unbroken on Senlac Hill in front of them. But now the figure of Anglo-Saxon England's last king could be seen on the skyline ahead, hunched over his shield, fatally injured by a random arrow which had struck him in the eye. His soldiers were now too few or too demoralized to maintain the line, and as the horsemen approached they began either to run or to prepare themselves for a last stand, ready to die with their king. An army fighting in the old English tradition on foot with spear, axe and shield had been outmanoeuvred and worn down by the combination of well-organized heavy cavalry and missile troops which had already brought the Normans victory over the Byzantines and Lombards, and was soon to carry them as far as Jerusalem. It was 14 October 1066, and unlike many other so-called 'turning points' in history, the significance of this one must have been very obvious to the men who saw it happen on that hill overlooking the English Channel. England was to change, profoundly and forever, as a result of that day's deeds. What was to become known as the Battle of Senlac Hill, or Hastings, was entering its final phase, and those weary horsemen – Normans, Frenchmen, Bretons, Flemings and others – were about to be transformed from the desperate adventurers who had followed Duke William of Normandy across the Channel into England's new ruling class. Not surprisingly they were convinced that the victory – and the land of England – had been given to them by God.

Despite their ferocity towards their enemies, and the greed for land and riches which had brought them across the sea, the Normans who led the invasion were a devoutly Christian people who had filled Normandy with splendid stone-built churches and abbeys, many of which survive to this day. Less than two centuries earlier the ancestors of many of them had been Vikings, pagan pirates who had forced the Frankish kings to grant them land in Normandy in exchange for peace. By 1066 they had enthusiastically adopted not only the faith and language of the Franks, but also the social system based on a pyramid of personal obligations, known to us today as feudalism, which had been developing since the centralized empire of Charlemagne had disintegrated in the late ninth century AD. Their leader William was Duke of Normandy, holding his duchy – at least in theory – as a vassal of the King of France, and presiding in his turn over a hierarchy of barons, knights, freemen and serfs, all holding their land from a superior in exchange for service of some kind, whether it be military, labour or food rents. But the Normans and their allies had retained something of their Viking ruthlessness, as the English were soon to discover. William, now King of England, dispossessed most of the native elite and distributed their lands among his own followers, imposing on this blank slate an exceptionally thorough and rigid version of the Frankish feudal system. In order to overawe the populace, he and his followers built – or rather forced the common people themselves to build for them – castles in every population centre and strategic location, and garrisoned them with foreign soldiers. Dissent was suppressed in a series of campaigns that even William himself, on his deathbed, acknowledged to have been excessively brutal.

But although King Harold's army had not been a match for the latest Continental techniques, England itself could not be so easily destroyed. It was a prosperous country of perhaps two million people, with a long tradition of efficient government and a thriving Christian culture in close contact with the rest of Europe. The conquerors cannot have numbered many more than 7,000, and although they retained their military traditions, their system of government and for a few centuries their French language, the process of absorbing them must have begun almost immediately after 1066. Seventy years later, when their grandchildren and great-grandchildren prepared to go to war in the upheavals of King Stephen's reign which were later to become known as the 'Anarchy', they still looked back to the events of 1066 as their origin and their inspiration. They may even have known men who had fought at Hastings, as Stephen himself surely had as a young man, and there is no doubt that the knightly class would have identified themselves with the victors on that day. Many of them still owned land in Normandy as well as in England. But they were no longer purely Normans.

One of the legacies which these Anglo-Normans had taken over from the Anglo-Saxons was the poisoned chalice of relations with the non-English inhabitants of northern and western Britain, the Welsh and the Scots, often generically but misleadingly referred to as 'Celts'. The former especially claimed to represent the original inhabitants of the island who had been driven into the far west centuries earlier by Saxon invaders. Although they were often forced to acknowledge English overlordship, their various kingdoms still maintained their de facto independence, and hostilities along the border were frequent. The kings of Scotland already had close relations with both English and Normans, but much of the mountainous periphery of the country remained outside their control, and the border with England was sufficiently undefined to give rise to frequent clashes. When the grip of the Norman kings on England slackened in the civil wars after 1135, it was not the downtrodden English who seized the opportunity, but the Celtic kingdoms. Their role in what was to become known as the Anarchy of Stephen's reign is often treated as peripheral, but it is the aim of this book to give it the attention it deserves. Thus the Welsh and Scottish military systems will be given as much prominence as that of the Anglo-Normans, and the campaigns on and beyond the borders of Stephen's realm will receive – where the sources allow – as much attention as the squabbles of the barons in England itself.

Introduction:
Scholars and Sources

The student of the wars of Stephen's reign is not short of source material, though the situation regarding Wales and Scotland is on the whole less favourable. The following are the main narrative sources used for this account, while others are mentioned in the text where they are particularly relevant. Widely available English editions are referenced in the Bibliography. For biographical notes on these and the other contemporary chroniclers, see the section on 'Who Was Who in the Anarchy' on pages 157–72.

Most prominent among the sources hostile to Stephen is the *Historia Novella* of William of Malmesbury, which unfortunately finishes in 1142, but is exceptionally useful for the early part of our period. William seems to have known men like Robert of Gloucester and Bishop Roger of Salisbury personally, and claims to have been an eyewitness to many of the events he describes. Despite his close links to the Earl of Gloucester he is relatively impartial, and readily acknowledges Stephen's virtues as well as his faults. His knowledge is, however, largely restricted to the south-west of England, and he ignores, for example, the momentous events of 1138 in the north.

The *Gesta Stephani* consists of two books, covering the period before and after 1148 respectively. Its author is unknown, and it is by no means certain that the two books were written by the same person; the second is far more critical of Stephen than its predecessor. Their translator K.R. Potter nevertheless believes that there was a single author, and has argued persuasively that he can be identified with Bishop Robert of Bath, who was a dedicated supporter of Stephen for most of his reign, but by 1153 had joined the court of his rival Henry Plantagenet. The work is our most detailed source for the military operations of the reign, although like William of Malmesbury its author focuses mainly on south-western England, paying particular attention to events in Bristol. His real aim was apparently didactic rather than what we would think of as scholarly – to use Stephen's career to illustrate the consequences of sin and repentance – but he does provide a wealth of detail on military matters, although his use of classical Latin terminology can be confusing. Thus, for example, we read of Stephen's '*legionarii*' coming to the relief of Exeter. Above all, the author of the *Gesta* was a humane man whose distress at the sufferings inflicted by the fighting on the ordinary people is a recurring theme.

Henry of Huntingdon's *Historia Anglorum* covers the reign of Stephen fairly briefly, but Henry specialises in set-piece battle accounts, and his East Anglian perspective is a useful corrective to the West Country bias of William of Malmesbury and the *Gesta Stephani*. Henry's account of the Battle of Lincoln, for example, is especially valuable because of his close links with Lincoln and its cathedral. He is also an essential authority for the Battle of the Standard. He is a consciously literary writer, and often breaks into verse or ascribes to his characters long and elaborate speeches which can hardly have been recorded verbatim, but he also provides much information which is not found elsewhere.

Also originating in eastern England was a version of the *Anglo-Saxon Chronicle* maintained by the monastery at Peterborough, which continued to be updated until 1154. This source clearly has little sympathy with the Anglo-Norman aristocracy, and devotes much space to the crimes committed by them in the absence of strong royal control. It is the origin of perhaps the most famous quotation on the subject of the 'Anarchy', when people 'said openly that Christ and His saints slept'.

The *Descriptio Cambriae* or *Description of Wales*, and *Topographia Hibernica* or *Topography of Ireland* by Gerald de Barri, otherwise known as Giraldus Cambrensis or Gerald of Wales, are our main sources for Wales and Ireland respectively. Gerald was writing in the latter part of the reign of Stephen's successor, Henry II, and most of his work does not deal directly with the events of Stephen's reign, but he is an essential source for the Welsh armies of the period, and he has much to say on military matters generally.

The *Orkneyinga Saga*, an anonymous saga history of the earls of Orkney composed in Iceland in the thirteenth century, is our main source for events in the far north of Britain from the foundation of the earldom in the ninth century until about the year 1200. No other source for events in Scotland in this period goes into so much detail. The Icelandic sagas are not strictly speaking history at all, but rather a mixture of myth, genealogy and biographies of eminent characters, replete with the gory details of battles and killings which their audiences obviously appreciated. But if some of the earlier chapters of the *Orkneyinga Saga* deal with people and events which are mainly mythical, those covering the twelfth century are relatively close in time to when the saga was composed, and are generally regarded as fairly reliable.

Charters and other contemporary records also survive in significant quantities, and their evidence is discussed in modern works such as those by Chibnall, Crouch and King. The anarchy which supposedly overtook England in the reign of Stephen is a subject which has been well covered by both academic historians such as these, and more popular writers. Part of its appeal is perhaps the very unfamiliarity of the breakdown of government in a well ordered kingdom like England – the idea that 'it shouldn't happen here'. To what extent it did happen, and why, are matters that will be touched on in this book, but its real subjects are the men and women who fought in its conflicts and suffered from its cruelties. Whether there really was anarchy, and if so whose fault it was, have long been debated among scholars. If this 'Anarchy' (customarily capitalised to distinguish the events of Stephen's reign from the concept in general) was something genuinely unique in English history, then it would be logical to seek unique factors to blame for it. The character of Stephen himself has often received its share of the blame. Certainly contemporary chroniclers – even those generally favourable to his cause – could be exasperated by him. To the author of the Peterborough manuscript of the *Anglo-Saxon Chronicle* he was 'a mild man, gentle and good, and did no justice', with the result that his barons did not fear him and disregarded the oaths that they had sworn. Both William of Malmesbury and the *Gesta Stephani*, from opposite sides of the political divide, agree that Stephen failed to keep his promises to uphold justice, stamp out corruption among royal officials, protect the Church and relieve the people from the most oppressive aspects of the forest law. Henry of Huntingdon relates the principal vows that the king made at his coronation, but adds sourly 'and there were others, but he did not keep any of them'. It is only to be expected that the king's admirers would attribute his failures to bad advice from his councillors, but William of Malmesbury does the same, admitting that Stephen was a 'kindly man', who if only he had obtained the throne legitimately and had ignored 'the whispers of the ill-disposed', could have been a successful ruler. Other historians have chosen to blame other individuals – notably J.H. Round, whose 1892 work *Geoffrey de Mandeville* characterized its subject as the archetypal unruly and treacherous baron, loyal to no cause but his own.

However, as David Crouch points out, the events of Stephen's reign did not involve anarchy at all in the generally-understood sense of 'the dissolution of the social or political order'. The large number of surviving 'private' charters drawn up between individual nobles might suggest that they felt able to issue them without reference to the king, but they also imply that they were trying to regularise relations with their neighbours according to established laws and customs. Men might disagree about who the king or queen should be, but no one questioned the assumption that England should have a single ruler, nor that this ruler should be drawn from the dynasty of William the Conqueror. The nobles might act as if they were autonomous rulers, as Earl Ranulf of Chester did in the north of England, but it can be argued that this was forced on them by the king's inability to defend them, and that this autonomy was almost without exception relinquished voluntarily when strong royal government was restored in the following reign. They might fight over possession of a particular town or castle, but that someone should hold it, as a vassal of whichever ruler they favoured and as a part of the feudal hierarchy established by the Norman Conquest, was not in dispute. In that sense early twelfth-century Scotland was far more anarchic than England at its worst. To see something approaching real anarchy in this period we need to look at what was happening in the far north, where the power struggles in the Earldom of Orkney, and the undefined relationship between that polity and its neighbour on the Scottish mainland, led to a bloodbath unparalleled in the Anglo-Norman world (see Chapter 12).

Chapter 1

Stephen and the English Succession

When William the Conqueror died in 1087 he was succeeded on the throne of England, not by his eldest son Robert 'Curthose', but by his second son, William II 'Rufus'. The laws of succession were less rigid at that time than they were to become in later centuries, and it was acceptable for a monarch to choose as his heir any member of his family who showed the necessary ability. William I had quarrelled with Robert, and hoped that he would be satisfied with the consolation prize of the Duchy of Normandy. In the event Robert unsuccessfully challenged Rufus for the throne, and was to do so again in the reign of Rufus' successor, Henry I. When Rufus died in 1100, in what was alleged to be a hunting accident in the New Forest, the Conqueror's third son Henry happened to be nearby, and seized his opportunity with decisive speed. He rode at once to Winchester, where he seized the treasury, and then on to Westminster, where he had himself crowned before Robert could mobilize his supporters. Henry also attempted to legitimize his rule in the eyes of the English themselves, as well as his Scottish neighbours, by marrying Edith, the daughter of King Malcolm and Queen Margaret of Scotland, who through her mother was a descendant of Anglo-Saxon royalty – a move which obviously improved relations between the two kingdoms, but was to give rise to unexpected problems after Henry's death. It appears that Edith – who once she arrived in England took the throne name of Queen Matilda – had once lived with her aunt in an English nunnery, where she had disguised herself in a nun's veil to escape the unwanted attentions of certain Norman knights. Consequently, although she had never taken a nun's vows, it was widely rumoured that she had done so. This of course would have made her subsequent marriage invalid, and provided a convenient excuse for some who later wished to claim that her and Henry's children were illegitimate. (The reader will soon notice the remarkable lack of variety in women's names in this period. Henry I, his successor Stephen, and their contemporary David I of Scotland, were all married to queens named Matilda. None of these should be confused with

Henry's daughter [and Stephen's cousin] Matilda, whose first marriage was to the Holy Roman Emperor Henry V, and so is generally referred to, even after his death, as the Empress. William the Conqueror's wife, Stephen's grandmother, had also been a Matilda. Several others appear in minor roles in the story. Men's names are slightly more varied, but Williams, Henrys and Roberts all recur frequently enough to risk causing confusion. The appendix on 'Who Was Who in the Anarchy' on pages 157–72 may help to clarify matters.) Meanwhile Robert Curthose, politically outmanoeuvred, resorted once again to armed force, but in 1106 he was captured by his brother at the Battle of Tinchebrai in Normandy. Henry, who had now reunited England and Normandy under his own rule, kept him in prison for the rest of his life.

Most writers on the subject have traced the origins of the troubles of Stephen's reign to the death of Henry I's heir – and only legitimate son – William in 1120. Henry was returning to England with his fleet after a successful campaign against the French, but one vessel, the *Blanche Nef* or *White Ship* belonging to Thomas fitz Stephen, who claimed that his father had ferried the Conqueror to England in 1066, started later than the others. Although exceptionally large, this ship must have closely resembled those illustrated on the Bayeux Tapestry – basically a Viking longship, propelled by both sail and oars. On board were about 300 of the Anglo-Norman aristocracy, including William and two of the king's numerous illegitimate children, Richard and Matilda. They were mostly young, and were said to have become drunk and disorderly, even jeering at some priests who came to bless the voyage. According to the chronicler Orderic Vitalis they forced Thomas fitz Stephen and his crew to row as fast as they could to overtake the king's party; the master, crew and helmsman were also accused of being drunk, though as none of the chroniclers were eyewitnesses this must have been guesswork. In any case the ship struck a rock and capsized, and even though the disaster occurred within earshot of the shore and the king's ships, only one man of all those on board survived. It was November, and although the weather was fine the water must have been very cold. We are told that Thomas fitz Stephen almost lived long enough to be rescued, but on being told that Prince William was among the missing he deliberately chose death by drowning. He was probably wise. King Henry, when his courtiers found the courage to tell him, was devastated. For the kingdom, as well as for Henry personally, this was a terrible loss. But more important for the fate of England in the long term were the people who had survived. William's wife, Matilda of Anjou, was travelling on another ship, but the couple had been married for little more than a year, and they had as yet no children of their own. She never remarried and eventually became a nun. Henry's legitimate daughter, Matilda, was safe in Germany with her husband, the Holy Roman Emperor Henry V. Another prominent member of the royal family, the king's nephew Stephen of Blois, along with some of his companions, had disembarked from the *White Ship* at the last moment, though his sister Lucia, who was married to the Earl of Chester, was drowned. According to Orderic Stephen was unwell, but a number of monks had gone ashore at the same time, and it may have been obvious to anyone who had remained sober that the vessel was heading for trouble.

Stephen was the son of Count Stephen-Henry of Blois and his wife Adela, who was the sister of Henry I of England. Stephen-Henry had been one of the most powerful magnates of his day, but his career was a chequered one. He had been one of the leaders of the First Crusade, but had deserted at the Siege of Antioch in 1098 and returned home with premature tales of the crusaders' defeat. When his former comrades went on to beat the Turks and capture Jerusalem, Stephen-Henry faced disgrace, but was persuaded by his wife to return to the Holy Land in an attempt to redeem his reputation. He was killed fighting bravely at the Second Battle of Ramla in 1102. Stephen's older brother Theobald became Count of Blois, and Stephen was sent to the court of his uncle Henry I to be educated. As a grandson of William the Conqueror he was by no means an outsider, and in fact was a great favourite of the king, who granted him, among other lands and honours, the County of Mortain on the western border of Normandy. In 1125 Stephen married Matilda, the daughter of Count Eustace III of Boulogne, through whom he inherited the title of Count of Boulogne on the death of her father. This Matilda was also a woman of strong character and considerable political and diplomatic ability, whose support was later to be vital to Stephen's kingship. The couple had three children who died in infancy, and three who survived to adulthood. The oldest of these, Eustace, eventually became his father's heir to the throne of England.

Henry never fully recovered from his grief at the loss of his son and, it was said, never smiled again. But he was well aware that despite the personal tragedy he needed to take steps to ensure a peaceful succession. William would have been in many ways the ideal king; he was descended not only from the Conqueror but, through his mother Queen Matilda, from the Anglo-Saxon and Scottish royal houses as well. But there would be no more such heirs, as the queen had died two years earlier. Henry did marry again, to Adeliza of Louvain, but this marriage produced no offspring. William of Malmesbury assures us that the numerous extra-marital affairs for which the king was notorious were carried on not for pleasure but 'for the sake of issue', but his twenty or so illegitimate children could not be considered for the succession even by the relatively flexible rules of the twelfth century. When his son-in-law the Holy Roman Emperor died in 1125, it must have seemed to Henry as though his problems had been solved. He recalled the widowed Empress Matilda to Normandy, and persuaded his barons to take an oath to support her claim to the throne on his death. The implication of this oath, which was followed by several others in the same vein over the next few years, is that the accession of a woman, while legal, was sufficiently controversial to require careful preparation. One of the signatories, Bishop Roger of Salisbury, later stated that he had sworn only on condition that Henry would not arrange another marriage for Matilda without the barons' consent. The logic of this is obvious; monarchs in this period had an indispensable role as military commanders, which no one would have considered appropriate for a woman. Therefore, by agreeing to support Matilda, the barons were also committing themselves to fight under the command of any future consort that she might have. So when, in 1128, Henry married her off to Geoffrey, the 15-year-old son of Count Fulk V of Anjou, some of those who had taken the oath may well have felt that they had been tricked. An alliance with the County of Anjou, which was situated on Normandy's southern border, against their mutual enemy the French was always an important policy objective for Henry, who had arranged the short-lived marriage of his son William to Fulk's daughter Matilda ten years before. Modern writers often refer to the Empress Matilda's party in the war with Stephen as 'the Angevins', and this convention is occasionally followed here for convenience. But it is really applicable only with hindsight, as the struggle led eventually to the succession of Matilda and Geoffrey's son Henry as King of England as well as Count of Anjou. The Norman nobility regarded the Angevins as traditional rivals, and it is likely that at the time the marriage reduced rather than enhanced the Empress Matilda's appeal as a future queen. In fact the couple were not particularly happy, and not long after the wedding Matilda left Geoffrey and returned to Normandy, where she remained until 1131. In September of that year Henry arranged a reconciliation, but the couple's first child, Henry Plantagenet, was not born until about 1133.

It is highly likely that King Henry, who was well aware of the unpopularity of his daughter's marriage, was hoping that by the time he died his grandson and namesake would be old enough to rule, perhaps with his mother acting as regent. But by this time the king himself did not have long to live. He spent the last three years of his reign in Normandy – distracted, according to the chronicler Henry of Huntingdon, by 'various disputes' involving Matilda and Geoffrey, which so annoyed him that some people suggested that they had helped to undermine his health. William of Malmesbury concurs that Geoffrey had threatened and insulted the king. The latter was in any case 67 years old, a considerable age for the time, and had endured a hard life of constant travel and campaigning. The Huntingdon chronicler tells how towards the end of November 1135 the king went hunting in the Forest of Lyons near Rouen, and on his return ate a dish of lampreys, a food which he enjoyed but which his doctors had warned him to avoid. This stirred up a 'destructive humour' and gave him a chill, followed by a fever, of which he died on 1 December. This story has become very well known, but Henry of Huntingdon is the only contemporary chronicler to implicate the lampreys, which were a popular dish among the medieval upper classes, and are still eaten today without ill effects. William of Malmesbury quotes a letter sent to the Pope by Archbishop Hugh of Rouen, who was present at the death, and who mentions only a 'sudden illness'. Whatever the fatal affliction was it allowed the king time to make his peace with God and his preparations for the succession. The Archbishop also said that, in front of witnesses including his son Robert of Gloucester and Hugh himself, Henry had 'assigned all his lands on both sides of the sea to his daughter in lawful and lasting succession'.

It seems likely that he had made some pronouncement on the subject, because a peaceful and uninterrupted succession was vital for the prosperity of the kingdom. According to the account in the *Gesta Stephani*, it was only the tough personality of King Henry that had kept the turbulent population of England in line so far. Now suddenly the country, 'formerly the seat of justice, the habitation of peace, the height of piety,' became 'a home of perversity, a haunt of strife, a training-ground of disorder, and a teacher of every kind of rebellion . . . each man, seized by a strange passion for violence, raged cruelly against his neighbour and reckoned himself the more glorious the more guiltily he attacked the innocent'. The modern historian will look for more convincing reasons for the outbreak of disorder than the removal of the influence of a single man, and we should be aware that for the author of the *Gesta*, concerned to establish Stephen as a rightful king, it was desirable to exaggerate the chaos which preceded his seizure of power. Nevertheless, it is clear that people did have grievances which they hoped to resolve before a successor could impose his own rule. Henry of Huntingdon attempts to give a balanced account of the character of the late king, admitting that many people admired him for his wisdom, his wealth and his military skill, but that others recalled his greed, which led him to impose excessive taxes, his cruelty to his opponents, and his extra-marital affairs. He comments on the fate of the man hired to extract Henry's brain as part of the embalming process, who despite all his precautions caught a fatal infection from the decaying corpse, that 'he was the last of many whom King Henry put to death'. But, the chronicler concludes, all ought to admit that the king's firm rule had brought peace, and that the events which followed his death were worse than any of his tyrannies.

That, however, was hindsight. On the face of things Henry's daughter Matilda was the obvious successor, being her father's nominee as well as – the rumours about her validity of her parents' marriage notwithstanding – his only surviving legitimate child. But no succession in this period was ever straightforward. As we have seen, there was a dispute over the throne after the death of each of the first three Norman kings. And in contrast to the situation in 1100, when the news of the old king's death became known at the end of 1135 none of the possible contenders for the English throne was actually in England. Matilda and her husband were living in Anjou. Much closer was Henry's nephew Stephen, whose county of Boulogne was just across the Channel and furthermore had close trading links with London. Other possible candidates included Stephen's older brother Theobald, Count of Blois, and Henry's illegitimate son Earl Robert of Gloucester, but both rejected the urgings of their supporters; Theobald already had extensive commitments on the Continent, while Robert, no doubt aware that his illegitimacy would be an insuperable obstacle in the eyes of the Church, preferred to support the cause of his half-sister Matilda. It is interesting to speculate on whether Robert Curthose might have revived his claim for the third time, but he had died in prison at Gloucester only the year before. Stories soon began to circulate that the old king had changed his mind on his deathbed and disinherited Matilda. This must have seemed plausible to many, as it was common knowledge that he disliked her husband – even William of Malmesbury admits as much. An East Anglian baron named Hugh Bigod, whose treachery was later to become notorious, even swore on oath, along with two other knights, that he had heard Henry name Stephen as his preferred heir and release those who had sworn to support Matilda from their oaths. Modern commentators, like Stephen's contemporaries, disagree about whether Hugh's claim can be believed. David Crouch and Jim Bradbury suggest that it can, pointing to the fact that the Archbishop of Rouen among others in Henry's inner circle seems to have believed it, and in fact later argued Stephen's case before the Pope. Bradbury also points out that there is no evidence that Hugh ever made any deal with Stephen or received any reward from him – though of course he might have expected one even in the absence of a prior agreement to that effect. To Chibnall all these tales are 'later justifications' for what amounted to a *coup d'état*, and it is possible to concur without necessarily regarding Stephen's grab for the throne as treacherous or unprincipled. In Edmund King's view Hugh

Bigod's testimony was useful to Stephen, but hardly decisive, since most people accepted that the original oaths that the barons had sworn to Matilda had been made under duress and so were not legally binding.

The real reason for Stephen's success is that he was the first to move, and that – like his predecessor Henry – he moved quickly and ruthlessly. Crouch argues that he must have had a plan already in place in anticipation of Henry's demise, and was acting with the support of his brother Theobald, who must have feared that if Matilda and Geoffrey secured England and Normandy his county of Blois would be encircled by a huge Angevin power bloc. As soon as the news of Henry's death reached him, Stephen set sail from Wissant in the Pas de Calais, taking with him only a small group of knights, as he did not wish to delay the enterprise while he collected an army. We are not told exactly where he landed in England, but he rode swiftly to London, where the relieved citizens greeted him with joy and acclaimed him king. The *Gesta Stephani* says that an agreement was made according to which the Londoners would support him as long as he lived in return for his promise of protection. According to the same source the citizens actually claimed the traditional privilege of appointing a successor to the throne, and although it is unlikely that this privilege was recognized outside the city, or even universally inside it, it is equally unlikely that Stephen was disposed to dispute it. He quickly cemented his position by taking action against a band of pillagers who were raiding the surrounding countryside under the leadership of a man who once been King Henry's doorkeeper. Stephen now had under his command not only the militia of London but a large number of knights who had flocked to join him, and with this force he killed or captured many of the bandits, bringing their ringleader back in chains to be hanged. Stephen then led his growing army to Winchester, where he was welcomed by his younger brother Henry, who was the bishop there. It was, says the *Gesta*, Bishop Henry who persuaded an initially reluctant William de Pont de l'Arche, the former king's treasurer, to hand over the keys of the castle and the treasury which it contained. This was a particularly important gain as Henry I, though often criticised by his enemies as a grasping miser, had at least left the treasury full. Bishop Henry also negotiated the support of Archbishop William of Canterbury in exchange for a promise from Stephen to restore and uphold the privileges of the Church. So on 22 December 1135 Stephen was anointed by the Archbishop and proclaimed King of England. Henry I had been dead for little more than three weeks.

William of Malmesbury emphasizes that the ceremony was poorly attended, with few nobles, no abbots and only three bishops present – those of Canterbury, Winchester and Salisbury. Given the speed of Stephen's coup, however, this is not surprising. At Easter 1136 he held his court at Oxford, and there he received the allegiance of most of the English barons. The *Gesta Stephani* says that they accepted Stephen as king 'gladly and respectfully', although this may have been due largely to his generosity in giving gifts and grants of land – a course of action which had been followed by most of his predecessors, including Henry I. During this period he promised reforms in numerous areas, including forest law, the laws governing female inheritance, and the abolition of the Danegeld, a long-obsolete tax originally imposed to pay off Viking invaders. In the event none of these promises was kept, though this failure is more likely to have been a result, rather than a cause, of the civil strife that was to follow. Nevertheless, whatever the legality of the proceedings, the fact that Stephen had been anointed as king with the holy oil was not something that could be disregarded. Even at the lowest point of his fortunes, neither his bitterest opponents nor the least sympathetic among the chroniclers were ever able to argue that he was not the king. But above all, to most people in England, what mattered was not the technicalities of the succession but the desperate need for someone to impose their authority before the country fell further into anarchy. The author of the *Gesta Stephani* begins his account of the chaos which followed Henry's death by telling how the '*ferae*', the wild beasts, which had formerly swarmed in thousands, were rapidly exterminated, to the extent that it soon became a rare event to catch sight of one of the few survivors. There was more logic to this killing than might at first appear. Henry, like his Norman predecessors, had been very keen on hunting and had set aside large tracts of land for the preservation of deer, but most of these were not strictly wild animals at all. Parks and forests throughout the kingdom had been stocked with fallow deer, not a native species but a recent introduction from the Mediterranean, which were enclosed within fences and ditches and often artificially fed in winter. They were protected from poachers by the notorious forest laws which had been introduced by the Conqueror, and which according to the *Anglo-Saxon Chronicle* punished anyone who killed the king's deer with blinding. Clearly the setting-aside of so much land for these animals had given rise to resentment, and being enclosed and semi-tame they made easy targets for anyone wishing to put the land to a different use, or simply looking for a source of free meat. It is possible that more exotic creatures might also have been caught up in the massacre, because we hear no more of the lions, leopards, lynxes and camels that Henry I had kept in semi-natural conditions in his walled park at Woodstock (James, 1990).

Then, says the *Gesta*, having wiped out the animals, the 'English' turned on each other. It is noteworthy, however, that there is no record of any organized uprising on the part of the people who might have been expected to be most oppressed by Henry and his laws. This is unlikely to be because the churchmen who wrote the histories of the times did not notice them; the sufferings of the common people are a common theme in their accounts. But this was an age long before any detectable national or class consciousness among the mass of the people. Most of the real 'English', the ordinary people at the bottom of the feudal pyramid, apparently accepted their lot. Although they may have shot a few deer for the pot, and there are isolated reports from Stephen's reign of small parties of them attacking their social superiors if they could catch them at a disadvantage, we have no reason to suppose that they undertook any real armed resistance. This might at first seem surprising, but it is likely that the popular stereotype of downtrodden Anglo-Saxons harking back to a pre-conquest golden age under their own rulers owes more to nineteenth-century nationalist ideas, and to Walter Scott's influential novel *Ivanhoe*, than to any evidence from the Middle Ages. It is true that Matthew Paris, writing in the thirteenth century, says that when the Anglo-Saxon nobility were deprived of their lands after 1066 they had taken to the forests and lived as outlaws: 'Ashamed to beg, ignorant of how to dig, they and their sons and brothers took refuge in the woods. They robbed and they raided rapaciously, but only when they were lacking in game and other victuals.' But this sounds more like a matter of personal survival than organized resistance. If there had ever been a 'golden age' of liberty and equality among the Anglo-Saxons – which is unlikely – it was certainly too far in the past to have inspired popular discontent in the 1130s. As early as the reign of Alfred the Great, the king's biographer Asser had criticised the ruling class for their indifference towards the welfare of the common people, and to judge from the few records that survive, a common language and culture had not prevented the Anglo-Saxon thegns of the eleventh century from living increasingly luxurious lives at the expense of the peasantry. A twelfth-century life of Saint Kenelm relates how an arrogant lady refused to allow her tenants a day's holiday on the feast day of the saint, while the life of Saint Wulfstan, Bishop of Worcester in the late eleventh century, describes an obviously familiar stereotype of an English thegn who spent his days drinking and playing at dice in the shade of a tree while his serfs sweated in the fields. Aelfric of Eynsham, whose Latin textbook or *Colloquy* was written around the year 1000, provides a fictional dialogue with a ploughman whose life was clearly no better than those of his descendants under the Normans. He has to work incessantly, even in the worst weather, 'for fear of my lord', but his most heartfelt complaint is not the work itself but the fact that he is not the one who benefits from it: 'It is hard work, sir, because I am not free.' The complaints that are preserved in the chronicles of the Anarchy relate to specific acts of oppression such as forced labour for castle building, and to the damage caused at times by the breakdown of law and order, rather than to any detectable resentment of Norman rule as such. In the aftermath of the rout at Winchester in 1141 some of Robert of Gloucester's knights 'fell into the hands of peasants and were terribly beaten', in the words of the *Gesta Stephani*. Agricultural tools could be turned into fairly effective improvised weapons – Jordan Fantosme, writing of the wars of Henry II in 1170s, describes peasants killing Flemish mercenaries 'with fork and flail'. But these peasants were no doubt among those whose crops and houses had recently been burnt by the warring armies, and their victims were probably attacked not because they were Normans, or lords, but because by fighting among themselves they had failed in the principal duty of any lord, native or foreign, which was to keep the peace.

Chapter 2

Disorder in the West Country

The men who did rise in revolt on Henry I's death were all members of the Anglo-Norman elite. The first was Robert of Bampton, 'a knight not of the lowest birth' according to the *Gesta*, but an alleged drunkard who had a grudge against Glastonbury Abbey (whose abbot was Stephen's brother, the Bishop of Winchester) on account of a legal dispute over land. After Henry's death Robert had garrisoned his castle at Bampton in North Devon with knights and archers, and from there he launched a series of plundering expeditions against his neighbours. When Stephen arrived in England Robert's victims lodged a complaint against him at court, so he was summoned and ordered to hand over his castle to a royal garrison. He appeared to accept the king's verdict 'with a cheerful and smiling countenance', and returned to Bampton with an escort of royal knights, to whom he was to surrender the castle on arrival. But en route he contrived to spend the night at one of his other manors, where his servants wined and dined the king's men lavishly. Then, when they were asleep, he mounted a horse and escaped. He reached Bampton and immediately put it into a state of defence, victualling it with supplies stolen from his neighbours, while Stephen's knights had to return to their master and confess that they had been made fools of. Stephen immediately gathered what the *Gesta* describes as a 'strong force' and marched to Bampton, but for reasons which are not explained the instigator of the revolt was no longer there. Robert seems to have decided to fight a sort of guerrilla campaign outside the stronghold, wandering from one place to another and sometimes joining other enemies of the king to make war on him, until eventually he 'met a dreadful end among strangers'. The *Gesta* gives no further details, but Robert's rebellion does not seem to have been part of a wider conspiracy, or even to have been properly planned at all. The leaderless garrison at Bampton held out briefly, but soon after their arrival Stephen's men caught one of them trying to escape and hanged him within sight of the walls, declaring that the same fate would befall all the defenders if they did not surrender at once. They immediately did so and their lives were spared, though according to the *Gesta* they were sent into exile, some of them eventually entering the service of King David of Scotland.

But even before the surrender of Bampton Stephen had received news of another crisis. A deputation from Exeter arrived to report that another dissident, Baldwin de Redvers, was behaving in a highly provocative manner. He had occupied the royal castle at Exeter and was forcing the citizens to provision it, swaggering about the town with an armed retinue and demanding the allegiance of everyone living there and in the surrounding villages. Again, it is difficult to detect any logical military or political agenda behind Baldwin's actions. He may not have believed that the new king was secure enough to undertake decisive action in response, but he certainly did not control sufficient forces to challenge Stephen in battle if he did respond. Baldwin was one of the leading barons of the kingdom, and one of the very few who had not attended Stephen's court at Easter in 1136, and so he had never acknowledged him as king. He had apparently tried to approach Stephen when he realized that Robert of Gloucester had done so, but had left it too late and the king had refused to meet him. Whether this was a motive for the rebellion is not clear; historians have often speculated about the involvement of Robert of Gloucester and others who were later to form the Empress Matilda's party, but proof is lacking. Stephen did, in any case, react with his characteristic speed and determination. As soon as the news reached him of what was happening in Exeter he despatched a force of 200 mounted knights, ordering them to ride through the night and take the city by surprise.

This was fortunate for the citizens, because Baldwin, who had learned of their complaint to the king, sent his men out of the castle the next morning to punish them by burning the town. But before they could do much damage the banners of Stephen's knights could be seen approaching. Seeing what was happening, the royal knights galloped headlong through the open gates and sent the garrison fleeing back to the castle. Shortly afterwards Stephen himself arrived with the main army, to receive a rapturous greeting from the citizens. Baldwin's garrison, however, was numerous and determined, and the ensuing siege was fought ferociously on both sides. The castle, says the *Gesta Stephani*, was set on a very high mound, still surrounded by the walls and limestone towers constructed centuries before by the Romans, and more recently strengthened using the latest building techniques. Stone castles, in fact, were still relatively uncommon in England, but this was one of the best. Stephen managed to capture an important outwork and destroy the bridge which connected the castle to the town. He built high wooden siege works outside the walls from which his archers and slingers could annoy the men on the battlements, and bombarded them with missiles thrown by heavy engines, while other troops dug tunnels to undermine the walls. The defenders, however, 'cared nothing' for all the resources ranged against them, but retaliated with arrows and thrown spears, and made unexpected sorties from hidden postern gates to inflict losses on their opponents. With Stephen unable to break in, the siege turned into a test of endurance. The king had one success when the garrison at nearby Plympton, which was also held for Baldwin, approached him with an offer of surrender. Two hundred knights supported by archers were sent to Plympton, whereupon the garrison – 'utter cowards' in the view of the author of the *Gesta* – handed over the castle without resistance. The fortifications were destroyed, and the huge herds of cattle and sheep which grazed in the neighbourhood were rounded up and taken to Stephen at Exeter to provision his army.

Most of the nobility of the West Country now came to offer or renew their allegiance to the king. However, one man, Alfred fitz Judhael of Totnes, remained loyal to Baldwin. Because his own castle was too dilapidated to stand a siege, Alfred abandoned it and went to join Baldwin at Exeter. He somehow managed to get his men into the town, where they mingled with Stephen's soldiers. The *Gesta* says that as they all wore the same mail armour it was difficult to distinguish them, and it is also likely that the place was full of other newly-arrived contingents, most of whom had come in response to a summons from the king. But Alfred had got a message to Baldwin, who launched a surprise sortie and succeeded in bringing his allies safely inside the castle walls. According to the *Gesta* Stephen's commanders were angry at the way in which they had been fooled, but the king took the news with good humour, saying that he was quite happy for all his enemies to shut themselves up together in one place.

Nevertheless the siege continued for three months, until the two wells inside the castle suddenly ran dry. The author of the *Gesta* ascribes this to divine intervention, arguing that it had never happened before even in the hottest weather, but the summer of 1136 had apparently been unusually dry. The defenders still had large stores of wine, which they now had to use for everything; making bread, boiling their food, and extinguishing the fires which broke out when the besiegers hurled flaming torches over the walls. It is not clear whether Baldwin was still in the castle – certainly he escaped before it fell – but when the wine also ran out, two leading men went to meet Stephen and seek surrender terms. The king refused to offer terms – encouraged, says the *Gesta*, by his brother Bishop Henry, who had seen from the wasted faces and shrunken lips of the emissaries that they were suffering from extreme thirst, and so put forward the rather unchristian argument that clemency was unnecessary since they would soon be forced to surrender unconditionally. Baldwin's wife then came to beg for mercy with floods of tears, but although Stephen spoke to her kindly he also sent her away. But then the king's own leading followers gathered together to change his mind, arguing that as Baldwin had not formally given his allegiance to Stephen the defenders were not technically traitors, and that in any case they were only showing loyalty to their own lord. So Stephen finally relented, and allowed them to go free with all their possessions as long as they handed over the castle. It was said that as the emaciated garrison filed out, the first thing that any of them did was to look for something to drink. Baldwin himself was already gone, but soon afterwards he turned up at another of his castles, at Carisbrooke on the Isle of Wight, where he collected a fleet of ships and turned to a career of piracy in the English Channel. But Stephen was close on his heels, commandeering a fleet of his own at Southampton and crossing the Solent to attack Carisbrooke. Baldwin had allegedly paid careful attention to the water supply this time, but the drought continued and soon the springs failed once again, reinforcing the chronicler's conviction that God was not on his side. Baldwin apparently tried to reach an accommodation with the king, but was rebuffed and fled once more, this time abandoning England and seeking asylum at the court of Count Geoffrey of Anjou. With hindsight this was an ominous development, as even though the Empress Matilda's party had not yet made a move against Stephen, their very existence was a magnet for disaffected men like Baldwin.

For the time being the West Country was quiet, but there was also unrest in East Anglia, where Hugh Bigod and Bishop Nigel of Ely had their strongholds. It is interesting that these two widely-separated regions, which were to cause most trouble for Stephen throughout his reign, were already sources of unrest even before his principal opponents, Matilda and Robert of Gloucester, declared against him. Hugh Bigod was the man whose testimony had provided Stephen with his justification for taking the throne, but he was far from a loyal adherent of the king. At some point after Stephen's accession he had taken possession of Norwich Castle; he handed it over without a fight when Stephen came to demand its return, but retained the rest of his castles which provided him with a significant power base for future defiance. It seems that Bishop Nigel also attempted an abortive revolt about this time, but this too quickly petered out when the king arrived with his army. By March 1137 Stephen felt secure enough in England to turn his attention to Normandy.

Chapter 3

A 'Land Full of Castles'

The comments of the Peterborough version of the *Anglo-Saxon Chronicle* under the year 1137 have given us the classic image of the reign of Stephen: 'Every powerful man made his castles and held them against (the king), and filled the land full of castles. They greatly oppressed the wretched men of the land with castle-work; then when the castles were made, they filled them with devils and evil men.'

And yet the castle was a relatively new feature in the English landscape. Fortified towns had been known since the Roman period, and some towns, such as Exeter and Bath, still retained parts of their Roman walls. In the ninth century Alfred the Great had introduced a system of defended 'burghs' which provided the people with refuges against invading Vikings, but castles as we know them had only begun to appear in northern France during the tenth century. They differed from earlier fortifications in that they were not intended to protect communities directly, but merely to house an armed garrison in the service of a lord. This lord may have been the king or other supreme civil power in the country, but could equally well be a local magnate, who may or may not have had permission from his overlord to build and garrison his castle. They were often a symptom of weak government and decentralized power, not only in England but also in France, where the first appearance of castles coincided with the decline of the Carolingian Empire. Conversely, when centralized government was restored, for example on the accession of Henry II in England, its first act was often to order the destruction of 'adulterine' castles, those that had been fortified without the permission of the monarch. A castle might be situated inside a town, walled or otherwise, but frequently stood on its own, though sometimes – as happened at Ludlow in Shropshire for example – a town might later grow up around what had originally been an isolated castle. It may have been built on a site of strategic value – for example to guard a ford – but could alternatively be sited in a central location to control the territory of the man who built it, or even to counter the influence of a rival's castle. It was usually a freestanding building, but during the wars of the Anarchy hastily-built fortifications were often added on to existing buildings.

These were usually churches or priories, the only solid stone edifices to be found in most settlements, but this practice inevitably led to damage to Church property and attracted the disapproval of the churchmen who wrote the chronicles of the time.

Although these strongholds were often justified as designed to protect the local populace from attack, they were seldom big enough to allow the people and their livestock to take refuge inside them, as Iron Age hillforts and Anglo-Saxon burghs had been, and people often saw them not as offering security but rather as instruments of oppression. Castles were unpopular with the common people not only because of the forced labour required to build them, and because they might provide a refuge from which robber barons could commit their depredations, as the Peterborough chronicler recognized, but also because they attracted armies to attack them. And armies would not only requisition supplies from the surrounding area, but would often deliberately destroy crops and villages in order to starve the defenders or persuade them to come out and fight. Bradbury quotes Jordan Fantosme, the chronicler of the Anglo-Scottish war of the 1170s, as the source of the saying 'First destroy the land, and then the enemy', but there is no doubt that the principle was already well known to Stephen and his opponents.

Castles had proliferated in England immediately after the Norman Conquest, and there may have been as many as 600 in the country by the end of the eleventh century. Most of these had originally been built on the orders of William I to overawe potentially disaffected towns, guard river crossings or act as supply bases for his campaigns. In the interests of speed and cheapness of construction they were generally made of earth and timber rather than stone, although a few in exceptionally important locations, such as the Tower of London and Chepstow on the vulnerable border with Wales, were built in stone from the beginning. The most common design was the 'motte and bailey', which consisted of an earth mound (the 'motte') surmounted by a wooden tower, and an enclosed courtyard or 'bailey'. Both motte and bailey were generally circular, or roughly so. The earth mounds survive in many places where the fortifications themselves have disappeared, and can sometimes give a better impression of the twelfth-century defences than better-known sites which have been extensively rebuilt in later centuries; there is an excellent example of Anglo-Norman earthworks at Stafford, although they were not tested in battle as the castle here was not attacked during Stephen's reign. Wooden fortifications were of course vulnerable to attack by fire as well as by heavy missiles thrown from siege engines, and by the 1130s many were being rebuilt in stone, with the central wooden tower replaced by a massive

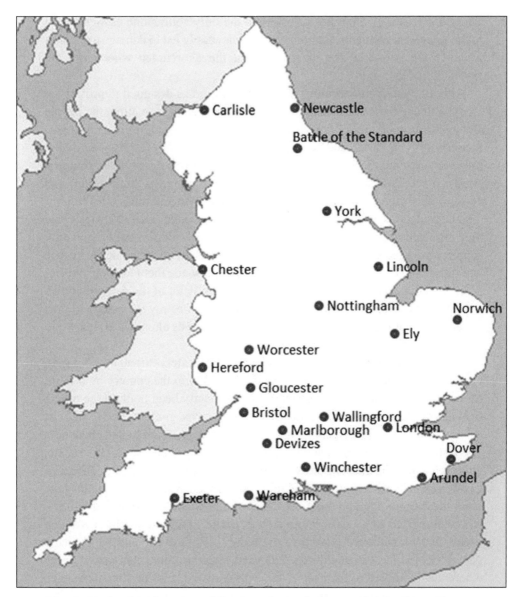

Map 1. England in the reign of Stephen. (www.thehistoryofengland.co.uk)

rectangular stone building known as a 'donjon' (the more familiar modern term, 'keep', dates from Tudor times).

Even in the early Middle Ages, defence was not the only function of a castle. In many cases the display of the owner's wealth and power, whether to intimidate the locals or to impress his peers, must have been equally important. North Norfolk, for example, was relatively peaceful during the Anarchy, but was nevertheless the scene of some outstanding examples of castle-building. Francis Pryor (2006) has described the activities of the de Warenne family at Castle Acre in terms which we associate more with the eighteenth century than the twelfth: the entire area, it appears, was landscaped during the 1140s in order to afford the visitor the most impressive view possible of the stone castle and its associated priory. This even included diverting the old straight Roman road known as the Peddar's Way so that it approached the site via the priory, with the aim, so archaeologists believe, of emphasising the piety of the de Warennes as well as their secular power. Castle Rising, not far away near the eastern shore of the Wash, is another example of expensive castle-building which appears to have had little if any practical military function. It is surrounded by an earth rampart which is too high to be overlooked from the donjon, and so if anything would provide cover to an attacker rather than presenting an obstacle.

Most castles, however, were functional, and were formidable obstacles for the siege technology of the day. There were essentially three ways to capture a castle. The most obvious – and the least expensive in money and lives – was to induce the garrison to surrender. To do so in the face of overwhelming odds appears not to have been incompatible with the Normans' sense of honour, and it was common for a pragmatic agreement to be made between the parties according to which a castle would be surrendered if a relieving army had not arrived before a specified date. The resistance of the garrison could be further undermined by starvation, and if an initial assault failed it was usual to impose a blockade, very often assisted by the building of siege works to protect the besiegers and provide a platform for siege engines. An unorthodox but fairly common variant on the negotiated approach was to capture the castellan himself, or someone whose life he valued, and use threats to force him to order his men to surrender. Stephen made frequent use of this ploy, as in the case of three bishops in 1139, and of Geoffrey de Mandeville in 1143, who were unexpectedly arrested at court and only released in exchange for handing over the castles which they controlled. Perhaps surprisingly, there are several instances on record of a besieged baron being caught outside the walls of his stronghold during hostilities; for example the *Gesta Stephani* tells of a Gloucestershire knight named Robert Musard, who in 1146 'left his castle unsuspectingly or rather, to confess the truth, foolishly', and was captured by Philip of Gloucester. Philip put a rope around his neck and forced him to surrender the castle under threat of hanging. Some victims, however, were made of sterner stuff. At around the same time Roger of Berkeley was captured by Walter of Hereford, stripped, bound, and three times subjected to a mock hanging within view of the walls of his castle. On the last occasion he was allowed to fall heavily to the ground, where he lay 'half dead', but he still refused to yield. At that the besiegers gave up, but they took the unfortunate Roger away with them and threw him into a dungeon. A similar failure is recorded in the *Histoire de Guillaume le Marechal*, the biography of William Marshal, later 1st Earl of Pembroke. According to this story William was sent to Stephen in 1152 as a hostage for the good behaviour of his father, John Marshal, but the latter failed to hand over his castle at Newbury as promised, and instead began to strengthen the defences. Stephen blockaded the castle and threatened to hang William, who would have been about 6 years old at the time, but his father replied rather callously that 'I still have the hammer and the anvil with which to forge still more and better sons!' As John no doubt knew, Stephen was not the sort of man to carry out the cold-blooded murder of a child. The king then threatened instead to shoot the boy into the castle from a stone-throwing engine. Of course this was also a bluff, and William survived to become perhaps the most famous knight in English history.

Alternatively the place could be taken by a more conventional assault, but as long as the defences were intact this was likely to be a very risky strategy. At Winchcombe in 1144 Stephen's men climbed up the mound under the cover of 'clouds of arrows', so demoralizing the defenders that they surrendered at once, although on this occasion the garrison was very small, most of their comrades having already fled at the king's approach. The *Gesta Stephani* describes a version on this tactic which was used by the king at Harptree in 1138. Stephen marched past the castle with a large army, giving the impression that he was advancing on Bristol. The garrison, which presumably was too small to challenge him directly, came out and shadowed him, following on his flank in the hope of finding an opportunity to attack. But Stephen suddenly turned and galloped back to the castle with his horsemen. Very few defenders had been left there, and they were unable to prevent the king's men setting fire to the gates and swarming over the walls with scaling ladders.

The third method of attack was simply to demolish the building, usually by undermining it or by throwing heavy projectiles at the walls. We read in the chronicles of various types of siege engines, but the terminology is not always very clear. The *Gesta Stephani*, for example, refers rather vaguely to machines 'of various types' ('*machinas diversi generis*') at Stephen's siege of Exeter; some high, for observing the interior of the castle, others low, designed to attack or undermine the walls. These sound like towers and battering rams rather than stone-throwers, and although the chronicler refers to slingers on foot hurling stones, it is possible that the king had no larger missile weapons on this occasion. However, the same source, describing the siege of Faringdon in 1145, tells how the garrison were annoyed not only by arrows shot over the walls by archers, but by stones hurled from '*machinae*'; in fact in this case it was the bombardment alone that persuaded the defenders to surrender. At this date the stone throwers were almost certainly what were known as mangonels or *petrariae* – devices consisting of a long wooden beam on a pivot, with a sling or cup at one end to hold the projectile, and powered by men (or not infrequently women) pulling on ropes fixed to the other end. The Romans had favoured machines operated by the torsion power of twisted animal hair or sinew, such as the two-armed '*ballista*' and the one-armed '*onager*', but although the names remained in use, and the torsion principle was to enjoy a revival later in the Middle Ages, the devices themselves had apparently fallen out of favour in the West after the end of the Roman Empire. Perhaps, as David Nicolle suggests, they were too complex to make and keep in action, and the supply of sinew required the slaughter of more livestock than the reduced economic circumstances of the so-called Dark Ages would permit.

The mangonel was a Chinese invention, introduced into Europe via the Middle East around the seventh century AD, perhaps by invaders from Central Asia such as the Avars. It was simpler to build and operate than the old torsion machines, and could be made in a wide variety of sizes from small and mobile wheeled versions operated by one or two men, up to giant engines with teams of twenty or more, which could throw 60kg stones to ranges of well over a hundred metres. Some time around the end of the twelfth century we start to hear of a new and more powerful stone-throwing engine, the trebuchet, which was powered by a heavy counterweight – usually a wooden box filled with earth and stones – and could throw a much heavier missile with greater force. Trebuchets made it possible to physically destroy stone fortifications in a way that was not feasible with the lighter mangonels. They were probably a Middle Eastern invention, and as Nicolle suggests it is likely that the first such machine seen in England was one brought by Louis of France in 1216. The armies of Stephen's reign, therefore, were operating at a time when the technology for attacking castles had fallen temporarily behind the defence. They might have been able to bombard defenders into submission with stone throwing engines, but actually knocking down castle walls was probably beyond them.

At Castle Cary in 1138 the *Gesta* says that Stephen's '*balistis*' threw fire as well as stones ('*ignem et lapidum*'). We do not know exactly how this fire was delivered, but it appears that the employment of incendiary weapons was increasing at this time, perhaps as a result of experience gained during the Crusades, since the Lateran Council of 1139 went to the trouble of banning their use against fellow Christians – a ban which was evidently as ineffective as its better-known pronouncement against archery. A famous story about Geoffrey of Anjou suggests that his armies may have been in advance of those in England as far as incendiary weapons were concerned, though this might just be an accident of our sources. According to the *Historia Gaufredi Ducis*, while Geoffrey was besieging Montreuil-Bellay in 1151 a party of monks visited his camp to find him reading a book, which he put aside out of politeness. An elderly monk picked up the book and found that it was a copy of *De Re Militari* by the classical Roman writer Vegetius, specifically a chapter in which the author explains how to capture a timber-reinforced tower. Seeing his visitor engrossed, Geoffrey told him that if he waited until the next day he would see what he had read being put into practice. The monk must have been curious enough to do so, as the chronicle continues with what is obviously an eyewitness account. The besiegers made an iron jar, held together with iron bands and filled with an inflammable mixture of nut oil and hemp seeds, then hung it in a furnace by a chain until it was glowing red hot. The chain was then cooled with water, and the jar pulled out and somehow attached to the throwing arm of a mangonel. The target was a barricade of strong timbers that the garrison had erected to block a breach in the wall. When the jar struck them it burst, and the boiling oil inside caught fire. The flames destroyed three houses as well as the barricade, forcing the defenders to run for their lives, and in the confusion Geoffrey's men burst into the castle and captured it. This particular incendiary device sounds rather crude by comparison with the petroleum-based 'Greek Fire' that makes its appearance in Western Europe around the end of the twelfth century, but it was obviously effective against wooden fortifications. It is possible that it was a novelty in 1151, and we do not know if Stephen or his advisors had read Vegetius, but the story illustrates the sort of techniques that might have been available to them. Chibnall has pointed out that copies of *De Re Militari* were not uncommon in monastic libraries (there were at least two in Normandy), perhaps because it can be interpreted in religious terms as an allegory of the war between virtue and sin.

Fortifications could also be attacked by mining underneath them, or even by more sophisticated engineering techniques. When Stephen was planning to attack Bristol in 1138 he quickly realized that the defences were impregnable to conventional siege operations, so he called a council of war to discuss how to proceed. One suggestion was to dam the rivers which flowed into the sea on either side of the town with rocks, timber and turf, thus blocking the harbour and preventing supplies from reaching the garrison, with the added advantage that with luck the rising waters would flood the place. The author of the *Gesta Stephani*, who knew the area well, seems to have thought that this plan could have succeeded, because he accuses those who argued against it of being secret opponents of the king. But Stephen was persuaded that it was impossible to 'block up the unfathomable sea', and so the attempt was never made.

Chapter 4

The Armies of England

The core of English, and to a lesser extent Scottish, armies in the early twelfth century was the armoured horseman or knight, generally referred to at the time by the Latin term '*miles*', or soldier. Though not necessarily all of Norman or Anglo-Norman descent, these men fought in what had come to be regarded as the classic Norman style. Essentially they were heavy cavalry, protected by coats of mail and large shields, whose close-order charge had dominated the battlefields of Europe ever since their victory over the forces of the Pope at Civitate in 1053. It was men like these who had defeated the English at Hastings in 1066 and the Byzantines at Durazzo in 1081, and had repeatedly overcome the formidable Turkish mounted archers during the First Crusade. Their weapons were designed for combat at close quarters: the lance and the sword, plus occasionally an axe or mace. Knights were raised and maintained by the system we have come to know as 'feudalism'. In theory the whole kingdom was held to belong to the king, who kept a proportion of the land as his own estates, the 'royal demesne', and distributed the remainder to his leading barons, or tenants-in-chief, who established themselves in the villages in manors, each with its own smaller demesne and its own sub-tenants. Originally the manors held by each baron had been scattered throughout the country in order to prevent them from consolidating their own regional power bases, but there had long been a tendency, which accelerated in Stephen's reign, for men to reorganize their holdings into just such locally-based strongholds.

The majority of the land was designated for military service, and was divided into a specified number of knights' fees. A baron would therefore be responsible for supplying a number of fully-equipped knights for the king's army when required. The actual terms of service varied, but a typical period for which a knight was expected to serve was forty days. The individual knights might be maintained in one of two ways. Especially in the early post-conquest period many magnates kept their own household troops, who were fed and housed at their lord's expense and so were available to march at short notice as well as serving as bodyguards or castle garrisons for their masters. This practice became less common as time went on, but even in the reign of Henry II, his 1181 Assize of Arms envisages barons possessing enough weapons and armour to equip their household employees to make up any shortfall in the number of knights for which they were assessed. More usual was sub-infeudation, which involved the tenants-in-chief granting land to lesser knights on similar terms to those on which they held their land from the monarch. These men might hold only a single knight's fee, in which case the terms required them to serve in person, or they might be responsible for providing yet others by a further layer of subinfeudation. Sometimes these layers of obligation led to a clash of loyalties, with men attempting to serve two or more masters at the same time. Matthew Strickland quotes the case of David Olifard, who held his fief at Sawtry in Huntingdonshire from Earl Henry, the son of King David of Scotland, who was Olifard's godfather. When Stephen confiscated Huntingdon in 1138 and gave it to a new earl, Simon de Senlis, Olifard found himself summoned to fight alongside Simon on the side of Stephen, although his sympathies lay with the other camp. At the Battle of Winchester in 1141 he changed sides and helped King David to escape, as a result of which Simon took away his fief. Olifard fled to Scotland, where he received lands from a grateful David. Some men of knightly rank also served as mercenaries for pay, but these men generally had an unsavoury reputation. William of Malmesbury says that as soon as Stephen took the throne 'knights of all kinds hastened to the king, as also those more lightly armed, especially from Flanders and Brittany. They were a class of men full of greed and violence.'

There is no contemporary record of the total number of knights in England in Stephen's reign, but a fairly good indication is provided by the *Cartae Baronum* collected by Henry II in 1166. After the chaos of the preceding reign the king needed to establish what military forces were available to him, so he instructed all his tenants-in-chief to report in writing all the sub-tenancies which they had on their lands, both before and after the death of Henry I, and the number of knights owed. In many cases the respondents used a formula such as 'on the day when King Henry your grandfather was alive and dead', which gives us a snapshot of the situation at the very beginning of Stephen's reign. As the returns were later used as the basis for levying a tax they were kept by the Exchequer, which enabled J.H. Round to calculate that the total number of knights in the English lands under the control of Henry I was probably slightly less than 5,000. It is unlikely that all of these were ever in the field at one time, and of course they were never all available to Stephen, but this does give an approximate upper limit for the size of armies in this period, and helps to explain how relatively small forces of a few hundred knights could be decisive in battles like The Standard and Lincoln. As for the overall size of armies, including the less highly regarded but indispensable foot soldiers, we also lack reliable contemporary figures, but the 7,000 men deployed by the Conqueror at Hastings, though regarded at the time as exceptional, might provide a benchmark for estimating the strength of the largest armies, like the one which Stephen led to York early in 1136. As churchmen, the chroniclers tell us less than we would like to know of how these armies were commanded and controlled in battle, but their narratives show that they were capable of some fairly sophisticated deployments. Orderic Vitalis was well aware of the importance of discipline in an army: he remarks of the Angevin force which invaded Normandy in 1136 that the great magnates 'ought to have led separate squadrons in a properly levied army', and ascribes their failure to the fact that they neglected this vital command function.

We are told, or can deduce, rather more about the tactics and equipment of the individual fighting man. The typical knight of the wars of Steven's reign would not have looked very different from his predecessors at Hastings, like those familiar to us from the depictions on the Bayeux Tapestry. His hair was no longer cut short, but he wore the same type of iron helmet, fitted with a nasal to provide partial protection for the face. The helmet was often still made in sections and riveted together like the old-fashioned 'spangenhelm', though one-piece versions were becoming more popular as metalworking techniques improved. Body armour consisted of a 'hauberk' or coat of mail constructed from interlocking iron rings. By this date the hauberk was usually knee length, with full-length sleeves and a mail hood or coif to protect the neck; mail gauntlets and separate leg defences were coming into use by the middle of the century, but were probably still uncommon. By the end of the twelfth century it was also customary for knights to wear a gown or surcoat over their armour; this was originally a Middle-Eastern practice adopted by the Crusaders, perhaps as protection from the sun or, when helmets with full faceplates became popular later on, as an aid to identification. The first depiction of such a surcoat is believed to be on a seal of Count Waleran de Beaumont of Meulan dating from about 1141, but in England during our period the fashion was probably restricted to a handful of the most eminent noblemen. Mail provides a good defence against drawing cuts made, for example, with the edge of a sword, but it can be pierced by a sharp, pointed weapon which is able to thrust between the rings, and the rings themselves can cause injury if driven into the wearer's flesh. Therefore it was usual to wear a thick padded garment underneath. This was known as a 'gambeson' or 'aketon' (the latter term being derived from the Arabic *al-qutun*, 'cotton'), and could be made either of layers of deerskin or other leather, or of linen stuffed with cotton or similar soft material. The outer layer was often painted with pitch for waterproofing and additional durability. Thirteenth-century gambesons, which probably did not differ significantly from earlier versions, are well illustrated in Embleton (2000). Contemporary records of this type of armour are scanty, and being made of organic materials it is generally invisible archaeologically, so that some modern writers have doubted whether it was used by mail-armoured warriors in some earlier periods – notably the Vikings. However, even brief experience with a reproduction coat of mail will show that mail on its own or on top of unpadded fabric is very uncomfortable to wear, and offers inadequate protection against both thrusts and blows. Gerald de Barri, writing of the 1180s, describes the 'heavy' armour of his time as being made 'partly out of cloth and partly of iron', which seems to confirm that the best protection was considered to be a composite of different materials. The real value of the mail is as a sort of hard 'skin' over the soft armour, preventing the latter being cut to pieces by sharp edges, and with luck the flexibility of both materials would allow the armour to 'give' slightly under the impact of a missile, preventing it from penetrating far enough to wound the wearer. Contemporary illustrations show that poorer foot soldiers, and perhaps some mounted sergeants, often wore a gambeson without the mail, which is a far better option than mail without the gambeson, as it would offer almost as good protection while being much cheaper to make and lighter to wear.

We have conflicting evidence about how effective knightly armour actually was. At one extreme epics like *The Song of Roland*, the most famous of the French *Chansons de Geste* which were so popular in this period, are full of heroic blows with lance or sword which smash through armour and leave its wearers dead on the field. Such exploits were not all fictional: the Syrian knight Usama ibn Munqidh, for example, describes a skirmish during the Crusades in which a Muslim warrior named Yaqut the Tall charged two Franks who were riding side by side, and knocked both men and their horses to the ground with a single lance thrust. The same writer also tells of a lance blow which killed a Christian knight by breaking his mail hauberk and driving a section of the iron links into his stomach, while according to Orderic Vitalis, Anseau de Garlande, who was the commander of a French army and so likely to have been wearing the best-quality armour, was killed instantly by a lance at Le Puiset in 1118. On the other hand, no contemporary Anglo-Norman writer doubted the value of armour. The *Histoire de Guillaume le Marechal* makes this point in describing an incident in 1141 in which a group of knights under Earl Patrick of Salisbury, who were not expecting trouble and so were not wearing their armour, suffered heavy casualties in an encounter with John the Marshal. What Gerald de Barri described as 'the sheer mass of iron which they wear' is repeatedly cited as the main advantage that the Norman elite enjoyed over more lightly-equipped opponents, whether the latter were poor soldiers unable to afford mail or warriors in the Celtic tradition, who deliberately sacrificed protection for mobility. When fighting on an open level field, says Gerald, 'I have no doubt at all that you must pit armour against armour and weight against weight'. This metaphor, though, points to the real reason why mail armour was not suitable for all conditions. It was heavy: no complete twelfth-century examples survive, but Strickland quotes weights for shorter fourteenth-century coats ranging from 20lbs to 31lbs (10kg to 15.5kg). The weight could vary depending on the length of the hauberk, the size of the rings, and whether or not it was reinforced in vulnerable places by an extra layer, but taking into account the gambeson, shield and helmet a knight's burden could easily exceed 50lbs (25kg). Modern re-enactors often point out that this is less than a present-day infantryman is expected to carry into action, but writers like Gerald confirm what we would expect, that at least when fighting on foot it was enough to slow men down and put them at a disadvantage in rough or hilly terrain. Where we read of dismounted knights in pitched battles, as at The Standard and Lincoln, they are standing on the defensive, so restricted mobility is unlikely to have been a serious issue, but things would be very different if attempting to pursue Welsh raiders, for example, in their native forests. It might be thought that the weight of the armour would be of less significance for a knight fighting on horseback, but even then it might lead to a loss of speed that could be fatal if the knight had to retreat, which is no doubt why armour was often discarded by men fleeing from a lost battle. For example, Ailred of Rievaulx tells how Prince Henry, the son of the Scottish king, gave his expensive hauberk to a poor peasant while escaping from the debacle at The Standard in 1138. This is presented as an example of the earl's generosity, but it is likely that he was simply glad to get rid of the weight. The flexible construction which is one of the advantages of mail can also be a drawback, as the weight can shift awkwardly unless it is carefully constrained by straps and belts. Hill and Freiberg describe it as 'slippery', so that it required time and practice – and ideally the assistance of a squire – to put on or take off. This is why a character in the *Histoire de*

Guillaume le Marechal (quoted by Strickland, 1996) always put on his hauberk when already mounted, rather than before mounting as was the usual practice: he explained that he was wary of being caught on foot by a surprise attack while in his armour, which he could neither shed in a hurry nor run quickly enough while wearing to get to his horse. The possession of fine armour could also identify a fugitive as a wealthy magnate, and put him at risk of either being seized for ransom or simply attacked by disgruntled commoners who blamed him for the damage caused by war, as happened after the rout at Winchester in 1141.

Like his armour, the knight's shield had changed little since Hastings. It was of the type known today as a 'kite' shield (the term is not contemporary), long enough to protect a man on foot from neck to knee, and either flat or slightly curved laterally to provide improved coverage for the torso. This type is often considered to be a horseman's shield, but it had become almost universal even among men who fought on foot. In fact the earliest representations of kite shields, dating from the late tenth century, are shown being carried by infantrymen (Heath, 1980). From surviving thirteenth-century examples we know that a kite shield could be made from a single piece of wood, though some might have been constructed by gluing planks side by side like earlier Anglo-Saxon round shields. A covering of leather, canvas or parchment was probably added for additional resistance to penetration. A round metal boss was often riveted onto the front of the shield. Most modern commentators regard this as an item of decorative value only, as the shield was now carried strapped to the forearm rather than by the single central handgrip which the boss was originally designed to protect, but it could still have functioned as an offensive weapon. The author has a reconstructed kite shield which weighs around 8lbs (4kg), and is light enough to be punched forward into an opponent's face, as well as 'flipped' up to strike with the pointed lower section. Nevertheless, the usual grip for this type of shield, consisting of a strap through which the left forearm is passed rather than a central grip held in the fist, does make it less suitable for rapid manoeuvring than the earlier round types. It also prevents the shield being held out and used as a weapon with the edge foremost, a move which many modern re-enactors have demonstrated. But the Norman style of fighting on foot relied on solid, close-order formations rather than individual combat, and here the ability of the kite shield to protect most of the body without the user having to move it around would have been invaluable. Re-enactment experience suggests in particular that a slicing attack to the rear of the leg with the 'back' edge of a two-edged sword, which had once – to judge by the sagas – been a favourite tactic of the Vikings, could be fairly easily frustrated by a kite shield.

The knight carried a straight, double-edged sword which was similar in design to that used by his Viking and Anglo-Saxon predecessors, but the addition of a heavy disc-shaped pommel, which acted as a counterweight to the blade, made it better balanced and suited to a wider range of techniques. We are accustomed to thinking of a medieval sword as being used in a rather unsophisticated manner to deliver powerful cutting blows, and it seems that this is what the people of the time expected of their heroes. The *Song of Roland* describes numerous single combats with the sword, most of which are resolved by tremendous blows which cut through armour, helmets and bodies alike. But although twelfth-century knights might have liked to see themselves this way, this is not what their swords were really designed to do. In balance and overall design they would have been optimised for rather more subtle moves; for example a swift drawing cut to the side of an opponent's neck, a target which had been left unprotected by the old-fashioned mail shirts worn by the Vikings. This could have been a factor in the addition during the eleventh century of a mail hood to the hauberk, to protect the knight's head and neck. Significantly perhaps, the word 'hauberk' itself derives from the Old English 'hals burg', or neck defence. Later medieval fighting manuals distinguish between the two edges of a double-edged sword by using terms like 'front' and 'back' or 'long' and 'short', which can be confusing as physically they are identical. The 'back' or 'short' edge refers to the one facing towards the swordsman's arm when he is holding the weapon vertically in front of him. The opposite edge, or 'front', is naturally the one with which most blows are struck, but the 'back' is almost as useful. For example, it can be used to reach around behind an opponent's legs and cut his hamstrings, or by turning the sword hand and thrusting over the enemy's shield it can deliver a downwards cut. This latter technique is especially effective, as if it does not put the victim out of action immediately it puts the 'front' edge in a good position to cut upwards at his neck. We should therefore envisage the knights of the twelfth century making use of a range of sophisticated fighting techniques, rather than the mindless violence sometimes associated with the early medieval art of war.

The sword was still wielded in one hand, usually in conjunction with a shield; the 'great sword' or 'war sword', with a hilt long enough for it to be held with both hands, began to appear about a century after our period. It should be noted also that these swords were not designed for parrying blows in the style often seen in films, and were probably used for this purpose only in emergencies. A blade which is sharpened on both sides is too easily damaged to be employed in this way. A single-edged weapon with a thicker and stronger 'back' is more suitable for parrying, but although 'backswords' and 'falchions' of this type may have been in use by the twelfth century, and similar seaxes descended from Anglo-Saxon or Viking prototypes almost certainly were, they were not knightly weapons. A guard for the hand is obviously also desirable when using a sword to parry or block attacks, but the cross-pieces on twelfth-century hilts, though longer than their Viking predecessors, were still inadequate for this purpose, though they might have stopped the user's hand from sliding onto his own blade. There were no doubt several reasons why proper guards were not developed in this era: they were difficult to make; by forcing the user to hold the hilt in a certain way they might have reduced the versatility of a two-edged weapon; and in any case they were not needed, since the typical fighting position was with the shield forward, protecting the hand.

The other characteristic knightly weapon, the lance, has received less attention from modern scholars than the sword – inevitably perhaps, since the wooden shafts were perishable and so there is a scarcity of surviving examples to study. From depictions in art, including the Bayeux Tapestry, we can conclude that the shaft of the lance was probably between 7ft and 9ft (2.13m and 2.74m) in length, though the same cautions regarding artistic techniques and conventions apply as for bow lengths (see below). The small iron lance head was socketed and secured with nails, making it robust enough to withstand the impact of a mounted charge, though battle accounts – both factual and fictional – make it clear that the shaft would routinely break, obliging the knight to resort to his sword. In the *Song of Roland* Count Oliver is described as using the broken shaft of his lance as an improvised club because in the thick of the fight he does not have time to draw his sword, and though the story is fictional this was presumably a predicament that the poem's twelfth-century audience would have recognized. The commonest wood for shafts was probably ash, as it had been in Anglo-Saxon times, although Wace also mentions pine, which would be lighter though not quite so robust. There were two principal techniques for using the lance from horseback, though some modern writers have perhaps exaggerated their significance. Most ancient horsemen had wielded their spears overarm, but by the twelfth century Western knights are usually shown in art charging with the lance 'couched', or held close to the body in an underarm grip, with the rear of the shaft tucked under the elbow for added security. This, for example, is how Robert of Gloucester is depicted in a copy of Geoffrey of Monmouth's history made in Normandy around 1150 (see Gravett 1993). The Bayeux

Tapestry shows the Normans at Hastings using both methods, which suggests that the 'couched' style had become standard in the intervening three-quarters of a century. The principal advantages of using a lance overarm were that it could strike over an enemy's shield at his head or face, and that it was possible to throw it without warning the opponent by changing your grip. However, the striking power of the underarm attack, which could transmit the momentum of the horse as well as its rider, would obviously be much greater. Holding the point low in an underarm grip would also be most suitable for attacking the chest of an enemy's horse, a tactic which, unchivalrous as it was considered to be under the later rules of the tournament, was commonly used in twelfth-century battles. The situation may not be quite so straightforward, however. At Hastings William's cavalry were attacking up a steep hill which would have robbed their charge of much of its momentum, and perhaps obliged them to throw their lances in order to reach the Englishmen sheltering behind their shields, so the Tapestry might not be depicting their usual tactics when fighting other horsemen. Conversely, illustrations from Spain as late as the thirteenth century show the overarm position still in use. No doubt tactics continued to be adapted to particular circumstances, though as lances became heavier later in the Middle Ages, throwing them would have been a less practical proposition. The real secret of the Norman cavalry's success was not the method of holding the lance as such, but the fact that their charge using these weapons could be delivered in close order, presenting the enemy with a wall of lance points which he would not be able to penetrate, whereas swinging a sword would require a considerably looser formation.

When used on foot the lance or spear appears in our sources mainly as a defensive weapon, employed for example by the dismounted knights at The Standard and Lincoln to stop charges by either cavalry or faster moving light infantry. Non-noble infantrymen armed principally with spears were probably more numerous than the occasional note in our sources might suggest. By the time of Henry II's Assize of Arms of 1181 all freemen in the kingdom were being expected to equip themselves for military service, and Henry's regulations set out the equipment which they had to possess, depending on a man's wealth and social standing. Anyone who had goods or rents worth 16 marks or more, or who held a knight's fee, was to arm himself as a knight; those worth at least 10 marks had to provide mail armour, helmet and spear, while the poorer classes were to have only helmet, spear and gambeson. We have brief mentions of the presence of spearmen at Hastings and The Standard, and although they are not depicted in the Bayeux Tapestry, they do appear in other illustrated sources such as the Bury Bible. This book was produced at

Bury St Edmunds some time in the 1130s, and is now in Corpus Christi College, Cambridge. It is of particular interest as it contains two of the very few illustrations of fighting men contemporary with the reign of Stephen. One picture depicts the fall of Jerusalem as foretold by Jeremiah, but could well have been inspired by one of Stephen's sieges. The city walls are being defended by men in full mail armour, but two of the three attackers shown are unarmoured, though equipped with helmets and large kite shields. One of them is throwing a missile of some sort, while the other charges at the city gate with levelled spear and his shield held over his head. A third man, clad in mail, is swinging a two-handed axe. He may of course be intended to represent a knight, but an axeman in another picture is unarmoured and lacks even a helmet.

Such axe-wielders might alternatively have been professional mercenaries, or as Ian Heath suggests could represent the members of a town militia. We know from Orderic's account of the Battle of Lincoln that some of the citizens there were armed with axes, and the *Gesta Stephani* mentions Londoners with helmets and coats of mail. In England and Scotland long two-handed axes of Danish type continued in use throughout the twelfth century, and on occasion even Norman knights did not disdain to wield them. The most famous example is Stephen himself at the Battle of Lincoln, who was captured while fighting with what Orderic calls a 'Norse axe', which had been given to him by a citizen of Lincoln after his sword broke. Bradbury suggests that this was an indication of the sort of obsolete equipment used by the poorer men of Lincoln, but it was not the only such axe in the king's army that day. An illustration in two copies of Henry of Huntingdon's chronicle shows Baldwin fitz Gilbert leaning on a similar weapon while giving his speech before the battle, which suggests that it was a fairly familiar item of equipment even among the Norman elite. A heavy axe could only be wielded when dismounted, but it would be more effective against armour than a sword, as well as having a longer reach. Gerald de Barri, in his *Topographia Hibernica*, refers to the Irish habit of carrying long-handled axes everywhere, as others might carry a staff. He calls this an 'evil custom', and argues that an axe lends itself to treachery and surprise attacks because it is always ready for action as it 'has not to be unsheathed like a sword, or bent as a bow, or poised as a spear. Without further preparation, beyond being raised a little, it inflicts a mortal blow.' Gerald's distrust of the Irish is very evident in this passage, but his general point seems valid. Perhaps because they were so easily brought into action we often hear of axes being used for assassinations, as in the case of Walter de Pinkney in 1144, as well as several of the victims of the Orkney pirate Svein Asleifsson.

The Normans, of course, had encountered this weapon at Hastings and had every reason to treat it with respect. An example of the sort of wounds it could inflict comes from the Irish *Song of Dermot and the Earl*, which describes how at the Battle of Dublin 1171 the Orkney berserk Eoan Mear ('John the Mad') cut off a knight's leg with a single blow. Its only disadvantages were, firstly, that the wooden shaft was vulnerable to being cut by a sword stroke, as is shown happening on the Bayeux Tapestry, and secondly that it required two hands and so could not be combined with a shield. But it was far from an unsophisticated device for chopping at people's heads. The shaft as well as the head can be employed as an offensive weapon as well as to block incoming blows or missiles, which is why a character in the Icelandic *Fostbraetha Saga* claims that his axe will also serve as his shield and mail hauberk. The shape of the axehead also enabled it to be used for hooking an opponent's shield or parts of his body, while some twelfth-century axeheads from Scotland and Ireland have a blade which projects upwards to form a point parallel to the shaft, which could presumably be used for thrusting as well as cutting in the same manner as a later medieval polearm.

The knight's other main weapon was his horse, which provided him with mobility on campaign as well as speed and striking power on the battlefield. Medieval war horses were known by various names according to their function and price. The most expensive were 'destriers', which were trained for the tournament and may have been too expensive to have been routinely ridden into battle. They were traditionally stallions, which are notoriously difficult to control, but display a natural aggression which was considered to be an asset in battle. The 'courser' was considerably cheaper and perhaps lighter in build, and seems to have been the usual mount of the armoured knight, while 'rounceys' were general-purpose riding horses used for day-to-day travelling as well as in combat by sergeants and other non-knightly horsemen. Evidence from a variety of sources, including the illustrations on the Bayeux Tapestry and surviving sets of later medieval horse armour, suggest that the average height of a warhorse was just under fifteen hands, about the same size as a hunter of today. It was sufficiently agile, as well as sufficiently under control, to carry out difficult manoeuvres in battle; although it is not attested from the wars of Stephen's day, most scholars today would accept that the 'feigned flight' which the Normans carried out at Hastings and elsewhere was within the realms of possibility for a twelfth-century knight. To judge from illustrations the knight rode with straight legs, angled lightly forward for stability, and was held upright by a saddle with a high cantle at the rear and pommel at the front. This was useful in preventing him from being unhorsed by a blow, but could itself be a danger; William I suffered a fatal injury when his horse threw him against the pommel of his saddle. Because the knight was held so firmly in the saddle it was unusual for him to be unhorsed by a lance thrust, though he would inevitably fall if the saddle girth broke – a fate which occurs several times in the *Song of Roland*. A more common way of forcing a man to dismount was of course by killing his horse, which could be achieved either by a lance thrust or by missiles. Writing of the Battle of Borgtheroulde in 1124, Orderic Vitalis says that the royalist archers were ordered to shoot at the horses rather than the rebel knights, as a result of which many of the latter were unhorsed and captured. The same writer tells us that 700 horses were killed at the siege of Chaumont in 1098. Armour for war horses does not appear until the late twelfth century, but it is nevertheless likely that the impact of ordinary arrows would annoy and frighten the animals, causing them to become uncontrollable and throw their riders, rather than kill them outright, though they might later die from loss of blood. In contrast Strickland (1996) quotes the example of the Battle of Lincoln in 1217, where the horses were killed en masse 'like pigs', so that the joke was current that their aristocratic riders had been instantly converted into infantrymen. But here the attackers were crossbowmen, whose more powerful weapons probably could kill horses so quickly as to bring their riders to the ground on the spot.

The remark about knights becoming infantry through the loss of their horses was a popular jibe because fighting on horseback was the mark of the upper classes. It was generally the less well-equipped, non-knightly components of a twelfth-century army who marched and fought on foot, though as we have seen knights could dismount to fight, and conversely it is possible that men of lower rank might serve as cavalry. Ian Heath quotes the Norman *Inquest of Bayeux* of 1133, which specifies that a man holding less than a knight's fee should serve on horseback with lance, shield and sword, and deduces that such men, known as sergeants from the Latin '*servientes*', or servants, might have been the inspiration for illustrations such as those in the Bayeux Tapestry showing armed horsemen without armour. However, the sources for Stephen's English wars do not mention such troops, and it is likely that by that time, although sergeants of non-knightly rank did fight alongside their social superiors, they were not equipped significantly differently from the knights. Exactly how foot soldiers were recruited has been the subject of much scholarly debate, with many arguing that the old Anglo-Saxon '*fyrd*' system was retained intact by the Normans. The *fyrd* was a sort of territorial army, originally raised to fight the Danes, in which all free men were obliged to serve if summoned.

By the twelfth century the term '*fyrd*' no longer appears, but it seems to have been generally accepted that the free male population aged between 15 and 60 was subject to call-up when required. The earliest surviving legal framework for this dates from the reign of Henry II, but in view of the similarities with the old *fyrd* system it is likely that there had been some sort of continuity in the intervening period. We can therefore assume that some at least of the infantrymen in the armies of Stephen and his opponents were obliged to serve on a similar basis. More prominent in contemporary accounts, however, were mercenaries, including the 'more lightly armed' of those whom William of Malmesbury describes as coming from Brittany and Flanders to join Stephen. It is noteworthy that in his discussion of tactics and their suitability for use against the Welsh, Gerald de Barri lumps together 'Flemings, Normans, French routiers and Brabancon mercenaries' as disciplined, steady troops, in contrast to the Welsh. Brabant, on the coast of what is now Belgium, was a well-known source of mercenaries in this period, to the extent that such troops were often referred to as 'Brabancons' regardless of their actual origin. 'Routiers' were itinerant soldiers of fortune of very diverse backgrounds, known mainly for their greed and cruelty towards helpless civilians. It is of course quite likely that men would behave badly in a foreign country, surrounded by people of a different language and culture who must have seemed to them very alien, but it is also possible that foreign soldiers provided convenient scapegoats for crimes committed by others. Whatever the reason, mercenaries from the Continent received the blame for much of the damage caused to the country during the Anarchy, and they were expelled en masse by Henry II at its conclusion.

The most common infantry weapons were spears, swords and bows. In earlier centuries swords had been very expensive weapons, wielded only by the few who were able to afford them, but by the twelfth century advances in metalworking had made them cheaper and more widely available, so that they were no longer associated exclusively with the upper classes. However, the weapon which appears most often in the sources for Stephen's wars is the bow; in fact detached forces are sometimes described as consisting of 'knights and archers', as if infantry with other weapons were either not present or not considered to be important. Men of the knightly class did not usually employ bows for warfare, but this was not because these weapons were ineffective. Rather, the principal focus of the knight was fighting on horseback, even if in practice he often dismounted, and the English bow – unlike the shorter and handier composite bow of Asia – was not primarily a cavalry weapon. In any case, because the knights' offensive tactics relied on moving together in close formation, they would not have wished to risk the cohesion of these formations and the impact of the concerted charge by allowing individuals to pause to shoot. That is not to say that bows were never shot from horseback. They were routinely used by mounted aristocrats while hunting – William of Malmesbury says that William the Conqueror could draw his bow while at full gallop – and there are a few hints in the sources that mounted archers occasionally appeared on the battlefield. A single such figure is shown on the Bayeux Tapestry, and William of Jumieges refers to them at the Battle of Bourgtheroulde, which was fought in Normandy in 1124. However, we do not know whether the latter actually fought from horseback or whether, like the mounted longbowmen of later English armies, they rode into position and then dismounted to shoot. According to Robert of Torigny, in 1139 Earl Robert of Gloucester broke out of Arundel with an escort of ten knights and ten '*equestribus sagittariis*', 'equestrian archers', but in this case the purpose of mounting such a small contingent was surely so that they could keep up with the knights.

Few scholars today would accept Sir Charles Oman's thesis that the bows used in England before the adoption of the Welsh longbow under Edward I were short and lacking in power, but the exact nature of the weapons which saw service in the wars of the twelfth century remains obscure. Some writers have continued to argue that twelfth-century bows, though far from useless, were shorter and hence less powerful than the classic longbows of the fourteenth century onwards. In support of this the complete yew bow excavated at Waterford in Ireland in the 1980s has been frequently cited (e.g. Wadge 2012). Dating from around the end of the twelfth century, it is very short at 49in (1.25m), but it is not necessarily relevant to English practice, since it is known that the Irish had a tradition of using short bows: 'as short as half a bow of England' according to one source from 1397 (Heath). Medieval illustrations – notably the short weapons shown being drawn to the chest in the Bayeux Tapestry – are also sometimes cited in support not only of a later increase in bow lengths, but of a radical change in the late thirteenth century from the relatively weak draw to the chest to the more powerful one to the mouth or ear. However, Matthew Strickland (in Strickland & Hardy), in a chapter on 'The Iconography of the Bow', has argued persuasively that the stylized artwork of the early medieval era, heavily influenced by classical models, should not be compared with the more realistic portrayals which appear from the fourteenth century onwards. Artists used a variety of techniques to avoid obscuring their subjects' faces with the details of strings and arrow shafts, and the draw to the chest – though undoubtedly used on occasion in real life – was one of them. The apparent development in the proportions of the bow and the method of drawing it is therefore more in artistic styles than in the bows themselves.

More useful for assessing the effectiveness of archery are excavated medieval arrowheads, which naturally survive much better than the wooden bows or arrow shafts. Excavations on the site of a Norman castle at Goltho in Lincolnshire, estimated to date from some time before 1150, revealed a mixture of lozenge-shaped arrowheads and long pointed ones of the type which would later be referred to as 'bodkins' (Wadge). The former design had been in common use since pre-Conquest times, and could be considered as a general purpose arrowhead useful for warfare and hunting. The bodkin types, however, appear optimised for penetrating mail, and so are likely to be more purely military. Examination of socketed arrowheads should in theory enable us to estimate the thickness of the shafts they were fitted to, and hence the power of the bows that shot them, as a more powerful bow generally requires a thicker shaft to withstand the stress imposed by the string as the arrow is discharged. Unfortunately this is not an exact science, as so much depends on the wood used for the shaft, and such technical details as whether or not it was 'barrelled', or made thicker in the middle and tapered towards the ends. In any case most finds are not in good enough condition to enable precise measurement; the best the excavators could calculate for the Goltho arrows was that the two largest might have fitted shafts of about 10mm diameter, while the smallest was around 6mm. Finds from other early medieval sites such as Thetford in Norfolk and Wharram Percy in Yorkshire appear to confirm that arrows came in two broad size categories, with the thinner shafts, between 6mm and 8mm, being more commonly associated with small barbed heads, and the thicker ones, in the region of 10mm or 11mm, more likely to be found with military bodkin types (Wadge). This implies that there was already a class of what we might call military bows (or in later parlance 'longbows') which had higher draw weights than those used mainly for hunting. This seems logical, as military weapons were more likely to encounter armoured targets, but there was probably not a rigid distinction, and each archer probably used a bow suited to his own strength and ability.

Of course what we would like to know is what sort of draw weight a 10mm-thick shaft represents. Were these bows comparable in power to those used at Crécy, for example, or was Oman right to argue that archery before the fourteenth century was relatively ineffective? Ailred of Rievaulx describes the Galwegians at the Battle of the Standard as being struck by so many arrows that they resembled hedgehogs, but still on their feet and slashing about them in fury. The implication is clearly that the English bows were not powerful enough to kill a man outright. But as discussed below (page 70), the Galwegians might not have been quite as unprotected as we are led to believe. Several important Anglo-Norman lords, including Payne fitz John and Geoffrey de Mandeville, were killed by single arrow wounds while on campaign, and therefore presumably wearing armour, though most of these wounds appear to have been to the unprotected face. We are specifically told by William of Malmesbury that Henry I, who was once struck by an arrow while fighting the Welsh, was protected by his hauberk. In none of these cases do we have the data that would be required for a scientific assessment of the effectiveness of the bow, such as the range or the exact nature of the target area. It is even possible that in some cases, such as the death of Geoffrey de Mandeville, the weapon involved was a crossbow.

The most effective defence against archery for men lacking mail hauberks would seem to be a shield. And yet modern re-enactors and experimental archaeologists have conducted a number of tests on ancient and medieval shields, most of which have led to the conclusion that they were fairly easily defeated by arrows. For example Hilary Travis reports on tests which employed a bow of only 35lbs (17.5kg) draw weight against a reconstructed Roman shield made of 10mm thick plywood faced with linen (and so similar in thickness and materials, if not in shape, to a Norman shield) at ranges up to 60ft (18.28m). The arrows penetrated without difficulty, passing completely through at 30ft (9.14m), and leading the experimenter to conclude that Roman shields 'offered little protection against a close, flat-shot, direct arrow strike', though they might have slowed it enough to prevent it seriously wounding a mail-clad man behind it (Travis & Travis 2014). This test was carried out at very close range, and the shield was not covered with leather, which would have offered more resistance than the linen, but on the other hand the bow was relatively light. Godehardt et al likewise succeeded in penetrating a Roman '*scutum*' with a bow of around 50lbs (25kg) weight, concluding that a series of hits would quickly render the shield useless (in Molloy 2007). A verse quoted in *Heimskringla*, the Icelandic saga history of the kings of Norway, describing the Norwegian King Eystein's victory over a group of knights in Yorkshire in 1151, does imply that archery could be effective despite the opponent's use of shields to protect themselves: 'the arrow-shower like snow-drift flew, And the shield-covered foemen slew.' Conversely the Bayeux Tapestry shows multiple arrows sticking in the shields of English warriors who are obviously not *hors de combat*. Clearly much would have depended on unquantifiable factors such as the range, the strength of the archer, the construction of the shield and the angle at which the arrow struck. All that can be said with certainty is that archers were a highly-valued component of any army of the period, and as we shall see, at least one battle, at The Standard in 1138, was decided mainly by their shooting.

As mentioned above, at least some of the missile weapons used in Stephen's reign were probably crossbows, even though most of the evidence for these weapons in England dates from the reign of Henry II and his successors. The crossbow had been known in western Europe since early in the previous century, and the *Carmen de Hastingae Proelio* describes its use by the Normans at Hastings. The famous account by the Byzantine princess Anna Comnena (quoted in Strickland & Hardy) gives details of the crossbows used by the Franks in the First Crusade. These were simple wooden bows drawn by lying down with both feet on the bow itself and pulling back with both arms. The string was then hooked onto a latch, which was released by pulling a trigger. It appears that devices such as levers, belt hooks and stirrups for the feet, introduced to facilitate drawing the heavier later medieval versions, were not yet in use. This laborious method of drawing the crossbow made it slower to shoot and less suitable for mobile warfare than the ordinary bow, but in compensation it was possible for a man to manage a considerably higher draw weight. Anna Comnena describes the effects of this 'diabolical machine', which could send a bolt through shields, armour and even city walls: so great was its impact that 'the unfortunate man who is struck by it dies without feeling the blow'. Unlike ordinary arrows, crossbow bolts do seem to have been able to demolish shields fairly consistently. The *Carmen de Hastingae Proelio* specifically tells us that shields are no use against them, and that at Hastings the shields of the English were destroyed 'as if by a hailstorm'. This was an exceptional case, however, because Harold's army was standing on the defensive for most of the day, allowing plenty of time for the Norman missiles to take effect. The *Carmen* admits that the process required 'countless blows', and a similar opportunity did not arise in any of the battles of Stephen's reign. It is usually supposed that the high draw weight of a crossbow would give it a greater range than other bows, but Mike Loades (Loades 2013) disputes this, citing modern tests in which he was involved. Apparently the weight and poor aerodynamic properties of the crossbow's shorter bolt meant that it would lose velocity much more quickly than a longer arrow, so that it was ineffective beyond about 80 yards (73m). The main use of the crossbow was in sieges, when the user would usually have less need to shoot rapidly to prevent a charging enemy from overrunning him, and could make use of cover when loading and shooting. Because a crossbow, unlike an ordinary bow, could be left drawn and ready to shoot until the archer was ready, and could then be discharged with a minimum of movement simply by releasing a trigger, it was especially useful for men whom we would call snipers, detailed to pick off individual high-value targets. The highest value 'target' of the age was of course Henry II's son, Richard 'the Lionheart', who was fatally wounded by a crossbowman at the siege of Chalus in 1199.

Missile weapons generally were clearly regarded with disfavour by many of the ruling elite, though this was probably a testimony to their effectiveness, which enabled a low-born archer to kill his betters despite the armour in which they covered themselves. A surprising number of eminent men did meet their deaths by arrows or crossbow bolts during this period, whether in battle, or deliberately targeted by enemy sharpshooters, or in more dubious circumstances. Miles of Gloucester, for example, was shot in the chest by one of his companions while hunting deer on Christmas Eve 1143, a fate suspiciously similar to that which had befallen William Rufus in the New Forest in 1100. Hunting was obviously a dangerous activity, but that must have made it even more convenient as a way of disposing of a rival. Henry I had once ordered, presumably in an attempt to encourage archery, that a man who accidentally killed another while practising should not be charged with murder. But by the 1130s attitudes seem to have changed. The Lateran Council held in Rome in 1139 under the auspices of Pope Innocent II attempted to mitigate the effects of warfare, extending the prohibitions on fighting incorporated in the 'Peace of God', and prohibiting arson and attacks on non-combatants. It also singled out the 'murderous art of crossbowmen and archers, which is hateful to God', forbidding the use of their weapons against fellow Christians. Needless to say, all these pronouncements were routinely disregarded, despite the threat of excommunication for offenders. But four decades later Henry II was still legislating against archery, specifying in a decree of 1175 that no one was to carry bows and arrows in England east of the River Severn. Presumably he considered that on the Welsh Marches, west of the Severn, the need to defend against Welsh raids outweighed the potential risks of arming the people with such dangerous weapons. However, six years later, in his famous English Assize of Arms, Henry ignored the bow altogether, stating that non-knightly freemen were to be armed only with spears. It is clear that this was not because he regarded bows as ineffective, because in a similar decree for his Angevin and Norman territories, issued at Le Mans in 1180, he had ordered that the poorer classes should arm themselves with bows. The most plausible explanation of this inconsistency is that in England the prominence of archery in the wars of his predecessor's reign and more recent revolts against Henry himself, its association with mercenary troops, and perhaps its use as a means of attempted assassination, had left it with an unsavoury reputation. In fact John of Hexham says that Henry singled out archery in his final peace agreement with Stephen in 1153, when he insisted that all 'mercenary soldiers and archers of foreign nations' should be expelled from the kingdom.

Although the bow and crossbow were predominant, other missile weapons were also in use, at least in siege warfare. We frequently hear of men throwing spears from castle walls, and the Bury Bible shows troops in armour – so obviously not poor men who possessed no other weapons – apparently throwing stones. The *Gesta Stephani* says that at the siege of Exeter in 1136 Stephen had a corps of 'innumerable' slingers, who made the defenders' lives intolerable with a rain of stones. The appearance of these slingers was apparently unusual, since the *Gesta* goes on to explain that the king had hired them from an unspecified 'distant region', but they are occasionally mentioned in English sources at least as late as the beginning of the fourteenth century. In 1303 Edward I raised slingers from Sherwood Forest in Nottinghamshire, which might give a clue to the origin of Stephen's contingent. According to Matthew Paris, if slingers accompanied a field army they were always placed in front – perhaps because being lightly-equipped, lower-class soldiers they were considered expendable. They did, however, have their advantages. In most places there would be an endless supply of stones to use as ammunition, and a sling used by a skilled practitioner could inflict serious damage even on armoured men. Froissart, describing their effects in Spain in the wars of the fourteenth century, refers to iron helmets being split in half. However, we do not hear of slingers being used in pitched battles in this period, probably because it was recognized that their missiles, although annoying in a protracted bombardment, were not capable of stopping a charge. Archers solved this problem by deploying behind or within bodies of spearmen or dismounted knights, but a sling would need too much space for this tactic to be viable.

The Laws of War and the Peace of God
Despite the formidable array of weaponry which could be deployed, battle casualties among the nobility in Stephen's wars were surprisingly light. After the pitched battles at Lincoln and Winchester we read of numerous prisoners being taken – including the king himself at Lincoln and Robert of Gloucester at Winchester – but not of large numbers of knights killed. This is in sharp

contrast to the mass slaughter of non-knightly participants on the losing side, such as the city militia at Lincoln. When prominent figures in the wars did lose their lives, it was generally at the hands of ordinary foot soldiers, such as the archer who shot Geoffrey de Mandeville in 1143, or the man who decapitated Robert Marmion in the following year. In his account of the Battle of Bremule, fought between Henry I and Louis VI of France in 1119, Orderic Vitalis offers an explanation for the low knightly casualties which are such a striking feature of the period. Apart from the fact that the knights were all protected by armour, he says, they deliberately spared each other 'out of fear of God and fellowship in arms'. This sense of 'fellowship' among a small and inter-related class of men may have been a genuine factor, and it is interesting to note that such restraint does not appear in war against cultural outsiders such as the Welsh and the Scots, but Orderic ignores what must surely have been a more important consideration, which was the value of the ransom that could be demanded from the family and followers of a wealthy prisoner. The custom of demanding ransom money was increasingly popular in the twelfth century, and in subsequent decades was to give rise to the craze for tournaments. At that time the tournament was not a closely-regulated sport involving jousting in the lists, but a sort of ritualized warfare in which the objective was to capture other participants and release them in exchange for large amounts of money, which many knights made into a successful career.

Several contemporary sources quote references to rules which were supposed to govern conflict, at least between rival Christians. Henry of Huntingdon, for example, says that after the Battle of Lincoln the victors sacked the city 'according to the law that governs hostilities'. These isolated references cannot be taken as evidence for a formal set of written laws, and certainly nothing of this sort has survived. There was, however, general agreement that there were rules, for example governing the fair treatment of garrisons which surrendered on terms. The chroniclers, who were invariably priests or monks, deplored such actions as the massacre of non-combatants and the destruction of churches – though unfortunately they all too often had to record them – as being contrary to what was understood to be the will of God. But attempts to put this vague agreement on a more formal basis were not successful. The movement within the Catholic Church known as the Peace and/or Truce of God began on the Continent in the tenth century, and is usually interpreted as a reaction against the disorder which followed the collapse of the Carolingian Empire. It was promulgated by various church synods, and given Papal sanction at the Council of Clermont in 1095, at which Pope Urban II launched the First Crusade. The Peace of God was intended to be a permanent prohibition on fighting and applied, for example, to Sundays and feast days, and to the vicinity of churches and other holy places. Women, the clergy and men working in the fields were not to be attacked under any circumstances. Its protection was gradually extended until by the middle of the twelfth century it was theoretically forbidden to fight at all from nightfall on Wednesdays to dawn on Mondays, on the Church's feast days, or during Lent or Advent – altogether on more than three days out of every four in the year. In theory the penalty for breaking these rules was excommunication, but in practice – like the Lateran Council's bans on bows and crossbows – they were unenforceable, and there are few if any indications that either Stephen or his opponents ever took them seriously. The Battle of Lincoln, for example, was fought on one of the holiest days in the calendar, being the Feast of the Purification of St Mary as well as a Sunday.

Heraldry

Heraldry, in the sense of a device borne on a shield which was identified with a particular individual and his family, is popularly associated with the medieval knight, but was in its infancy in this period. The earliest evidence of a formal system of heraldry is generally thought to be the blue shield decorated with golden lions which John of Marmoutier says was given to Geoffrey of Anjou when he was knighted by Henry I in 1128. A version of this design was depicted on Geoffrey's tomb when he died in 1151, and it was later associated with his illegitimate grandson William Longespee, suggesting that it was regarded as Geoffrey's personal property and could be inherited by his descendants (Slater). The seals of a few other leading figures of Stephen's reign show their owners carrying shields with devices of the sort later used in the system of heraldry, and in some cases the same or similar devices were later adopted by their families, but there is no evidence that they were permanently associated with their bearers as early as the mid-twelfth century. It is noteworthy that although the seals of Waleran of Meulan and his son Robert both show shields decorated with what appear to be simple geometrical patterns (apparently chequered in Waleran's case), they are quite different from each other. Among ordinary knights and non-noble soldiers shield patterns were presumably a matter of individual choice, and many if not most shields may have borne no decorations or insignia at all. The faces of the shields depicted in the Bury Bible are all plain, as is that on Stephen's great seal, and most of those in the famous illustration of the king at the Battle of Lincoln in the chronicle of Henry of Huntingdon. The slightly later Winchester Bible, believed to have been completed in the 1160s, shows a number of simple patterns such as crosses and chevrons, while chevrons also appear in an illustration of Henry I's knights in the chronicle of John of Worcester, and on the shield carried by one figure in Henry of Huntingdon's picture.

It is usually supposed that heraldry was introduced alongside the full face-guards and enclosed helmets which began to appear later in the twelfth century, so that leaders could be identified on the battlefield even when their faces were not visible. However, identification had been a problem even with the earlier nasal helmets, as is shown by the incident at Hastings reported by William of Poitiers when William the Conqueror was forced to lift his helmet to counter rumours that he was dead. The author of the *Gesta Stephani* remarks that at the siege of Exeter 'among so many clad in mail it was impossible easily to distinguish one from another', which certainly suggests that the use of shield devices to identify individual knights or their followings was not yet common.

Chapter 5

Wales Liberated

The risings in the south-west of England may have been closer to home, and Normandy may have seemed of more immediate importance both as the Anglo-Norman homeland and as a source of wealth and manpower, but the worst setback to Stephen in the first two years of his reign occurred in Wales. Politically the situation in that country was already extremely volatile. Anglo-Norman chroniclers tended to write as if they owned the place; the author of the *Gesta Stephani*, for example, tells how the Norman conquerors of England had 'added it to their dominion', and elsewhere refers to the Welsh as rebelling against their 'masters'. But in fact the country was by no means conquered, even if its leaders had intermittently acknowledged a vague English overlordship since the days of the Anglo-Saxon kings. William I had established some of his most powerful barons along the frontier at Chester, Shrewsbury and Hereford as semi-autonomous marcher lords (they alone could build castles without royal permission, for example), with the aim of controlling the Welsh and gradually extending their authority westwards. Another Norman lordship at Pembroke in the far south-west of Wales, in the region which the Welsh knew as Dyfed, held one of the country's few extensive tracts of good agricultural land and had largely been occupied by Flemish settlers under Norman overlordship. But elsewhere native Welsh principalities retained their independence. Most eminent among these were Deheubarth in the south-west, Powys adjoining the English counties of Shropshire and Cheshire in the centre of the country, and Gwynedd in the north-west. Between Deheubarth and the English border in the south-east lay the smaller principalities of Brycheiniog, Morgannwg and Gwent. These larger entities were subdivided into '*cantrefs*', of which there were around fifty altogether, each led by its own minor prince or '*uchelwr*'. Not only the major principalities but even the *cantrefs* within each of them were frequently in dispute with one another, and mutual raiding, especially for cattle, was endemic; indeed their own chronicler Gerald de Barri identified their disunity as the greatest vulnerability of the Welsh.

The *Gesta* says that as soon as Henry I died, and in parallel with the disturbances which were breaking out in England, armed bands of Welshmen began to attack the Norman-occupied areas in the south. Their raids culminated in a battle fought in January 1136 on the coastal plain, probably on the Gower Peninsula not far from Swansea, in which 516 Norman troops, both knights and infantry, were surrounded and massacred. The Welsh annals name the commander at this battle as Hywell ap Meredudd of Brycheiniog ('ap' means 'son of', like the Anglo-Norman 'fitz'). Encouraged by this victory, the whole south of the country rose against the English. Then in the spring a column of troops marched into Wales from Hereford under the command of Richard fitz Gilbert de Clare, the lord of Cardigan. His castle at Cardigan on the west coast of Wales, which was presumably his objective, guarded the valuable anchorage at the mouth of the River Teifi as well as the northern approaches to Pembroke. Exactly what Richard's intentions were is unclear, and the author of the *Gesta* reports a rumour that he was actually planning a war against the king, who had refused his request for a grant of land as a reward for his assistance at Exeter. It is equally possible, of course, that he was concerned about the threat posed by the Welsh uprising to his own lordship. But it seems that it was by accident that about the middle of April he ran into a Welsh army led by Iorwerth and Morgan, two sons of Owain of Gwynllwg, and was killed while passing through a wood at Coed Grwyne, near Abergavenny on the borders of Brycheiniog and Gwent; the *Gesta* says that Richard 'alone of his company' died, which certainly does not suggest a determined attack, though it might of course have been a carefully-targeted assassination. Gerald de Barri gives a rather different account, according to which Richard had sent back most of his escort and ridden unarmed into the forest, accompanied by a singer and a fiddler to announce his arrival. The only rational explanation for this is that he was worried about random attacks by bandits or Welsh partisans, but believed that he would be safe if he identified himself and made it plain that he was coming in peace. In this he was seriously mistaken, because Gerald says that Iorwerth ambushed him in order to steal his baggage, killing Richard and most of his companions. Whatever the circumstances, the outcome of Richard's death was a general uprising of nearly all the leading Welsh princes. The first to move was Gruffydd ap Rhys of Deheubarth, who had always resented the establishment of Cardigan Castle in what had traditionally been his predecessors' territory. He rode north to Gwynedd to ask for the assistance of his father-in-law, Gruffydd ap Cynan, leaving his wife Gwenllian in command at home.

Unfortunately Gwenllian was not content to wait for reinforcements from her father, but instead raised her own army, and together with her sons Morgan and Maelgwn attacked the Norman castle at Kidwelly, south of Carmarthen. They were outmanoeuvred and their camp captured, allegedly thanks to the treachery of a local Welsh chief, and Maelgwn was killed by Norman troops. Gwenllian and Morgan were taken prisoner and executed as traitors. If Gruffydd ap Cynan had been wavering, the news of this disaster made up his mind. He sent an army from Gwynedd marching south under his sons Owain and Cadwaladr to join in the attack on Cardigan. They captured the Norman castles at Llanfihangel and Aberystwyth, rounded up large numbers of cattle and other loot, and took this back to Gwynedd before returning in September, this time accompanied by Gruffydd ap Rhys with the men of Deheubarth. Meanwhile Stephen had made two rather half-hearted attempts to restore his authority in Wales, neither of which achieved anything significant. Baldwin fitz Gilbert, Richard's younger brother, was despatched to defend his brother's land, and according to the *Gesta Stephani* was provided by the king with a large sum of money to raise fresh troops. He recruited 500 archers and an unknown number of knights and advanced to Brecon. But when he discovered that the Welsh under the command of Morgan ap Owain, one of his brother's killers, were in the field 'in countless numbers', and that they had blocked the roads by felling trees across them, he appears to have lost his nerve. He advanced no further, but waited in Brecon until his money ran out, then retreated. Another minor marcher lord, Robert fitz Harold of Ewyas, showed more courage. He fought his way as far as the castle at Carmarthen, which guarded the eastern frontier of Pembrokeshire, but finding himself isolated he left a garrison there and rode back to England with a small escort to raise more troops. He never returned, apparently because of a shortage of money, and eventually the Welsh overwhelmed the garrison and destroyed the castle.

Welsh Armies

The author of the *Gesta* deals with events in Wales only in the first year or so of Stephen's reign, when the country was in open rebellion. He shares his countrymen's characteristic prejudices against the Welsh, describing them as '*bestialium*', or animal-like, and ascribing the productivity of the country purely to the Normans who had colonized it since the conquest. He adds that it was mainly a land of woods and pasture, devoted to raising livestock rather than to the arable farming that the Normans equated with civilization. Hence the inhabitants were semi-nomadic, naturally swift-footed and warlike, but unreliable, changing their allegiances as often as they changed their abodes. They were 'addicted to every crime', and of course they had a 'deadly hatred' for the English. Much of what we know more reliably about the twelfth-century

Welsh comes from Gerald de Barri, whose *Description of Wales*, written about 1193, was probably the first serious ethnographic study to have been published since classical times. Though written fifty years after the wars of Stephen's reign, it is the nearest that we have to a contemporary account, and it is unlikely that much had changed in military matters; in fact the author emphasizes that much of the difference between the Anglo-Normans and the Welsh was due to what he presents as the primitive and unchanging nature of Welsh society. Another difference was the Welsh language, which remains a source of pride to this day, but which few English people have ever regarded as worth studying. Gerald was one of the first to argue that it was descended from the language spoken by the original Britons, though he also tried – not very convincingly – to establish a close relationship with Greek. At the time he wrote Gerald was employed in the service of Henry II, and part of his work is devoted to a discussion of how the English could best combat Welsh tactics, but as a native Welshman he was naturally more sympathetic to the people than most of his contemporaries, and indeed his career later suffered because of suspicions that he was too pro-Welsh.

In essence, however, Gerald confirms the impression given by the *Gesta Stephani*. Although there are fertile farmlands in Anglesey and the south, he says, most of the country is mountainous and more suitable for raising cattle than cereals. Hence the people live on meat and milk rather than bread. Their only cereal crop is oats, which are relatively easy to cultivate, and because they are not obliged to spend all their time labouring in the fields, and have almost no commerce or industry, the men can dedicate their lives to training for war. Warfare was not the preserve of a particular social class, but all free men possessed weapons and were eager to use them: 'Sound the trumpet for battle and the peasant will rush from his plough to pick up his weapons as quickly as the courtier from the court.' Gerald quotes Henry II himself as informing the Byzantine emperor that 'In one part of the island there is a race of people called the Welsh, who are so brave and untamed that, though unarmed themselves, they do not hesitate to do battle with fully armed opponents.' Their frugal lifestyle also prepared them for military life, as they were accustomed to going without food, and if they had nothing to eat one day they would wait patiently until the next. They were also used to being outdoors in bad weather and at night, and would take advantage of dark and stormy nights to spy on their enemies. Their clothing consisted only of a tunic and a light cloak which did not hamper their movements, and they often travelled barefoot or made crude boots from untanned leather. They cut their hair short or even shaved their heads completely, in order, says Gerald, to 'avoid the fate of Absalom', who according to the Second Book of Samuel was plucked off his mule when his head caught in the branches of a tree. Gerald quotes Julius Caesar's description of the Britons painting their faces for war, but he does not suggest that the Welsh of his day still did so.

Most Welsh warriors were lightly armed, partly because of the relative poverty of the country, but also in order to maintain their mobility in difficult terrain. Gerald describes them as wearing iron helmets and sometimes leg protectors, or greaves, but mentions only leather body armour, perhaps meaning hide-covered gambesons, which were worn as a substitute for mail; in fact contemporary illustrations tend to show Welshmen without any armour at all (Heath). Leaders, Gerald says, might go into battle mounted, but most men preferred to fight on foot, and even the horsemen would frequently dismount if the situation called for it. Instead of the Anglo-Norman kite shields the Welsh carried small round bucklers, which they traditionally used in conjunction with a sword. William le Breton, writing early in the thirteenth century, also mentions two-handed axes, which may have been adopted under Viking influence. However, by the time Gerald wrote the characteristic weapons of the Welsh infantry were long spears, which were especially favoured in the northern half of the country, and bows in the south. The men from Merioneth and Cynan were especially skilful with the spear. Despite its length this weapon could be thrown like a javelin, in which role it was extremely effective because of the penetrating power conferred by the weight of the long shaft. A famous passage in Gerald's earlier work, the *Journey Through Wales*, written around 1188, describes Welsh expertise with the bow. The men of Gwent, he says, are more experienced in warfare generally than their countrymen, as well as being better archers. He illustrates this with two anecdotes, the first of which took place at the siege of Abergavenny Castle in 1182. Two English soldiers were running to take cover in a tower while their Welsh pursuers shot at them with arrows. Several of these arrows struck the oak door of the tower, which was 'almost the space of a palm' ('*palmalis fere spissitudinis transpenetrarunt*', presumably meaning as thick as a man's palm is across, which would make it about 4in [10cm]), and went right through it, a feat so unusual that the arrows were left in the door afterwards to commemorate it. On another occasion a mounted knight was hit by an arrow which penetrated his thigh, despite the armour which covered it both inside and outside, then went through his wooden saddle and killed the horse. Another soldier was nailed to his saddle by arrows through each leg. Even a crossbow, Gerald adds, could hardly do more.

He goes on to describe the weapons that performed these feats, which were not made of yew, or horn, or '*alburnum*' (a term usually translated as 'sapwood', though what it means in this context is not clear), nor even polished to give them a pleasing finish, as presumably his English readers would have expected. Instead the Welsh cut them from the stunted elm trees which grew on the hillsides, and left them rough and unpolished. Nevertheless they could not only shoot a long distance but also inflict serious wounds at close range. (This passage has been translated in various ways, giving rise to some confusion. Thorpe, in the Penguin Classics edition of the *Journey Through Wales*, has 'You could not shoot far with them'. However, the original Latin is fairly unambiguous: '*non tantum ad eminus missilia mittenda, sed etiam . . .*') Elm was in fact a popular wood for making bows in the Middle Ages, though regarded as slightly inferior to yew; according to one modern bowyer the difference is not so much in performance as in the fact that elm is less durable and more likely to break, which might explain why the Welsh craftsmen deliberately left their bows unfinished, in order to avoid weakening them by removing any more wood than was strictly necessary. There is no reason to suppose that either the bows or the expertise of the archers were new in Gerald's day, though we have only isolated references to Welsh archery in and before Stephen's reign. William of Malmesbury and the *Brut y Tywysogyon* both describe incidents (or possibly the same incident) in which Henry I was struck by an arrow while on campaign against the Welsh, though he was saved from injury by his hauberk. According to William of Malmesbury his assailant shot at him from a distance and then escaped; the king for some reason was insistent that it was an English traitor rather than a Welshman who had attacked him, but it was clear that his followers had automatically assumed otherwise (Strickland & Hardy). Payne fitz John was killed by a Welsh missile which struck him in the head in 1137, though we are not told what sort of missile this was, and it might have been a thrown spear rather than an arrow.

This image of the lightly-equipped Welsh skirmisher, however, was not the whole story. Every prince maintained his '*teulu*' or body of household retainers, recruited from young men of noble birth, many of whom were his relatives ('*teulu*' literally means 'family'). They wore armour and fought from horseback with lances and swords, but they may not always have been as well equipped as the typical Anglo-Norman knight, and they must usually have comprised a relatively small proportion of any Welsh army: Ian Heath argues that the average strength of a *teulu* was only around 120 men. In fact mounted men may not always have been present; the *Gesta Stephani* specifically says that the large Welsh contingent which accompanied Robert of Gloucester to Tetbury in 1144 consisted of men on foot. Welsh rulers also employed foreign mercenaries, principally from Ireland; during their dynastic quarrel in the 1140s Owain ap Gruffydd of Gwynedd and his brother Cadwaladr both hired several shiploads of 'Ostmen' (Norwegian Vikings) from Dublin.

In another work, the *Conquest of Ireland*, Gerald de Barri again contrasts the tactical methods of the Welsh and Irish on the one hand and the Normans on the other. The latter, he says, prefer to fight in open country and value heavy armour, whereas the Celts favour rough and wooded terrain, and consider armour to be a burden. They win by mobility, while their opponents win by standing firm. The Normans aim to capture knights for ransom, but the Welsh and Irish behead them. In the *Description of Wales* he adds that in battle the Welsh make the first attack with great ferocity, yelling and blowing trumpets before launching a headlong charge accompanied by a shower of javelins. However, if the enemy stands firm, they cannot sustain a protracted fight but immediately retreat: 'their sole idea of tactics is either to pursue their opponents, or else to run away from them'. But although it is easy enough to beat them in a single battle, it is much harder to win a long war against them, because they are not discouraged by defeat but will return to the fray undaunted. It is also dangerous to chase after Welsh troops even when they flee, as their archers are as expert as the Parthians at shooting behind them to pick off unwary pursuers. A very similar account is given of the tactics of Scottish armies (see pages 69–72), which has led some commentators to suggest that this image of the lightly-equipped, rashly-charging Celt versus the steady, disciplined Norman or Englishman is no more than a topos or a racial stereotype. It is, of course, a dichotomy that appears in numerous sources from Greek and Roman descriptions of the European Celts to the Battle of Culloden in 1746, but its widespread recurrence need not mean that it lacks any basis in fact. For the twelfth century we have the entirely independent accounts of Gerald de Barri for the Welsh and Irish and Ailred of Rievaulx and others for the Galwegians and other Scots, and in both cases we have a plausible explanation based on the economies of the societies concerned and their geographical location. That people living in mountainous, high-rainfall areas which favoured cattle-raising rather than arable farming were necessarily poorer or more 'primitive' is certainly an unfair stereotype, but that their lifestyle would favour mobility and lightness of equipment is not at all unlikely.

The Battle of Crug Mawr

The failure of the counter-attacks of the summer of 1136 left the Normans in south-west Wales isolated in the face of the fresh invasion from the north. The total strength of the combined army of Gwynedd and Deheubarth is not known, but it must have considerably outnumbered the garrison at Cardigan. The decisive battle was fought on and around the hill now known as Banc-y-Warren, near the village of Penparc about two miles north-east of Cardigan. In medieval times this feature was called Crug Mawr, often translated as the 'Big Hill', although the word 'crug' also seems to have been used for a barrow or tumulus. In fact the place was a famous landmark long before the battle, and Gerald says that there was an ancient tumulus on the top which allegedly had magical powers. It might, therefore, have been deliberately chosen as a battlefield by one or both sides. The precise command arrangements of the armies are not clear; as is often the case with twelfth-century battles, we are given the names of the leading men without any indication of a precise chain of command. The Normans were Robert fitz Martin, lord of Cemais, Stephen, the constable of Cardigan Castle, and two brothers, William Carew and Maurice fitz Gerald. As Sir John Lloyd suggests in his *History of Wales*, the loss of Richard fitz Gilbert, who would have been in command if he had lived, may have been a contributory factor in the Norman defeat. Of the three named leaders on the Welsh side, Gruffydd ap Rhys was probably the oldest as well as the highest in rank, though he may have had no formal authority over the Gwynedd contingent under Owain and Cadwaladr.

All we know for certain about the Battle of Crug Mawr is that the Welsh allies put the Anglo-Norman army to flight. Several modern writers suggest that the victory was due to the superiority of the Welsh archers, and even that Crug Mawr 'marked the arrival of the longbow into medieval warfare' (battlefieldsofbritain.co.uk). Leonard James, for example, has attributed the Welsh victory to the ability of their archers to outrange the English, but this is not supported by any contemporary accounts. The theory appears to be based on the account of Welsh archery given by Gerald de Barri, who was writing fifty years later and was not specifically referring to this battle at all. In any case Gerald says that the men of Gwynedd, who must have comprised a large proportion of the army at Crug Mawr, were not archers but spearmen. The Welsh victory was probably attributable more to superior numbers, and perhaps their ability to outflank a Norman defensive position on the hill with their superior mobility, than to any advantage in weaponry. They pursued their enemies into the town of Cardigan and set fire to the buildings. Many of the English fled over a narrow bridge across the River Teifi, and were drowned when it collapsed under their weight. Others had taken refuge in the Church of the Holy Trinity and died when it caught fire. It may be significant that none of their commanders were killed or captured; possibly they had left the field before the general rout began, and their lack of resolution may even have been a factor in the Anglo-Norman defeat. Robert fitz Martin reached safety in the castle, but was trapped there, along with Richard fitz Gilbert's widow, by the triumphant Welsh.

Lloyd remarks that the Welsh victory would have had less long-term significance if it had been won during the lifetime of Henry I, because the beleaguered Anglo-Normans would have held out in the expectation of a relieving army arriving promptly from England. But they had less confidence in Stephen, a view in which they turned out to be fully justified. Several modern scholars have suggested that the king should have led an army into Wales himself in the summer, instead of sending unreliable subordinates like Baldwin fitz Gilbert or relying on weak and poorly-funded operations like that of Robert fitz Harold. At the time Stephen was fully occupied with the rebellion of Baldwin de Redvers and the siege of Exeter, but that, it can be argued, merely indicates his failure to grasp strategic priorities. David Crouch has pointed out that most of the great marcher lords who had responsibility for affairs in Wales were with the king at Exeter, and should at the very least have been released to do the job that they had been appointed for. Stephen's only recorded response to the catastrophe – quoted in the *Gesta Stephani* – was to decide not to waste more resources on trying to reconquer Wales, but to do nothing: to 'endure their insolent rebellion' and hope that they might fall out with each other or be weakened by famine. Both these things did happen, but it would be many years before the English position in Wales was restored to what it had been at Stephen's accession. Some of the marcher lords did attempt a more positive response on their own initiative. Robert of Gloucester went to South Wales and made what peace deals he could, notably securing the nominal allegiance of Morgan ap Owain in return for surrendering extensive lands on the frontier which he could probably not have held anyway. Miles of Gloucester led a mounted force from Brecon to relieve Cardigan and rescue Richard fitz Gilbert's wife, but he was unable to hold the town and quickly returned to safety in England. Payn fitz John made a similar march to relieve Carmarthen in the spring of 1137, but the attempt was abandoned after he was killed on the way, apparently the victim of another Welsh sniper. The *Gesta* says that like Richard fitz Gilbert he was the only one of his company to die. Shot in the head while 'pursuing the Welsh', he was perhaps the victim of a feigned flight designed to lure him into an ambush. Bearing in mind the similar fate of Richard, and the apparent targeting of Henry I mentioned above, it seems that it was a common, and evidently effective, Welsh practice in this war to pick off the leader of an enemy force before bringing it to battle.

Normandy

In March 1137, while the English position in Wales was collapsing, Stephen was en route to Normandy, which was under threat from the ambitions of Count Geoffrey of Anjou. The expeditionary force consisted of a contingent of Norman knights and a large force of Flemish mercenaries led by a commander of their own nationality, William of Ypres. The barons of Normandy had always been more unruly than those of England, and Stephen first had to suppress a number of minor local rebellions before he began negotiations with his brother Theobald and King Louis VI of France with the aim of consolidating his hold on the duchy. Theobald agreed not to contest Stephen's claims as King of England and Duke of Normandy, while the king's son Eustace did homage to Louis for Normandy, thus securing formal French recognition of his father's position. Stephen then advanced to deal with Geoffrey, who had invaded Normandy in May with a large army and inflicted considerable damage on the countryside. However, there were growing tensions within the royal army between the Normans and the Flemings, and when it arrived at Lisieux a fight broke out over a barrel of wine which some Flemish soldiers were accused of stealing. Several Norman barons then deserted, and although Stephen managed to restore order, it was clear that he was now too weak to confront the Angevin army in the field. He therefore made peace with Geoffrey, effectively buying him off for three years. The king then returned to England, where he was to remain for the rest of his reign. Henry of Huntingdon describes the campaign as an unqualified success, telling how Stephen 'thwarted the plots of his enemies, he destroyed enemy castles, he shone brilliantly among commanders'. But in fact, as often happened in Stephen's wars, he had failed to finish the job. The threat from Geoffrey of Anjou – and of course from his wife Matilda – had only been postponed.

Bedford

Soon after Stephen's return from Normandy he became embroiled in what was to be a long-running dispute over the castle of Bedford. This strategically-important site overlooking the crossing of the River Ouse had been strongly fortified by Henry I, who had entrusted it to Simon de Beauchamp. The *Gesta Stephani* describes the castle as a formidable construction, 'surrounded by a very lofty mound, encircled by a strong and high wall, [and] fortified with a strong and unshakeable keep'. At the time of Stephen's accession it was held by Simon's nephew Miles de Beauchamp, who had come to regard it as a hereditary possession. However, this view was evidently not shared by Stephen, who considered that as Simon had only been appointed to govern the place on Henry's behalf, it remained a royal castle which the king could dispose of as he wished. The legal rights and wrongs of the case are perhaps of less interest to us than the fact that even before Matilda made her bid for power the Norman barons were already encroaching on the rights of the king in order to build up their local power bases. Simon died in 1137, and Stephen arranged the marriage of his daughter to Hugh 'the Poor', the younger brother of Waleran and Robert de Beaumont, to whom he gave the title of Earl of Bedford. While holding his Christmas court, the king sent messengers to Miles de Beauchamp ordering him to hand over the castle to its new earl. But Miles, despite being promised substantial compensation, refused to do so. Stephen was furious, and although it was the middle of winter he lost no time in gathering an army and laying siege to Bedford.

The *Gesta* tells how Miles, who must have been expecting such a reaction, embarked on a ruthless scorched-earth campaign, confiscating all the supplies he could from the townspeople and the neighbouring countryside and collecting them inside the castle walls. When Stephen arrived he established a close blockade, with barons delegated to watch every entrance in order to prevent further supplies being brought in or the garrison making a sortie. He then posted archers opposite vulnerable points, ordering them to approach as close as they could to the walls and shoot constant volleys on a high trajectory to keep the sentries' heads down. The king then set about constructing siege engines. The *Gesta* describes these as being of 'different sorts', but all were designed to damage or break down the '*vallum*' and the '*murum*'. The latter term is customarily used for a castle or city wall, usually made of stone, while '*vallum*' more generally refers to an earthwork or wooden palisade, of the sort which the Roman legions had used to protect their camps. It is therefore possible that the *Gesta* is telling us that the perimeter of the castle was not entirely of stone, but at least in part consisted of something like an earthen bank topped with wooden stakes. But even if this was the case Stephen's engines evidently failed to inflict significant damage, because he soon realized that he could not take the place quickly, and left a force behind to continue the blockade while he left to deal with 'other affairs of the kingdom'. The siege continued for another five weeks, by which time the garrison was starving and agreed to surrender. Unfortunately for the king, however, this model operation was not to have lasting results, because by 1141 Miles was back in charge of Bedford and Hugh 'the Poor' had been evicted.

Chapter 6

Scotland Resurgent

The 'other affairs' which took Stephen away from Bedford included the first rumblings of trouble in Northumbria, where his authority was also being challenged – but this time not by dissident barons but by his most formidable external enemy, David I of Scotland. Hostilities between England and Scotland already had a long history. David was a younger son of the great Scottish king Malcolm Canmore and his second wife Queen Margaret, later canonised as Saint Margaret, who had ruled Scotland together for three decades until the deaths of both in 1093. Margaret was descended from the pre-Conquest royal house of England, and her brother Edgar was regarded by Anglo-Saxon loyalists until his death in about 1125 as the 'Aetheling', or legitimate heir to the English throne. Malcolm and Margaret had been responsible for far-reaching reforms in their kingdom, especially in religious affairs, where the Scottish church was obliged to conform much more closely to the practices of mainstream Roman Christianity. Inevitably, however, their main preoccupation was their relationship with the new Norman conquerors of England. In 1070, when the north of England had risen in revolt against William the Conqueror and a Danish army was operating in East Anglia, Malcolm raised an army and invaded England, apparently in support of Edgar the Aetheling's cause, but when it became clear that the uprising had failed and the Danes were prepared to make peace with William, the Scots withdrew. In 1072 William advanced into Scotland, but the two kings met at Abernethy and negotiated a peace deal by which Malcolm recognized William as King of England, and handed over hostages in exchange for a grant of some feudal estates in England whose revenue would maintain him on his visits to the English court. This was not, however, a treaty between equals. Since Anglo-Saxon times Scottish kings had generally acknowledged the vague overlordship of the English monarchs, and although this fell short of actually requiring the homage due to a feudal superior, the fact that Malcolm was envisaged as attending William's court, rather than vice versa, suggests that

William at least saw Malcolm as in some sense his vassal. In 1074 the Aetheling arrived in Scotland and tried again to win support for an attempt to regain the throne, but Malcolm and Margaret refused to help him, and eventually persuaded him to make his peace with William. At the same time the royal couple embarked on a policy of encouraging Anglo-Norman immigrants to settle in Scotland, their aim being to provide a counterbalance to the power of the local magnates, and to strengthen the Scottish monarchy by placing it at the pinnacle of the sort of feudal hierarchy that the Normans had imposed on England. They were also well aware of the military potential of the armoured Norman cavalry, and hoped to supplement the mercenaries who been serving in Scottish armies for the previous half-century with their own more reliable vassals.

After the accession of William Rufus in 1087 Anglo-Scottish relations became more volatile, at least in part because Norman settlers were now moving into parts of Cumberland and Northumberland that the Anglo-Saxon kings had only tenuously controlled and which their Scottish counterparts had traditionally regarded as part of their sphere of influence. Then in 1091 Rufus broke his father's agreement with Edgar the Aetheling, who was forced yet again to seek asylum in Scotland. Malcolm responded by marching south and besieging Durham, but when Rufus marched to meet him the two sides again made peace. It appears that either the Conqueror's promise to grant Malcolm estates in England had not been made good, or Rufus had reneged on it, because their restoration was again one of the terms of the agreement. Some historians have suggested that Malcolm was also offered Cumberland, only for William Rufus to immediately occupy Carlisle and build a castle there, which had the effect of blocking the Scottish king's access to the lands that he had just been promised. But whatever the location of the grants involved Malcolm obviously felt that he had been double-crossed, because in August 1093 he travelled to Rufus' court, which was then at Gloucester, to press his claims. Rufus apparently not only refused to meet Malcolm, but insulted him by suggesting that he should submit his claims to the assembled barons, implying that the English monarch regarded him as of no higher rank than the rest of his feudal vassals. Malcolm hurried back to Scotland to muster an army, and by the end of October he and his son and heir, Edward, were leading raiding parties across the border to harry Northumbria. But on 12 November, at Alnwick on the Northumbrian coast, the Scots were ambushed by a force of knights led by a local magnate, Robert de Mowbray. Malcolm was killed, and Edward, although he escaped from the field, died soon afterwards from his wounds. Queen Margaret, who was already ill, died at Edinburgh shortly after hearing the news. Subsequent events showed how the question of relations with England had polarised opinion in Scotland. Malcolm was succeeded by his brother Donald III, who favoured native Scots over the Anglo-Normans who had dominated his predecessor's court, and was consequently driven from the throne after only a year by Duncan II, a son of Malcolm Canmore by his first wife, who was supported by an English army. Although he was forced to promise not to bring in any more Englishmen, Duncan's reliance on foreign troops so infuriated his own people that he was assassinated after only six months, and Donald returned to power. Then in 1097 a younger son of Malcolm and Margaret, Edgar, invaded with the backing of another English army (commanded, according to the *Anglo-Saxon Chronicle*, by Edgar the Aetheling, once again briefly reconciled with William Rufus), captured Donald and established himself on the throne. Edgar reigned until 1107, and no doubt because he was happy to accept a subordinate position, relations with England were largely peaceful. In 1100 he married his sister Edith to William Rufus' successor, Henry I.

Malcolm and Margaret's youngest son David, who had been brought up at the English court for the last seven years following the deaths of his parents, then suddenly found himself, at the age of about 19, raised from relative obscurity to a position of importance there as the brother of the queen. In 1113 he married the widow of the Earl of Huntingdon, and Henry not only confirmed him in possession of the wealthy earldom, but persuaded David's brother Alexander I, who had succeeded Edgar as King of Scotland, to grant him even more extensive holdings in Scotland. In fact David seems to have spent a great deal of time in England even after he became king – though admittedly the only sources we have are English, and might give a biased impression of where his real interests lay. Certainly the Norman elite in England were in no doubt about the influence of Anglo-Norman culture on the Scottish king; according to the somewhat patronizing view of William of Malmesbury, the time he had spent in England had 'polished away the rust of his native barbarism'. When David inherited the throne from the childless Alexander in 1124, hopes were high for a permanent rapprochement between the two kingdoms.

The antagonism between England and Scotland goes back so far that we are inclined to take it for granted, but 'barbarism' seems a little harsh. After all, Scotland had been (at least nominally) a unified kingdom for much longer than England, and in the sixth and seventh centuries AD missionaries from Iona and elsewhere had played an important role in the conversion of the pagan English. The northern kingdom may have been geographically on the fringe of Europe, but it was by no means beyond the pale of Christian civilization.

Nevertheless it was often, like Wales, the butt of Anglo-Norman prejudice. The author of the *Gesta Stephani* describes it in terms very like those which he uses for Wales. Though well supplied with 'productive forests, milk and herds', its inhabitants are 'barbarous and filthy'. In war they prefer to rely on speed of movement rather than heavy armour, and though they are fearless they are also cruel, especially to foreigners. In fact there was an element of truth in both these apparently conflicting judgements, because David's kingdom was – even more than most medieval polities – a heterogeneous collection of diverse, and often mutually hostile, groups. To explain why this was so we need to consider briefly its earlier history. In the eighth century AD the territory corresponding to modern Scotland had been occupied by four distinct peoples. The south-east was inhabited by English-speakers and was intermittently under the control of English kings based in Northumbria, who fought a series of wars against the Picts further north. The Picts were supposed to be the descendants of the original inhabitants of the Roman era. They were ruled by kings who had their capital near present-day Inverness, and spoke a language which is now lost but was probably closely related to Welsh. Also Welsh-speaking was the kingdom of Strathclyde in the south-west, which maintained close relations with their fellow Celts further south. And in Dal Riata, on the west coast, were the Scots, whose language was more closely related to the Gaelic spoken in Ireland. Traditionally the Scots have been seen as invaders, who had gained a foothold during the migrations which followed the collapse of the Roman Empire. However, recent scholarship has cast doubt on this idea. Barry Cunliffe, for example, argues that there is no archaeological trace of an Irish invasion, and that seafaring communities speaking a common language might have existed on both sides of the Irish Sea for millennia (Cunliffe 2012). But whether they had arrived as conquerors or not, the Scots greatly expanded their influence in the early ninth century, at a time when their neighbours were being distracted and weakened by Viking attacks. By 840 the leader of the Scots, Kenneth mac Alpin, had overthrown the Pictish king and established a joint monarchy over most of what soon came to be known as 'Alba' or 'Scotia', with its centre of power in Strathtay, in the region of the modern city of Perth. Strathclyde was added to the Scottish kings' dominions in 945, and by the end of the tenth century the northern part of Northumbria, now known as Lothian, was also firmly under their control. It was presumably on the back of this dramatic success that the Gaelic language submerged Welsh and Pictish and became the predominant tongue of the whole country except the far south-east. But the ancient divisions still persisted, and in fact a large influx of Viking settlers had now added a fifth element to the mix.

Communities often described as Norse-Gaelic, combining elements of the original Scots-Irish or related groups with Scandinavian newcomers, occupied much of the Hebrides as well as Galloway. The latter comprised the far southwestern coastal region beyond the territory of Strathclyde, and early in the twelfth century it still retained its de facto independence under a line of self-styled kings. The '*ri*' or king of Galloway at the time of David's wars with Stephen was Fergus, a nobleman of unknown ancestry who first appears in written sources about 1136, but who is believed to have been married to an illegitimate daughter of Henry I of England (Oram 2000). Fergus' precise relationship with David is unclear, but although he was allied by marriage to the Anglo-Norman aristocracy, he provided troops for the Scottish army which invaded England in 1138. He may of course have considered himself to be acting on behalf of the Empress Matilda, who was probably his sister-in-law, but we have no record of any direct communication between them. Richard Oram suggests that David granted the fief of Annandale to Robert de Brus in 1124 as a buffer between the Scottish heartland and the growing power of Galloway, but the two powers did not confront each other directly until 1160, when a Scottish army invaded and deposed Fergus.

Elsewhere anti-David sentiment in Scotland coalesced around the figure of Malcolm mac Alasdair, an illegitimate son of King Alexander I and thus David's nephew, who had been a thorn in the king's side since his accession in 1124. His claim to the throne appears to have been supported by those Scots who regarded David as an outsider, and his Anglo-Norman favourites as a potential threat to the traditional order. In 1124, according to Orderic Vitalis, David defeated Malcolm in two battles, but he remained at large and made several further attempts to seize power. In the west of Scotland the old territory of Dal Riata, now known as Argyll, had come under Norse domination as part of the 'Kingdom of the Isles', and in the 1130s was ruled by a warlord of mixed Norse-Gaelic descent named Gillebrigte. Malcolm secured Gillebrigte's support by marrying his daughter, and from the scanty surviving records it appears that David was preoccupied with the Argyll frontier for several years in the late 1120s. Gillebrigte seems to have maintained his independence in the face of Scottish pressure, and after David's death was succeeded by his son, the famous 'Lord of the Isles' Somerled.

The far north of what is now Scotland had been similarly settled by the Norsemen, and was the domain of the Scandinavian Earls of Orkney and Caithness, who owed their allegiance to the kings of Norway. Though Orkney was less powerful than it had been under its famous Earl Thorfinn the Mighty, who died in 1064, and its once dreaded Vikings were now Christian, some of them still periodically raided south through the Hebrides. David's father Malcolm Canmore had cemented his relations with Orkney by marrying as his first wife Thorfinn's widow Ingibjorg, whose sons Paul and Erlend were joint earls from Thorfinn's death until 1098. But in that year they were overthrown with Norwegian help by Sigurd Magnusson, and relations with Scotland deteriorated. Beyond the southern frontier of Orkney and its dependent territory of Caithness on the Scottish mainland lay the region known as Moray. This was much more extensive than the modern county of the same name, and comprised most of the north-east and the central Highlands. There the descendants of a Dal Riatan clan known as the Cenel Loairn had established themselves as 'mormaers'. This title is sometimes translated as 'earls', but the mormaers enjoyed far greater autonomy than the earls of Norman England. Being related to the house of mac Alpin, they occasionally pursued their own claims to the Scottish throne, and in 1040 the most famous of their number, Macbeth, had killed King Duncan and taken the throne for himself. Shakespeare's famous characterization of Macbeth as a treacherous usurper reflects the views of much later chroniclers, but at the time he seems to have been a successful and popular ruler. In 1057, however, he was defeated in battle and killed by Duncan's son, Malcolm Canmore, with help from Siward, the English Earl of Northumbria. The people of Moray promptly proclaimed Macbeth's stepson Lulach as king, but in 1058 Lulach was killed in his turn, and Malcolm thus became the unchallenged ruler of Scotland.

But if the mormaers of Moray were ultimately unable to found their own royal dynasty, they remained determined to guard their de facto independence. Malcolm had to lead another punitive expedition into the turbulent region in 1078, and his son Alexander campaigned there in 1116. Nevertheless Moray was still far from subdued, and in 1130 a grandson of Lulach, Oengus of Moray, once again took the offensive and led an army south in alliance with Malcolm mac Alasdair to overthrow David. The attempt was narrowly defeated by the Constable of Scotland, an Englishman named Edward Siwardsson, at the Battle of Stracathro, which was fought in April of that year near Brechin in Angus. According to Orderic Vitalis, Oengus and Malcolm led 5,000 warriors to Stracathro, of whom 4,000 died in the battle. An Irish source adds that 1,000 Scots (presumably meaning men fighting for the king) were also killed. Oengus was among the casualties, and with Moray left leaderless David seized the opportunity to bring it under his control. Much of the territory was granted to foreign soldiers of fortune like the Flemish entrepreneur Freskin, who built castles and planted agricultural colonies in the fertile lowlands, but the more mountainous areas remained beyond their reach, and it was not until 1230 that the last resistance was finally crushed.

Malcolm mac Alasdair seems to have fought on for a few more years after his defeat at Stracathro, and a speech reported by Ailred of Rievaulx to have been made by Robert de Brus of Annandale at the Battle of the Standard in 1138 reveals that it was only with English help that the pretender was finally caught. 'In a previous year', he reminded the Scots, they had asked for assistance against Malcolm, and Walter Espec and other northern barons had answered the call, mustering at Carlisle with men and ships. They had waged war and 'terrified all your enemies' until Malcolm's own followers betrayed him, and the English knights brought him in chains to David. This otherwise undocumented campaign must presumably have taken place in 1134, in which year Malcolm was imprisoned in Roxburgh castle for the rest of his life.

Scottish Armies

With this background it is not surprising that Scottish armies tended to be a heterogeneous collection of semi-independent warbands, rather than coherent forces with a common tactical doctrine and a unified system of command. The contingents mentioned at the Battle of the Standard in 1138 included men from Lothian, 'Picts' from Galloway, 'Moravians', Normans, 'Danes', '*insulani*' or Islemen, Flemings and Germans. Richard of Hexham calls the men of Lothian 'English', which perhaps they still were in speech if no longer in political allegiance. They were raised from the fertile country along the south-east coast and the central lowlands, and made up the bulk of what was known as the 'Scottish Army' or 'Common Army'. Freemen, and even on occasion apparently serfs, were called up, usually on the basis of one man per ploughshare, although thirteenth- and fourteenth-century records show as many as three men per unit being obliged to serve in emergencies. In David's time they may still have been led by their local thanes, noblemen analogous to the thegns of Anglo-Saxon England. Being of humble origin most of the common army were poorly equipped, and few if any of the rank-and-file wore armour, a fact of which English propaganda took full advantage. For example Henry of Huntingdon describes Bishop Ralph at The Standard telling the assembled troops that the enemy 'do not know how to arm themselves in war', going on to ask 'What is there to doubt as we march forward against the unarmed and naked?' In fact it seems that Scottish lack of armour was not just a matter of poverty of resources, but that going into battle unprotected was actually a cultural preference, just as it may have been in Wales. For example, Ailred of Rievaulx claimed that one of David's mormaers, who as a man of high rank would surely have been able to afford a mail hauberk, boasted that although he wore no armour he would advance further than the mailed knights in the army.

This disdain for protection seemed as irrational to contemporary Anglo-Normans as it does to us, but of course there were sound tactical reasons for fighting lightly equipped in the rough and mountainous terrain of much of Scotland, just as there were in Wales. A note of caution is also necessary here, as we cannot be sure what exactly was meant by 'unarmoured'. Clearly a description like 'unarmed and naked' should not be taken literally, and it may be that in their desire to depict the Scots as outside the mainstream of European civilization some of the chroniclers exaggerated the situation. No doubt Anglo-Norman battlefield commanders would not have hesitated to do the same in the hope of boosting the morale of their own troops. There is reason to believe that at least some of the 'naked' Scots may have worn non-metallic protection similar to the gambesons which Norman knights wore beneath their mail, or at least that the linen shirts which they wore were treated in order to provide a similar level of protection. These might not even have been recognized as armour by those accustomed to the mail-clad armies of the south. Certainly this was the case in the sixteenth century: John Major, writing in 1521, describes the 'common people of the wild Scots' as wearing 'a linen garment manifoldly sewed and painted or daubed with pitch, with a covering of deerskin'. Leather armour was also known to the Norwegians, whose influence in northern and western Scotland was very strong during our period. For example, according to Saint Olaf's Saga many of the combatants at the Battle of Stiklarstadr in 1030 had worn coats of reindeer hide, and 'no weapon could cut or pierce them any more than if they were armour of ring mail . . .' (Heath).

Unfortunately for the Scots the climactic clash between the two military systems, the Battle of the Standard, was fought not on the heather-covered mountains but on an open plain in the lowlands of Yorkshire. Most of the contemporary descriptions of Scottish weaponry relate to the same battle. According to Henry of Huntingdon, the Lothian men who formed the first line of David's army were armed with javelins and long spears, but unfortunately there is some confusion here, as the other chroniclers say that it was the Galwegians who fought in the first line. A slightly later description by Ralph de Diceto, describing a campaign in 1173, refers to the Galwegians as carrying throwing spears in their right hands and long knives in their left, as well as 'long lances' which served as standards as well as weapons, so it seems quite likely that the armament of the Lothian and Galwegian contingents was similar, and even that the English found it difficult to tell them apart. Ian Heath implies that the use of long spears might foreshadow the 'schiltron' formation of the fourteenth century, but the schiltron as used at Bannockburn, for example, consisted of men in close order, advancing slowly shoulder to shoulder, or standing or kneeling on the defensive against cavalry behind a hedge of spears. At The Standard, as described below, the Scots relied on a wild rush without any attempt at formation-keeping, which must have negated any advantage they might have gained from the length of their spears.

The 'Moravians' at The Standard were the men from Moray, who were raised and commanded on a similar basis to their compatriots in Lothian, and probably similarly equipped. The 'Danes' were presumably the Scandinavian element among the Islemen from the Orkneys and Hebrides, who in fact were mostly of Norwegian descent. From the thirteenth to the sixteenth centuries this area produced the famous '*galloglaich*' or gallowglasses, who fought in the Irish wars. In contrast to the bulk of the Scots these men were protected by mail shirts and/or padded gambesons and wielded two-handed axes, and there are hints in our sources that this was already the case in the twelfth century. Gerald de Barri, for example, describes the Islemen at the Battle of Dublin in 1171 as 'in Danish fashion completely clad in iron', and their commander, Eoan Mear, was said to have killed as many as ten of his enemies with a Norse axe. The best guide we have to the appearance of these men comes from the 'Lewis chessmen' found at Uig on the Isle of Lewis in the 1830s, which date from the second half of the twelfth century. These were carved from walrus ivory, probably in Norway, but can probably be taken as representing fighting men of the period throughout the Scandinavian world. They wear nasal helmets and carry swords and spears, but differ from the classic image of Vikings in that some of them are clean shaven, and their shields – frequently emblazoned with crosses – are of the 'kite' variety associated with the Anglo-Normans rather than the traditional round shape. Nevertheless some of the figures are depicted biting the rims of their shields in classic berserker fashion – a mixture of old and new, Christian and pagan, which may accurately reflect the atmosphere of the time. According to the saga biographer of the Norwegian king Magnus Bareleg, when he and his men returned from an expedition to the Hebrides in 1093 many of them had adopted a form of local dress, with short tunics and bare legs, and this is likely to have become more common as time went on and the Norse and Celtic communities became more integrated. Old-style round shields must still have been in use among the more conservative warriors, and perhaps more widely for shipboard fighting, as their shape would have been more convenient for carrying mounted on the gunwales of a longship. Gerald de Barri describes the shields carried by the Orkney contingent at Dublin in 1171 as round and painted red, while the *Orkneyinga Saga* tells the tale of one Arni Hrafnsson, who ran away from a battle in Orkney and tried to take refuge in a church in Kirkwall, but became stuck in the doorway because he had forgotten that he still had his shield slung on his back. This must surely have been a large circular shield rather than a kite shield, which at its broadest point would not have been any wider than a man's shoulders.

Despite David's determined attempts to feudalize his realm, there were still relatively few knights' fees even in the southern part of the country, and the great majority of the heavy cavalry in the Scottish army were Anglo-Normans serving for pay. Macbeth had been the first to introduce Norman mercenaries as long ago as 1052, but their numbers had increased dramatically since David's accession, encouraged by the contacts which the new king had made while at the court of Henry I. These men would not have differed in equipment or style of fighting from their counterparts on the English side at The Standard, although their relatively small numbers prevented them from playing their usual decisive role.

Chapter 7

The Battle of the Standard

On 10 January 1138 a Scottish army under David's nephew William fitz Duncan crossed the River Tweed into Northumberland. This was not the first time since Stephen's accession that his kingdom had been invaded from the north. As early as the beginning of 1136 David had occupied five castles along the border, including Carlisle and Newcastle, but if he had had any plans to advance further they were thwarted by Stephen's rapid advance via York, with an army which Henry of Huntingdon says was 'greater than any in living memory in England'. David met him at Durham and made peace, although he was allowed to keep Carlisle. The campaign of 1138, however, was a far more serious affair. William fitz Duncan's first objectives were the Bishop of Durham's castle at Norham, some 10 miles up the river from Berwick-upon-Tweed – which was then held by the Scots – and the larger stronghold at Wark-on-Tweed, seven miles further upstream, which belonged to the Yorkshire baron Walter Espec and was being held by his nephew, Jordan de Bussey. Wark (which is not to be confused with Wark-on-Tyne, further south near Newcastle) was an important strategic objective, as it controlled not only a major river crossing but also the road which ran alongside the Tweed on the English bank. However, the Scots were unable to take it, even after David himself arrived and deployed siege engines against it. In fact the garrison not only refused to surrender but mounted successful sorties against the besiegers, on one occasion killing David's standard bearer and on another looting part of the Scottish baggage train. After three frustrating weeks David left a detachment behind to blockade Wark and marched south, taking an inland route through the hills of western Northumberland, seizing provisions and plunder from the countryside as he went. In describing this part of the campaign the English chroniclers related a shocking tale of atrocities which has ever since besmirched David's reputation as a civilized Christian king. Medieval armies often resorted to 'scorched earth' tactics, burning crops and houses and driving off livestock, partly to deprive the enemy of supplies, but also to force him to give battle in order to protect his subjects. The actions of the Scots in 1138, however, seem to have gone far beyond this. To Richard of Hexham they were 'an execrable army, more savage than any race of heathen', a charge which he supports by relating how they drove off not only cattle but the people of Northumberland 'like so much booty, the noble matrons and chaste virgins, together with other women. These – naked, fettered, herded together – by whips and thongs they drove before them, goading them with their spears and other weapons.' According to Walter Espec, quoted by Ailred of Rievaulx, 'The high born boys as well as girls were led into captivity.' As for those who were not fit to be employed as slaves, 'they slaughtered by the edge of the sword or transfixed with their spears the sick on their pallets, women pregnant and in labour; the babes in their cradles, and other innocents at the breast or in the bosom of their mothers, with the mothers themselves; and worn out old men and feeble old women, and the others who for any reason were disabled'. Henry of Huntingdon elaborates further, alleging that 'they ripped open pregnant women and tore out the unborn foetuses. They tossed children on the points of their lances. They dismembered priests on their altars . . .'

Some of these tales are surely exaggerated – for example Richard of Hexham goes on to claim that the Scottish soldiers slaughtered children, collected their blood in a stream and then drank it – but it is clear that the behaviour of the invaders shocked even an age which was accustomed to brutality. It is likely that David – who really did aspire to be a model Christian ruler – did not condone it, but had simply lost control of his troops. He appears to have accepted protection money from various towns and monastic houses in return for promises of immunity, but was not always able to persuade his men to respect these agreements. Fergus' Galwegians especially were not amenable to discipline, because they were not formally David's subjects but merely his allies. In fact John of Hexham tells how William fitz Duncan intervened personally to stop his own men from attacking Hexham and breaking into the monastery, and according to another local source, Richard of Hexham, relations between David and the Galwegians later became strained when the king tried to protect a woman whom they were attempting to abduct. Warfare in Scotland was traditionally waged with a ruthlessness that surpassed anything the Normans had done, but the root cause of these particular atrocities appears to have been the practice of taking slaves. Slavery, though dying out in England by the time of Domesday Book, remained an important part of the economy in the Celtic lands, and it was probably the prospect of acquiring captives as well as other loot that motivated the Galwegians and others to fight in a war which was not theirs. The wholesale slaughter of the unfit was all too often a logical outcome of slave-raiding, as was attested in nineteenth-century East Africa, for example. It was uneconomic for an army in the field to feed non-combatants who could not work, and it was also considered necessary to deter those who had been enslaved from avoiding their fate by pretending not to be able to march.

Stephen, who was still at Bedford when the invasion began, reacted quickly. He did not encounter David's army on his march north, perhaps because the Scots were keeping to the hills and avoiding the coastal plain where the superior English cavalry would have had the advantage, but by the end of February he had reached Wark and forced the besiegers to retire. He then crossed the Tweed and began to ravage the country on the Scottish side in the hope of forcing David to abandon his own depredations. According to the Hexham chroniclers the Scottish king did return home in a hurry, planning to lure the English into his stronghold at Roxburgh and trap them there, but Stephen was informed of the plan and withdrew in time. By the beginning of April he was back at Northampton. In a brief war of manoeuvre he had succeeded in thwarting the invasion with minimal loss to himself. However, the Scottish threat was by no means eliminated. In fact David had recrossed the border before the end of the month, plundering as far as the River Tyne. At the same time William fitz Duncan crossed the Pennines and raided the districts of Furness and Craven in what is now Lancashire. This was far to the south of any territory that David had claimed up until then, but William himself had inherited a claim to lands in the area, and David's biographer Richard Oram has argued that this campaign proves that his territorial ambitions now extended much further than the traditional Scottish interest in Northumberland and Cumberland.

Then on 10 June William encountered and defeated an English force at Clitheroe in the upper valley of the River Ribble. We have no details of this battle, but it clearly had a great effect on the morale of both sides. The defeated Englishmen had included a contingent of fully-armoured knights, and the Galwegians in the Scottish army were later to use their success against these to argue that they should lead the attack at The Standard, as they had proved that despite their lack of armour their charge could break the Normans. The nearest we have to an account of the fighting is the remark attributed by Ailred to a Galwegian chief at The Standard: 'What gain were their hauberks to the Gauls [i.e. the Normans] at Clitheroe? Did not these men [the Galwegians], unarmed as they say, compel them to throw away their hauberks, to forget their helmets, to leave behind their shields?' It is particularly unfortunate that we do not know the precise circumstances of this apparent rout, but it seems likely that the false conclusion reached by the victors resulted from the different nature of the terrain. Clitheroe is in a valley overlooked by the steep slopes of Pendle Hill about two miles to the south-east, and if the lightly-equipped Galwegians had managed to seize the hill and charge down it against the slower-moving knights, they might well have outmanoeuvred them and forced them to cast off their armour and flee. The ground around Northallerton, where the next battle was fought, would offer them no such advantage.

Meanwhile, on the English side the tiny garrison at Norham finally agreed to surrender, though Wark still remained defiant. But if David wished to consolidate his conquests in the north of England he would need to capture at least one of the major cities of the region, Durham or York. A local baron, Eustace fitz John, who held lands at Malton near York, now went over to the Scots with his forces. Eustace had been appointed by Henry I as keeper of the castle of Bamburgh, which was situated on the east coast of Northumberland about 15 miles south of the mouth of the Tweed, but Stephen had deprived him of this office, no doubt already doubting his loyalty. Perhaps it was at Eustace's instigation that David made Bamburgh the first objective of his latest invasion, but on discovering that it was garrisoned by a large force of knights and that the walls had recently been strengthened, he decided to bypass it and continue his advance southwards. As the Scots marched away, however, the garrison sallied out and attacked them. David's men rallied and drove the enemy back, breaking through the outer ramparts of the castle and killing around a hundred of the defenders. The keep still held out, but the chastened survivors took no further part in the war. By July David had crossed the River Tyne, where he rendezvoused with the raiding parties which had been campaigning in Cumberland, and gathered more recruits from Galloway. Richard of Hexham put the total number of troops at 26,000, which most modern scholars dismiss as impossibly large, but the figure does at least suggest that the size of the army was unusual. It swept on south past Durham, which was well fortified and would have taken too long to besiege, but it seems that the Scots deliberately laid waste the territory belonging to the Bishop – 'Saint Cuthbert's Land' as it was known at the time. A dispute over the bishopric of Durham was one of the ongoing causes of the hostility between David and Stephen. Then the invaders crossed the River Tees and marched up the broad valley of the River Swale, which runs between the high ground of the North York Moors on the east and the Pennines to the west. Their objective was York, now only 40 miles to the south-east. York would certainly have been a major prize for David. It was one of the great trading centres of Britain, and could have provided him with an income far greater than could be obtained from any city in Scotland, not to mention the potential of the rich agricultural land that surrounded it. But it was also the seat of an archbishop who claimed authority over the Scottish Church. This claim had often been disputed, but it must have been obvious to David that the issue would be settled once and for all if he could secure the appointment of his own nominee when the current English Archbishop Thurstan died.

At this moment of crisis Stephen was helpless to intervene. On his return from the north in April he had found himself facing threats from three different directions. Apart from the Scottish invasion, fighting had again broken out with Geoffrey of Anjou in Normandy, while the death of Payn fitz John in his skirmish with the Welsh had left a worsening power vacuum along the Welsh Marches. Stephen had confirmed Roger, the son of Miles of Gloucester, as Payn's successor in Herefordshire, but other local magnates, led by Geoffrey Talbot, disputed this and occupied the castle at Hereford. The king decided that the latter was the most serious threat in the short term, so from Northampton he marched to Gloucester and then on to Hereford. Two of his leading commanders, Waleran of Meulan and William of Ypres, were despatched to Normandy, while Archbishop Thurstan of York, who had come to Northampton to ask for the king's help against the Scots, was sent back with a small contingent of knights from the royal household and instructions to organize the defence himself. Stephen celebrated Whitsun at the end of May 1138 with a crown-wearing ceremony in Hereford cathedral (where the chair on which he sat can still be seen), within a stone's-throw of the rebel-held castle, but a few weeks later the garrison surrendered. John of Worcester, who praises the king as 'a pious and peaceable man', tells us that, as he had done at Exeter, he allowed the defenders to leave unmolested. Unfortunately Geoffrey Talbot was thus able to return after the king had left and set fire to the town, before taking refuge with his fellow dissidents in Bristol. Stephen went on to take Shrewsbury in Shropshire, where in an uncharacteristic display of ruthlessness he executed the captured garrison and its commander. It must have been around this time that the bombshell fell which was to lead the country from localized revolt into full-scale civil war. Messengers from Earl Robert of Gloucester, who was then in-Normandy, arrived with the news that the earl had announced his 'defiance' of Stephen, formally renouncing the homage which he had sworn after the king's accession. The reason, Stephen was told, was that he had himself invalidated the agreement by breaking his promises to Robert; there was also an unlikely allegation that the king had tried to have him assassinated. In any case, Stephen was informed, he was not really the rightful king, as he had himself previously sworn to uphold the claim of the Empress Matilda. In fact historians like Crouch have cast doubt on Robert's protestations of loyalty to Matilda, arguing that he had done nothing to promote her cause until after his break with the king, and that he perhaps saw her more as a weapon which he could use against Stephen than as the real reason for his rebellion.

Of course the timing of this defiance was not fortuitous. David's activities were well known in Normandy, as was the official line that the Scottish king had gone to war in support of his niece Matilda's claim to the English throne. Robert had made it even less likely that Stephen would be able to turn his attention north. Thurstan and the northern barons were on their own. Luckily they proved more than equal to the task. According to Richard of Hexham, the magnates who gathered at York in response to the Archbishop's summons were at first reluctant to trust each other, and it took all of Thurstan's authority and persuasiveness to forge a coalition. The Archbishop was in his seventies and in poor health, so he did not accompany the army himself, but appointed Bishop Ralph of Orkney, whose see was subject to York, as his representative. The precise command structure of the English forces is not entirely clear from the chronicles, but it appears that military command was shared between William of Aumale, whom Stephen had appointed as commander of the city of York, Bernard de Balliol, leading the king's household contingent, and Walter Espec, a veteran soldier whose extensive holdings in the theatre of war included the beleaguered castle at Wark-on-Tweed. The Peterborough chronicle mentions only William of Aumale, which might imply that he was considered to be the senior commander. Henry of Huntingdon also names a fourth member of the high command, Ilbert de Lacy. Contingents from as far south as Nottinghamshire and Derbyshire were summoned to join the host; many of them were led by their parish priests, which may be an indication of the improvised nature of the preparations. The army marched behind the banners of Saint Peter, the patron saint of the cathedral at York; Saint John of Beverley; and Saint Wilfrid of Ripon. Ailred also refers to a 'royal ensign', no doubt supplied by Stephen. This collection of flags was attached to a ship's mast topped with a silver box or pyx, containing the consecrated host, and mounted on a cart pulled by oxen to form a highly-visible rallying point. This practice was common in Italy, where such a cart was known as a '*caroccio*', and it was occasionally used elsewhere in Europe, but this is the only attested case of its appearance in Britain. Even before the two armies met, Thurstan had won the propaganda battle, successfully presenting the campaign as a holy war against heathen invaders. This was ironic in view of David's personal reputation as a benefactor of the Church, but the Scottish king's failure to discipline the wilder elements of his army had clearly played into English hands.

The English army advanced north from York to Thirsk, from where Bernard de Balliol and Robert de Brus, who as well as being Lord of Cleveland held Annandale from David and so had a foot in both camps, were sent forward to negotiate with the invaders. According to Ailred of Rievaulx the ambassadors offered to persuade Stephen to grant the Earldom of Northumberland to David's son Henry in return for peace. David considered the offer but was talked out of it by William fitz Duncan, whom Ailred regarded as 'the chief instigator' of the war, who accused Robert de Brus of being a traitor. Robert responded by formally renouncing his allegiance to David, and the conference broke up in acrimony. The ambassadors returned to Thirsk and led the English army some 10 miles further north to a site two miles beyond Northallerton, where they drew up their battle line to await the Scots. Here the road from the north ran along the top of a gentle ridge, with low-lying and marshy ground on either side. The English formed up in a solid block in front of their standard, with most of the knights dismounted to support the less well-armoured levies, who were a mixture of archers and spearmen. There is a modern monument beside the A167 which gives a general indication of the location of the site, but recent research has suggested that its placing is not quite accurate. The traditional site of the English battle line was on what is now known as Standard Hill, but The Battlefields Trust now argues, following Jim Bradbury, that it was probably on Red Hill further south. This seems logical as Scot Pits Lane, where local tradition claims that the Scottish dead were buried, lies between the two features, south of Standard Hill, and if the English line was on the latter it is hard to explain how the Scots could have got so far south.

Whichever site is correct, the terrain over which the battle was fought would have been similar. The area was probably open field in 1138, or perhaps partly common grazing, but either way it was open and fairly featureless, the hills being only very gentle rises on either side of Scot Pits Lane. The only other significant feature was an area of marsh called Cinnamire, now drained, on which the English left flank was secured. The Scottish army approached from the north early on 22 August, but because the morning was misty they did not see the English standard until they were fairly close to it – perhaps already on the crest of Standard Hill. David then deployed his troops, according to Ailred, in four lines. Although we cannot be sure of the exact numbers, all sources agree that they outnumbered the English, but no attempt was made to extend the line and outflank them. Possibly David was aware that the marshy ground on either side would have prevented this, but it is equally likely that the poor discipline of his army would have precluded any sophisticated tactics in any case. The Galwegians were in the first line – not for any sound tactical reason, but because they insisted on their right to the position of honour. Ailred says that the king had intended to lead with his mailed knights, who according to John of Worcester numbered only 200, thus opposing the heavily-equipped enemy with troops of similar strength. However, the Galwegians had argued forcefully that their lack of armour was not a disadvantage, as their victory at Clitheroe had proved that mail hauberks were a burden rather than a defence. The Scottish mormaer Malise of Strathearne then added his voice to the protest, saying that although he also wore no armour he would advance further than any of the mail-clad knights. At this one of the said knights, Alan de Percy, took offence and replied 'A great word hast thou spoken, which for thy life thou canst not make good this day'. Fearful that a fight might break out within his own army, the king agreed to the Galwegians' demand, placing his knights, with the archers, the Cumbrians and the men of Teviotdale, in the second line. This line, says Ailred, was placed under the command of Prince Henry, the king's son, who arranged it 'with great wisdom', perhaps using the knights to stiffen the archers and spearmen in the same way as the English were doing. Behind them were the men of Lothian, Lorne and the Isles, while the fourth line consisted of the troops from Moray, commanded by David himself, who also had beside him a number of picked knights as a bodyguard. (Henry of Huntingdon says that the Lothian men were in the front line, but this is contradicted by all the other sources.) The contingents from Lothian and Moray were mainly unarmoured spearmen, but it is likely that the Islemen included warriors equipped in Scandinavian style, with heavy axes and probably mail coats as well. The Scottish army clearly did not lack men capable of taking on the mailed Anglo-Norman knights, but David's flawed deployment had relegated them to a supporting role. What would have happened if these armoured warriors had advanced first and pinned the English while the more mobile Scottish contingents outflanked them, we can only speculate.

At his point in their narratives Ailred and Henry of Huntingdon both quote lengthy speeches which were said to have been made by the English commanders to their troops before the battle was joined. This of course was a standard feature of medieval battle accounts, and it is quite likely that it reflects genuine battlefield practice, but it is reasonable to assume that the actual words reflect the chronicler's view of the motives of the combatants rather than a word-for-word record of what was actually said. Interestingly, however, Ailred and Henry attribute what is essentially the same speech to different people: Ailred purports to quote Walter Espec (who happened to be the patron of Ailred's community at Rievaulx), while Henry puts more or less the same words into the mouth of Bishop Ralph. This makes it seem more likely that something of the sort was actually said, and perhaps repeated along the line for the benefit of those out of earshot, one of whom wrote it down, or at least remembered it, without being sure who had originally delivered the speech. It is worth examining as an illustration of how the Normans viewed themselves and their enemies. The 'illustrious nobles of England, Normans by birth', belonged to a race which had beaten the French, and conquered not only England but Apulia, Antioch and even Jerusalem. It was therefore a cause for shame that the Scots, who had also been subjected to them in the past, should now come armed into their country. This was especially so since the Scots were not even a properly-equipped army, but more like a mob of rioters, lacking armour, weapons and skill. This, the speaker assured them, had been deliberately brought about by God in order that the English could punish the invaders for the atrocities which they had committed. It was true, he went on, that the Scots were advancing eagerly to battle, and were not frightened by the countless banners which indicated the size of the Anglo-Norman force. But this was only because the enemy was so ignorant of war that they did not realize the advantages that the Normans' armour and training gave them: 'Your head is covered by a helmet, your breast by a hauberk, your shins by leggings [mail greaves?], your whole body by a shield. When the enemy looks carefully and finds that you are enclosed in steel, he cannot find where to strike . . . Of what avail, then, are ancestral glory, regular training, and military discipline, if, when you are few, you do not conquer the many?' (Ailred).

According to Henry of Huntingdon the bishop concluded by saying that he must now finish as the Scots were already attacking, and that he was delighted to see that they were doing so in 'scattered groups' instead of in disciplined formations. He then granted the troops absolution from their sins, and was answered with a great cry of 'Amen! Amen!' The charging Galwegians responded with what Ailred describes as a 'horrible yell', though Henry says that they called out their 'ancient rallying cry', 'Albani! Albani!' The English archers took a heavy toll of them as they came, but although Ailred describes Galwegians so stuck with arrows that they resembled hedgehogs, slashing the air with their swords in 'blind madness', missiles alone could not stop them. According to Ailred they struck the English line with such ferocity that the spearmen in the front rank were driven back, but the better-armoured knights stood their ground and the line held. Then, seeing that the initial shock had not broken the enemy as they had no doubt expected, the Galwegians abandoned their spears, drew their swords and attempted to duel at close quarters. In this they were equally unsuccessful because of their lack of armour, and all the time the English archers seem to have kept up the rain of arrows. This was presumably done at very close range from within the Anglo-Norman formation, perhaps from behind the shields of the knights and spearmen, as we have no indication that the archers had been deployed separately. Eventually two of the leaders of the Galwegians, Domnall and Ulgric, were killed, whereupon the survivors gave up the unequal contest and fled.

Henry of Huntingdon adds that the men of Lothian also retreated when their commander was shot. As we have seen he appears to have confused the Lothian men with the Galwegians, but it is not unlikely that the former had also joined in the attack, and perhaps been swept away when the Galwegians in front of them ran back through their ranks. It was probably at this stage that King David's son Henry led the small contingent of mounted knights on the Scottish side in a charge against the English line. They attacked so fiercely that what Ailred calls the 'unarmed men' among the English (presumably the less well-armoured spearmen and archers who had already borne the brunt of the Galwegians' attack) were scattered, and Henry broke right through them and threatened to overrun the English horse lines. Ailred says that Prince Henry's aim was to capture the enemy's horses so that they would not be able to escape – an optimistic assessment of the situation that suggests that he was not aware of the rout of the Galwegians when he began his charge. But Henry of Huntingdon emphasizes that the English knights once again stood firm, and that the Scots could not sustain a protracted fight against steady spearmen on foot. This implies that only a small number of them had broken through, while most of their companions had stalled in front of the line of dismounted knights. Their lances broken and their horses wounded, the Scots fell back. Henry ordered them to hide their banners so that they could disguise themselves as pursuing English knights, and by this stratagem he managed to get them to safety without further losses. But now the rest of the Scottish army, having seen a series of disasters unfolding in front of it, was wavering. Many of the men in the fourth line with David began to drift away in ever larger groups until the king was almost alone, at which point his closest companions persuaded him to mount a horse and escape.

The battle was over by mid-morning; John of Hexham says it took place between prime and tierce, in other words in the three hours or so after the time of prayer at dawn. The English casualties were apparently light; according to Henry of Huntingdon the brother of Ilbert de Lacy was the only knight to lose his life, though the lower-ranking infantry must have suffered more severely. The Scottish army was temporarily dispersed, but David managed to rally it and regroup at Carlisle. Henry of Huntingdon describes the victorious English hunting down fugitives in the woods and hedgerows, while others were said to have drowned trying to cross the River Tees. Henry gives a figure of more than 11,000 Scottish dead, but this must be an exaggeration, as Richard of Hexham says that only around 10,000 of the invaders failed to reach the rallying point at Carlisle, including no doubt a significant number who had simply gone home. John of Worcester adds that around fifty of the leading men of the Scottish army were captured, and that Prince Henry only got away on foot, accompanied by a single knight. Only nineteen of the surviving knights had retained their mail hauberks, the rest having thrown them away in order to escape more quickly. But surprisingly, in view of the decisiveness of the battle itself, the English commanders failed to follow it up. They did send a detachment to take Eustace fitz John's castle at Malton, in the Vale of Pickering 30 miles south-east of Northallerton, but otherwise they remained on the defensive. They may have had difficulty in keeping the army together once it had achieved the objective for which it had been raised, that of protecting York and the country further south from destructive raids. They may also have been aware that the enemy was still in the field in force, and that they could not guarantee another victory if they were attacked again in the rough and hilly country between Northallerton and Carlisle. On the other hand, the failure might have been a result of the essentially amateur nature of the army and its divided command. The English barons had successfully defended their own district, and they lacked any appreciation of the wider strategic situation. So David managed to extract his army unmolested, and even to resume the siege of the castle at Wark.

At this point there was an intervention from an unexpected quarter. Alberic, the Bishop of Ostia, was at York in his capacity as a Papal legate, sent to decide a dispute relating to the Bishops of Carlisle and Glasgow, and he began his journey north to Scotland in the aftermath of the battle. At Durham he negotiated the release of William Comyn, David's Chancellor, who had been captured by the English garrison during the retreat; he then went on to Carlisle, where he had an audience with David and persuaded him to agree to a truce. This was only a temporary ceasefire, during which the Scottish king promised not to assault Wark, though he continued to blockade it, and not to invade England again for six weeks. Alberic then went south to meet Stephen and persuade him to negotiate a formal peace. Meanwhile, the garrison at Wark was reduced to eating its horses and finally surrendered in November on instructions from Walter Espec. David allowed the soldiers to leave with honour, and even replaced the horses they had already eaten, but he made sure that the castle, which had been a threat to his communications throughout the campaign, was destroyed. Over the winter Alberic continued to work for a peace settlement. Stephen was at first reluctant to make concessions, but Richard of Hexham says that it was Queen Matilda who persuaded him. In April 1139 the queen arrived in Durham for a meeting with David and Henry, and the result of her diplomacy was a peace that was to last until the end of the reign. David and Henry were later to intervene in the civil war in England in support of the Empress, but only in their capacity as holders of English fiefs: no Scottish army came south again. But the treaty was less than a triumph for Stephen, even if it did free his hands to deal with the threats to his throne that were developing in the south.

In the north of England it must have seemed as though the victory at Northallerton had never happened, because the territory that the Scots had overrun in the summer, as far south as the River Tyne on the east coast and the Ribble on the west, was confirmed in their possession. The border now ran roughly eastwards from Newcastle upon Tyne to the edge of the Pennines south of Hexham, then south to the vicinity of Skipton and south-west to the mouth of the Ribble near Preston. David was also allowed to keep Carlisle Castle, which he extensively rebuilt as a royal residence. In theory this territory was not formally ceded to Scotland, but David's son Henry had to pay homage to Stephen for the Earldom of Northumberland, within which the English king retained a nominal presence in the castles at Bamburgh and Newcastle, while David himself controlled Cumberland, on the west coast, on similar terms. Prince Henry was compensated for his nominal subordination with the Earldom of Huntingdon and the lordship of Doncaster, which he also held as a vassal of Stephen, and which were to give the Scottish royal family a motive for meddling in southern English affairs until Stephen confiscated Huntingdon in 1141. Most importantly, the territory thus granted to David's family included the lead mines at Alston on the South Tyne River, in the hills east of Carlisle, where deposits of silver had been discovered a few years previously. Scotland had previously lacked a source of the precious metal, but David was now able to mint his own high-quality silver coinage, the first to be made from 'native' metal. This not only boosted the Scottish economy but enhanced its international standing, as silver coinage had come to be regarded throughout Europe as an important symbol of statehood.

It is noteworthy that during the negotiations David seems not to have mentioned the issue that ostensibly lay behind his invasion – the cause of his niece the Empress Matilda. Certainly he obtained no concessions on her behalf, but he was clearly well satisfied with what he had gained. Even if, officially, David and Henry held northern England as vassals of Stephen, they were soon treating it as if it were an integral part of the Scottish kingdom. Richard Oram quotes various charters dealing with matters in the region which were issued by them on their own authority, and make no mention of Stephen at all. Equally significantly, although the silver coins which David had struck at Carlisle at first used English dies, which must have helped to uphold the fiction that the Scottish king held northern England only as a vassal of Stephen, by 1141 David's own dies were being used in Cumberland and Northumberland as well as in Scotland itself. Most of the magnates of the region seem to have accepted the situation more or less willingly, notably Richard de Umfraville of Redesdale, one of the greatest landowners in the country, and his son Gilbert. And although David took over Stephen's personal estates in the region, he was careful to retain the local lords in their positions in exchange for pledges of loyalty to himself. Oram suggests that to many such men Scottish domination was preferable to the civil war that was afflicting the rest of England. Certainly William of Newburgh, writing towards the end of the twelfth century, felt that the benefits of David's rule had outweighed the damage caused by the Scottish army in the invasion of 1138.

Chapter 8

Matilda and Civil War in England

Back in England, the defection of Robert of Gloucester seems to have rekindled opposition to Stephen. Even though the earl was still in Normandy, the prospect of an invasion in support of his half-sister the Empress Matilda must have encouraged the dissidents in their defiance of the king, whether by men convinced of the justice of Matilda's cause or by those who simply sought personal gain by playing off the rival factions against each other. David Crouch argues that during 1138, despite the looming crisis, Stephen embarked on what amounted to a radical reform of the administrative apparatus established by his predecessor. Henry I had been a strong character who had been able to maintain a system of government based on sheriffs and justiciars appointed by, and answerable to, the king himself. But without his dominating personality this system worked less effectively, and Stephen attempted to replace it by a much more decentralized arrangement. The key to this was the role of the earls. Henry had recognized only seven earls in England, but by the end of 1138 Stephen had doubled this number. The award of new titles may have been partly a way of rewarding his followers, but the earls were also given wide administrative powers, including in at least some cases, according to Crouch, control over the sheriffs in their territories. Stephen was by no means an amateur in the art of government; before his accession he had already been one of the greatest magnates in England, with extensive lands to administer there in addition to his Continental possessions of Mortain and Boulogne. But this decentralizing policy was particularly unfortunate in the circumstances of his reign, because it encouraged men of doubtful loyalty to establish regional power bases too strong for the king to easily control. Furthermore, it combined with his famous generosity to bankrupt the exchequer. Stephen had always been eager to buy loyalty with gifts of manors, revenues, and even, as King says in the case of the earls, whole counties, thus sacrificing long-term solvency for short term popularity. In the subsequent reign Richard, the son of Stephen's old enemy Bishop Nigel of Ely, observed how the power of kings depends on sound financial foundations. It 'rises and falls as their portable wealth flows and ebbs. Those who lack it are a prey to their enemies, those who have it prey upon them.' There can be little doubt, as King points out, that the example Richard had in mind of a king who lacked the necessary wealth was Stephen. We do not have precise figures for his revenues or the size of his armies because the fiscal records of his reign do not survive, but it is noteworthy that what Henry of Huntingdon describes as his greatest army was that raised to confront the Scots at the very beginning of his reign, when he could still draw on the riches left to him by his predecessor.

Thus it was becoming increasingly difficult for the king to exert his power. The author of the *Gesta Stephani* likened the new spirit of rebellion to the mythical Hydra: 'when one head was cut off two or more grew in its place'. The people of Bristol, encouraged by the defiance of nearby Gloucester and led by Geoffrey Talbot, the instigator of the earlier trouble at Hereford, now began to terrorise the surrounding area. They not only drove off livestock and seized loot from the villages, but kidnapped and tortured wealthy men in order to obtain their treasure. The *Gesta* even accuses them of sending out parties of men disguised as peaceful travellers to lure unsuspecting merchants from less troubled areas to the city. Some time in 1138 Talbot led a surprise attack on the nearby city of Bath, intending to scale the walls with ladders, but the plot was discovered by the Bishop of Bath's soldiers and Geoffrey was captured. However, his men retaliated by inviting the bishop to a parley and treacherously seizing him, threatening to hang him unless their leader was released. The *Gesta Stephani* devotes considerable space to this episode, which is understandable if its anonymous author was the Bishop of Bath himself. In that case its description of the bishop as 'a simple-minded man', far too trusting for his own good, carries extra conviction. Geoffrey was released and went back to Bristol, but soon afterwards Stephen arrived in Bath at the head of an army. He criticised the bishop for allowing the rebel leader to go free, but accepted his excuse that he had done so under duress, then gave orders for the walls of Bath to be strengthened as a counter to the enemy stronghold. The king went on to Bristol and intended to attack it, but found it too strong, and his ambitious plan to dam the River Avon and flood it was opposed by his advisors as impractical. So he contented himself with ravaging the long-suffering countryside and taking two nearby castles, at Castle Cary and Harptree. He left a garrison in Bath which carried on a small-scale war against Bristol, but the city remained a focus of rebellion, and when in the following year Robert of Gloucester and the Empress arrived in the West Country Bristol was to become their main headquarters. The next time the king was to enter it would be as a prisoner.

In 1139 Ludlow Castle in Shropshire was the scene of another dispute between a royal appointee, in this case Robert fitz Miles, and Gilbert de Lacy, a relative of Geoffrey Talbot, who believed himself to have a hereditary right to the place. Gilbert had seized the castle by a *coup de main*, and in the early summer of 1139 Stephen arrived to besiege it. The siege is chiefly remembered for the account by Henry of Huntingdon of how Stephen personally rescued Prince Henry of Scotland, who by the terms of the peace deal between the two countries was accompanying the royal army in his new role as Earl of Huntingdon, from an attempt to capture him. The prince, we are told, was 'pulled off his horse by an iron hook'. This is often interpreted as referring to a 'crow', a device consisting of a long beam on a pivot with a hook at one end, which could be let down from the walls of a castle to catch unwary attackers on the ground below and hoist them inside. So perhaps Stephen and Henry rode too close to the walls when reconnoitring the defences, and only the king's presence of mind and quick reactions prevented an embarrassing diplomatic incident. Even the generally unsympathetic Huntingdon chronicler remarked on the king's bravery. Perhaps he grabbed the young prince as he was about to be hauled up into the air, and – even more fortunately for the royalist cause – the combined weight of the two men was too much for the device, and so Gilbert's men were cheated of an even more valuable haul. On the other hand Henry of Huntingdon is our only source for this famous incident, and he does not specifically mention any sort of engine, so it is possible that the circumstances were less dramatic. Nevertheless, we have here a glimpse of the personal courage and quick thinking that distinguished Stephen as a war leader. Unfortunately the sequel showed some of his failings equally clearly. He was, as Henry of Huntingdon says, very good at starting things, but he seldom followed them through to a conclusion. Finding the castle too strong to take quickly, Stephen left a detachment of his army to continue the blockade, and led the rest away to Oxford. Ludlow did eventually fall and was handed over to another of the king's nominees, Joce de Dinan, but Gilbert de Lacy remained at large and carried on his private war with the new castellan for several years. At some point before the end of Stephen's reign Gilbert was once more in possession of the castle, and his heirs continued to hold it under Henry II.

It was at Oxford in June 1139 that one of the most notorious episodes of the reign took place. Among the great men whom Stephen summoned to a council in the town were the three bishops who had controlled the exchequer and other aspects of civil administration since the time of Henry I: Roger of

The Great Tower of Ludlow Castle in Shropshire. Ludlow was besieged by Stephen in 1139, and was the scene of the famous incident in which Stephen saved the life of Prince Henry of Scotland. It is not certain whether the tower in its present form existed in 1139 or was built shortly afterwards, but its massive rectangular construction is typical of mid-twelfth century styles of fortification. Often referred to by the later term 'keep', such towers were generally known at the time as 'donjons', from which the modern word 'dungeon' is derived.

The east gate of Lincoln Castle. Lincoln had been a fortified site since Roman times, and was walled in stone as early as 1115. The approach from this side, between the castle and the cathedral, is less steep than from other directions, and it was probably against this gate that Stephen launched his main attack during the siege of 1141. (Flickr)

The west gate at Lincoln. The present gate tower dates from the thirteenth century, but traces of earlier stonework can still be seen. The remains of the original Roman gate were excavated on the same site in the nineteenth century. The Battle of Lincoln was probably fought on the flat ground beneath the walls on this side, although the site is now occupied by modern housing. (Flickr)

The west wall of the castle also formed the western defences of the city itself. It was here that the pro-royalist citizens of Lincoln were deployed at the start of the battle, perhaps to prevent a sortie by the rebels inside the castle. The slight overhanging lip on the outer face of the battlements is probably a thirteenth-century feature, intended to trap incoming missiles which might otherwise be deflected upwards into the faces of the defenders.

Now known as the Observatory Tower, the bastion on the motte at the south-eastern corner of Lincoln Castle dominates the approach from the town. The turret on the top post-dates the wars of Stephen's reign, but the rest of the defences would have appeared very similar in 1141. (Flickr, David)

The Lucy Tower, on the second of the castle's two mottes, is also slightly later than the siege of 1141, but replaces an earlier keep on the same motte. This is a design known as a 'shell keep', which takes the form of an enclosure or miniature curtain wall rather than a roofed building, and may follow the line of an original wooden palisade.

Saint George's Tower, Oxford. Oxford Castle controlled an important crossing of the River Thames and was fortified by Robert d'Oyly in the early 1070s. The original castle was of conventional motte-and-bailey design, but this tower, added later in the eleventh century, is not on the motte but closer to the river. It tapers from base to top for greater stability, a design perhaps made necessary by the relatively fragile limestone from which it was built. It is said to have been in this tower that the Empress Matilda lived during the siege of 1142. (Flickr, Anders Sandberg)

The original Norman motte at Oxford, with Saint George's tower in the bottom left corner of the picture. (Flickr, Bernard's Badger)

The side of Saint George's Tower overlooking the river. Matilda is alleged to have made her famous escape from one of the windows visible here, though other accounts have her leaving through a postern gate.

At Bedford, the scene of fierce fighting on several occasions in Stephen's reign and renowned for its immense earthen ramparts, only this mound – once part of the motte erected by Henry I – now remains. It is now an archaeological park and regularly hosts medieval re-enactments.

Tamworth Castle, on the border of Staffordshire and Warwickshire, was the stronghold of Earl Ranulf of Chester's inveterate enemy Robert Marmion. This was originally a typical wooden motte-and-bailey castle, but like many such fortifications it was rebuilt in stone at some point during our period. The gate tower at right is twelfth-century, and surviving masonry on the causeway leading to the tower has been dated to the Norman period. (Flickr, Dun.can)

The Great Tower at Kenilworth in Warwickshire was built in the 1120s by Henry I's Lord Chamberlain, Geoffrey de Clinton. De Clinton was a rival of Roger de Beaumont, Earl of nearby Warwick, but – perhaps because of its formidable construction – Kenilworth was not seriously attacked during the 'Anarchy'. The downward sloping sills at the bottom of the arrow slits on the top level of the tower were designed to allow an improved field of fire against attackers threatening the base of the wall. It is not known whether these are later improvements, but if they are original they may be the earliest surviving example of this design in England. The large windows below are later additions.

The first castle at Warwick was a motte-and-bailey design, built by William I as early as 1068 overlooking the River Avon. The original motte, seen here, was later incorporated into an enlarged curtain wall. The wife of Roger de Beaumont, Earl of Warwick, surrendered the castle to Henry Plantagenet in 1153, against her husband's wishes. (Wikipedia Commons)

Castle Rising in Norfolk, the stronghold of William d'Aubigny, Earl of Arundel, from 1138, is more of a fortified hall than a conventional tower or donjon. As the husband of Henry I's widow, William was socially ambitious, and he seems to have planned the castle from the beginning for display as much as for defence. It appears to have consciously imitated the design of Henry's royal castle at Norwich. It was also the site of a mint, authorized by Stephen in 1145. The earth rampart or bailey visible here is in fact one of three, which together form one of the most extensive surviving earthworks in Britain.

This view from outside the earth rampart at Castle Rising illustrates how poorly designed this building was as a military stronghold. The tower is not tall enough to overlook the rampart, so that the latter, far from protecting the castle, would provide cover behind which an attacker could approach to within bow range. The site is also overlooked by nearby high ground. The contrast with castles like Warwick or Tamworth, built on commanding eminences to provide a wide field of view and overawe the neighbouring towns, is striking. That d'Aubigny could undertake such a construction at this time suggests that he felt more secure than our traditional view of the 'Anarchy' would warrant.

The gatehouse at Castle Rising is nevertheless a fairly typical, and exceptionally well preserved, example of twelfth-century military architecture. It makes use of a forebuilding attached to the main structure to provide a covered approach to the doorway. Again the emphasis is on the visual impact, but this steep approach through an enclosed space would also be a daunting prospect for an attacker. (Flickr)

Salisbury, and his two nephews Alexander of Lincoln and Nigel of Ely. The king's advisors had previously warned that these men were excessively powerful, and were possibly plotting in favour of the Empress Matilda. They had also all built and garrisoned their own castles, of which the greatest was that of Roger of Salisbury at Devizes. William of Malmesbury describes them as 'obsessed with castle building', which even in an age when churchmen played a prominent role in secular affairs must have seemed suspicious. It is therefore quite likely that Stephen had already decided to take action against them, but Bishop Roger played into his hands by arriving at Oxford with an unruly contingent of armed retainers, who got involved in a brawl with the followers of some of the barons. Several men were killed, and Stephen arrested Roger and Alexander for the serious offence of breaking the peace of the king's court. Nigel, who had been staying in a nearby village, escaped to Devizes, which Bishop Roger had entrusted to his mistress Matilda of Ramsbury. Stephen pursued him and persuaded Matilda to surrender the castle by threatening to hang her son, Roger the Poor. He then proceeded to confiscate the other castles belonging to the three bishops. Naturally this attack on the Church caused great controversy, and a council was called at Winchester to debate it. Stephen risked being censured or even excommunicated, or alternatively the bishops could have sent an emissary to Rome to ask the Pope to intervene, but in the event none of these things happened. Henry of Winchester was strongly critical of his brother's actions, but according to William of Malmesbury Archbishop Hugh of Rouen intervened on Stephen's behalf, arguing that the bishops should have their castles restored only if they could prove that they were entitled to them by canon law. As they could not do so, it was wrong for them to keep them. According to the *Gesta Stephani* the king agreed to accept an unspecified penance, but apart from that the assembled clerics were obliged to accept the situation. The three bishops were released, and the king kept the castles, at least for the time being. Roger of Salisbury died soon afterwards and Alexander seems to have given no further trouble, but in Nigel of Ely Stephen had made a determined enemy for the future. Legally the king was no doubt in the right, and he had arguably strengthened his position by forestalling a potentially dangerous plot, but the most ominous legacy of the affair was the way in which he had succeeded in acquiring castles by arresting their owners while they were attending his court. He was encouraged to employ the same method on several later occasions, with much more damaging results.

The council concluded on 1 September 1139, but the king's relief must have been short-lived. At the end of the same month he received news that the

Empress Matilda and her brother Robert of Gloucester had arrived in England. Their first certain port of call was Arundel Castle in Sussex, which belonged to Henry I's widow, Adeliza of Louvain, and her new husband William d'Aubigny. Chroniclers give various dates for the arrival of Matilda's party in England – Robert de Torigni places it in August – so it is quite likely that they had been secretly in the country for some weeks before their appearance at Arundel, which is several miles inland, having landed on some quiet stretch of shore in order to evade the watch which the king had placed on the south coast ports. At about the same time the veteran troublemaker Baldwin de Redvers had landed on the coast further west, attacked Wareham, and then gone on to seize the royal castle at Corfe. This was no doubt a deliberate diversion, and it succeeded in its aim. Stephen marched quickly to blockade Corfe, only to abandon the siege as soon as the news arrived from Arundel. Adeliza had admitted Matilda and Robert into the castle, 'as guests' according to the *Gesta Stephani*, though she could hardly have been ignorant of their real purpose, since the same source admits that Robert had a 'strong body of troops' with him. William of Malmesbury, however, says that this army amounted to only 140 knights, a far smaller force than most people would have considered necessary for the conquest of a kingdom. The subsequent events and the motivations of the participants have always been a puzzle to historians. As the king's army approached his hideout, Robert took a small escort (William of Malmesbury mentions twelve knights, Robert of Torigny ten knights and ten mounted archers) and escaped, abandoning his sister and making for Bristol where he could rely on popular support. The *Gesta Stephani* relates a rumour (which the author himself claims not to believe) that Robert was intercepted en route by Bishop Henry of Winchester, who made a private agreement with him and let him go. Henry then marched to join Stephen at Arundel, where he persuaded the king to allow Matilda to leave unmolested and go to join her brother. Henry's opinion was that since Robert of Gloucester was the main threat, the king was wasting his time in front of Arundel, and that his enemies could be more easily dealt with if they were located in one place. This argument makes little sense from a strategic point of view, and it is hard to believe that Stephen could have been swayed by it, even though he had once used it himself to make light of being outmanoeuvred at Exeter. Adeliza meanwhile claimed that she had had no intention of succouring the king's enemies, but had merely given hospitality to some noble visitors who also happened to be her relatives by marriage. Eventually Stephen agreed not only to allow Matilda to leave, but even to provide her with an escort, which, says the *Gesta*, 'it is not the custom of honourable knights to refuse to anyone, even their bitterest enemy'.

But can it really have been through a sense of misplaced chivalry that Stephen missed the best opportunity he would ever have to prevent the looming civil war? Possibly. Matilda had not yet displayed any sign of open hostility, and he may have believed that a negotiated peace with her, if not with Robert, was a real possibility. So might Adeliza. It is also plausible, as Henry of Huntingdon suggests, that Stephen considered the castle at Arundel to be impregnable; we know from his actions at Bristol, Ludlow and elsewhere that he was easily discouraged by such fortresses, making some sort of agreement the only honourable option for ending the siege. Bishop Henry's conduct is harder to explain. It is of course possible that the author of the *Gesta* was right to disbelieve the story that he deliberately allowed Robert to escape, but the existence of such rumours shows that he had already attracted suspicions of disloyalty, and he was later to give his support, if only temporarily, to the Empress' party. William of Malmesbury goes further, reporting a claim by one of Matilda's envoys that the bishop had actually written 'frequent' letters inviting her to England.

Whatever the exact circumstances, the outcome of events at Arundel can hardly have been unexpected. Stephen had never succeeded in completely suppressing the opposition to him, and now several of the most prominent among the dissident barons marched to Gloucestershire with their followings to join Robert and Matilda. They included Miles of Gloucester, who the *Gesta* says brought with him 'beasts in countless quantities' stolen from farmers all over England; Brian fitz Count, the son of Alan, Count of Brittany and lord of Wallingford Castle, which commanded a strategic crossing of the Thames south of Oxford; and John the Marshal, who had been holding out against the king in Marlborough. Wallingford was now the nearest rebel stronghold to London and Stephen intended to make it his first target, but he was advised by his barons that it was well supplied and defended and could not be taken without heavy losses. He therefore built two counter-castles nearby to contain the garrison while he marched west to South Cerney, on the border with Gloucestershire, and captured the smaller castle there. Stephen followed this up by besieging Malmesbury, another of the strongholds which the *Gesta* describes as impregnable, but there was no occasion to put this particular claim to the test as Malmesbury was promptly surrendered by its commander, Robert fitz Hubert. The king now advanced on his next objective at Trowbridge, only to learn that Miles of Gloucester had led an army around his flank to Wallingford, surprised the royal garrisons in the counter-castles there, and killed or captured most of them. The author of the *Gesta* blames this reverse on the fact that one of Stephen's castles had been created by fortifying a local church, thus incurring the disapproval of God. The king refused to be diverted and began by constructing engines for the siege of Trowbridge, but when the place continued to hold out, his barons again persuaded him to blockade it rather than continue with siege operations. To this end another counter-castle was built at Devizes, and the two opposing garrisons settled down to raid each other's lands and plunder the intervening countryside until, in the words of the *Gesta*, it was reduced to a 'lamentable desert'.

Over the next few months the Empress' party consolidated its hold over the lower Severn valley and the southern part of the Welsh marches. Some of the local magnates, says William of Malmesbury, joined her out of goodwill and some under compulsion, while others simply sat tight in their castles to await events. In November Miles of Gloucester took Hereford, while another force from Gloucester attacked the city of Worcester, further upstream on the banks of the River Severn. Worcester was an obvious target as the king had recently given its earldom to Waleran of Meulan, one of his most eminent supporters, but it was also a commercial rival which the merchants of Gloucester may have been happy to see destroyed. The local chronicler John of Worcester naturally makes much of the sufferings of the town. The inhabitants had been expecting trouble ever since Matilda arrived in Gloucester, and had already taken many of their goods and even their families into the cathedral precincts for safety, so that there was hardly any room left for the monks, and their services could hardly be heard for the crying of the women and children. The expected attack came on 7 November, while the clergy were carrying the relics of Saint Oswald in procession through the streets, praying for divine assistance. The citizens did manage to beat off the first assault, but the attackers rallied, got over the walls on the north side, and set fire to the wooden buildings inside. In the confusion they looted the city and took away many prisoners for ransom. Stephen and Waleran, arriving soon afterwards, were of course furious, but as Robert of Gloucester carefully avoided giving battle they had no means of retaliation other than revenge attacks on the enemy's territory, which inflicted more damage on the long-suffering population.

If Stephen had planned to contain disaffection within the south-western corner of England, he was unsuccessful. It was noteworthy that the Welsh marcher lords, who had good reason to feel that the king had failed to support them over the past few years, mainly threw in their lot with the rebels, opening the way for the recruitment of the Welsh troops who were soon to take their place alongside Earl Robert's forces. Meanwhile in Cornwall the leading magnate, William fitz Richard, had handed over his castles to his new son-in-law, Reginald, an illegitimate son of Henry I, who promptly declared for

Matilda. Stephen led an army into the county in the summer of 1140, but as usual was unable to completely suppress the revolt. He appointed Alan of Penthievre as Earl of Cornwall and left him to finish the job, but with Matilda's support Reginald pursued a rival claim to the earldom, and hostilities between the two claimants dragged on inconclusively. Other disturbances arose in eastern England. At Ely Bishop Nigel fortified two castles and from them began to launch raids on his royalist neighbours. Ely, situated in the fens about 12 miles north of Cambridge, was in an excellent defensive position on an island surrounded by the River Great Ouse and its marshes, and had served as a base for Hereward the Wake in his resistance to William the Conqueror seventy years earlier. Stephen, however, showed exceptional resolve in dealing with Nigel's rebellion, perhaps aware of the danger posed by an enemy stronghold so close to the centres of royal power in south-eastern England. The only track across the marshes was watched by one of Nigel's castles, so the king built a bridge of boats, and with the aid of a loyal monk who knew of a secret fording place he brought his troops safely onto the island. Most of Nigel's knights were captured, but the bishop himself managed to escape and fled to join the Empress at Gloucester.

The Nature of the 'Anarchy'
It is at this point in his narrative that William of Malmesbury inserts his famous account of the suffering that this style of warfare inflicted on the country. 'There were many castles all over England,' he says, 'each defending its own district, or to be more truthful, plundering it.' The knights who held these castles robbed their own tenants of everything they could find, not sparing even the bishops and monks and their churches. They then resorted to kidnapping people and holding them to ransom, or torturing them to force them to hand over any gold or silver that they possessed. Robert fitz Hubert, who had established himself at Devizes after the evacuation of Malmesbury, was in need of money to hire mercenaries, and was accused of extorting it by smearing his victims with honey and tying them up in the sun, exposed to stinging insects. The Peterborough version of the *Anglo-Saxon Chronicle* tells a similar story, and elaborates further on the sort of ingenious tortures employed. Some, like shutting people in a dungeon with snakes and toads, seem like the stuff of wild rumour, but others are all too plausible. Victims might have knotted strings tightened round their heads, be choked with foul smoke, shut in chests full of sharp stones, loaded with chains, or hung by their thumbs with mail coats on their feet. According to the chronicle these illegal exactions were known as '*tenserie*' – perhaps literally 'protection money', from the French '*tenser*', to

protect. The chronicle goes even further than William in describing the chaos which had overtaken England, where people 'said openly that Christ and His saints slept'. The inhabitants of a village would flee at the approach of any strange riders, even if they numbered only two or three, because they expected them to be robbers. Such men would even plunder the graveyards, ignoring the threat of excommunication for sacrilege. Under these conditions it became impossible for the farmers to sow or harvest their corn, so that the price increased dramatically, while meat, cheese and butter were unobtainable and people began to suffer from starvation. With obvious hindsight, the Peterborough chronicler concludes that 'we suffered nineteen years for our sins'. Some caution, however, is necessary when considering this source. Another of the events of the reign which it reports as fact is the story that on an unspecified Good Friday the Jews of Norwich tortured and crucified a Christian boy called William, who was later sanctified as a martyr. This is the first of several stories of ritual murder carried out by the Jews, and it has become notorious because of its sinister role in their subsequent persecution and expulsion from England. It is, of course, complete invention. Whether it discredits the other atrocity stories repeated by the chronicle must be a matter of opinion, but it is a reminder that much of what the chroniclers tell us is no more than hearsay.

On the other hand a passage very similar to the Peterborough lament appears in the *Gesta Stephani*, this time describing events after the Battle of Wilton in 1143, and presumably referring mainly to the south-west of the country. Clearly the general picture was familiar from various times and places during the reign. The *Gesta* refers to a terrible famine, which forced people to eat dogs, horses, roots and other unpalatable foods, while many died and others, who still had the strength and money to travel, fled abroad. In some places in the autumn of 1143 villages could be found abandoned, the fields 'whitening with a magnificent harvest' which had ripened too late, because the peasants who should have gathered it in had fled or were already dead from starvation. Again we are told how innocent people, even monks, were robbed and beaten, but this time the culprits were alleged to be the foreign mercenaries who had flocked into the country to seek employment with the various combatants, and had been left to fend for themselves when the barons who had hired them ran out of funds. What is sometimes forgotten is that royal armies inflicted just as much 'collateral damage' as those of the barons, and that this was regarded at the time as a distasteful but unavoidable necessity. The *Gesta* describes how in 1149 Stephen called a council in London to decide on 'the easiest way of checking the continual disorder' in the kingdom. Eventually he decided to attack the various districts which were still under the control of his enemies, burn the crops and destroy 'every other means of supporting human life'. He acknowledged that this would be a tragedy for the people, but thought that one decisive campaign would be a lesser evil than the continual raiding and pillaging inflicted on them by the rebels.

Much of the devastation was clearly due to the activities of the various campaigning armies, but it is likely that low-level lawlessness also increased. There is a great deal of data on this subject from later centuries but, as usual when it comes to the activities of the lower classes, there is very little evidence from the twelfth century. It is just possible, however, that one of England's most enduring legends has its roots in this era. The oldest surviving ballads of Robin Hood date from the fifteenth century, although their language suggests that they must have originated a century or so earlier. In modern popular culture of course, the famous outlaw is seen as a contemporary of King Richard I and his brother John, placing him at the very end of the twelfth century, but the ballads give very little indication of the period in which they are supposed to be set. Most scholars place the 'real' Robin Hood – if there ever was one – in the early fourteenth century, but there are a few hints that the origin of the tales might be much earlier. The activities of outlaw bands led by dispossessed aristocrats, as Matthew Paris reminds us (see page 16), dated back to the time of the Norman Conquest. Several legal records from the thirteenth century mention a Robin Hood, suggesting that this had already become a well-known alias for an outlaw. The first written reference to 'rhymes of Robin Hood' is in fact in William Langland's poem *Piers Plowman*, which dates from the 1370s or 1380s: here Sloth, the useless priest, confesses that although he cannot say the Lord's Prayer properly, 'I kan rymes of Robin hood and Randolf Erl of Chestre'. There were three Randolfs or Ranulfs who held the title of Earl of Chester in the Middle Ages. Ranulf le Meschin, the third earl, who died in 1129, was Lord of Cumberland and effectively an autonomous ruler in north-western England under Henry I. The sixth earl, Ranulf de Blondeville, was a contemporary of King John and a witness to Magna Carta, but he was most active in the south Midlands and the south of England rather than the northern counties which have always been associated with the famous outlaw. More famous than either was the fourth earl, Ranulf de Gernon, who played a major role in the events of Stephen's reign, and was most active in the North and north Midlands. Of the three Ranulfs, he seems by far the most likely to have featured in a popular ballad. Of course Langland does not actually say that Ranulf and Robin featured in the same stories, but it is at least possible that they were somehow associated. Also perhaps relevant, if it derives from a genuine tradition, is the connection made by the sixteenth-century writer Anthony Munday between Robin and the Earldom of Huntingdon. This title was extinguished and recreated several times during the Middle Ages, but was most famously in dispute during the reign of Stephen. The question will probably never be satisfactorily resolved, and it is certain that whether or not the stories have a kernel of historical truth, Robin Hood as we know him is largely mythical. But it nevertheless remains a possibility that the tradition originated in the events of the Anarchy, and reflects an otherwise unrecorded popular response to the uncertainty of the times.

More generally, the damage to the life of the countryside caused by the wars has sometimes been exaggerated. The peasants, whose labour underpinned the activities of all classes, were remarkably resilient, and at least in normal times would have been able to produce a surplus of grain. In contrast to the situation at the beginning of the fourteenth century, twelfth-century England was relatively thinly populated and there was still uncultivated land available in many areas for the taking. The practice of making 'assarts', or clearings in forest land, is documented in several charters of the period. It was technically an offence, but in reality was regulated and usually 'punished' by a small fine, making it a practical way for men to increase the land under cultivation. M.M. Postan and others have discussed the question of crop yields in the Middle Ages, and concluded that, although the evidence is patchy, they probably declined steadily between the late twelfth and the late fourteenth centuries due to over-cultivation and a shortage of manure for fertiliser. It follows that in the 1140s we can expect them to have been considerably higher than they were in later and better-documented periods. The famines caused by war, therefore, are likely to have been short-lived. The first reliable data on grain prices comes from the Pipe Rolls of the reign of Henry II, from the 1160s onwards, but Postan has noted that the earliest records show much greater regional variations than those from the thirteenth century. This could be one of the legacies of Stephen's reign, when some areas suffered worse than others from raiding armies, and the lawless state of the country in general made it difficult to transport grain from regions with a surplus, but equally it implies that in places there was a surplus to be traded. Much modern scholarship has focused on the meaning of the term '*vastum*', or 'waste', which to us signifies destruction, as in the phrase 'to lay waste', but is often used in medieval documents to describe land which did not have a taxable value. The sheriffs' accounts of the late 1150s refer to large areas in most regions of the country as '*vastum*', and nineteenth and early twentieth-century writers took this to refer to war damage. The same assumption was made about the entries for Yorkshire in Domesday Book, where the extensive 'waste' was linked to William I's 'harrying of the north' in the aftermath of the conquest. However, since the 1970s historians like W.E. Wightman (for Yorkshire) and J.A. Green (for the Midlands) have established that the word was often used in cases where taxes could not be collected for administrative reasons, and did not necessarily imply that it had gone out of cultivation (Crouch). In any case it is not clear exactly how pasture or arable land could be made unusable in the long term. Burning the crops, slaughtering the plough oxen and even driving out or killing the farmers themselves might cause the loss of a harvest or two, but the land itself would not lose its fertility and could be quickly reoccupied. None of this, of course, diminishes the personal tragedy that the 'Anarchy' must have represented for many thousands of innocent people, but it does help to explain how society as a whole continued to function.

Chapter 9

Lincoln and its Aftermath

By the middle of 1140 it must have seemed to Stephen that the crises of the first few years of his reign had been at least contained, if not fully resolved. After their initial victories the Welsh had reverted to fighting amongst themselves as predicted; there was peace with Scotland, albeit at the cost of abandoning large parts of northern England; and Matilda and her supporters were confined to the south-west, beyond a devastated frontier zone. It was not unusual for a new monarch to have to fight to consolidate his power, and considering the difficulties raised by Stephen's dubious legitimacy, he might be thought to have escaped fairly lightly. But – not for the first nor the last time in his reign – a sudden reversal of fortune was to give his enemies fresh hope.

At some point during 1140, Lincoln Castle, which Stephen had granted – along with the earldom – to William d'Aubigny, was seized by William de Roumare and his half-brother, Earl Ranulf of Chester. The background to the event is obscure, but it has been conjectured that the king had promised Lincoln to William de Roumare but that William d'Aubigny had refused to give it up, or alternatively that Stephen had tried to resolve a dispute between the two men by taking the castle into royal control. The Peterborough chronicle glosses over all the complexities and describes the troubles that followed as 'a very great war between the king and Ranulf Earl of Chester', fought not because Ranulf had a genuine grievance, but because every concession he gained from Stephen further encouraged his ambition. Whatever the truth of the situation, William of Malmesbury tells us that Stephen had visited Lincoln before Christmas 1140 and come to an agreement with Ranulf and his brother, but that soon afterwards, when the king was in London, a deputation had arrived from the citizens of the city asking for his help. They claimed that the two brothers had again taken possession of the castle, which implies that this was contrary to the agreement that they had just made. So Stephen, 'unwilling to miss any chance of increasing his power' as William of Malmesbury puts it, returned to Lincoln and besieged the castle with a small force of knights and foot soldiers. He arrived while the garrison was still celebrating the feast of Christmas, probably around the beginning of January 1141. Seventeen unsuspecting knights were actually captured in the town where they had been carousing, but Ranulf somehow escaped from the blockade and went to his father-in-law Earl Robert of Gloucester for help. The latter, no doubt seeing an opportunity to decide the civil war once and for all, immediately raised an army to attack the king in his exposed position. Many barons who had been disinherited by Stephen in his various reallocations of castles and manors came to join Robert, and he led the army by an indirect route from Gloucester to Lincoln, keeping his objective secret from all but a few of his leading commanders. They stopped in the Derby area for a while to gather more troops, and came in sight of Lincoln in the early morning of 1 or 2 February, while Stephen was still preoccupied with attacking the castle, bombarding it with what the *Gesta Stephani* calls '*balistis*' and other kinds of siege engines.

William of Malmesbury describes the rebels as crossing a river named Trenta, but this must be a mistake, as the Trent flows about 12 miles to the west of Lincoln. In fact the river involved was the Witham, which runs just south of the city. Not unusually for the time of year it was in flood, and William says that Robert's army had to swim across, while Henry of Huntingdon has them wading through an 'almost impassable' marsh. It was evidently a daring operation, and one that the royalists may not have expected their opponents to undertake. The city of Lincoln is situated on top of a hill rising out of what is otherwise an extensive area of flat countryside. The approach from the south is particularly steep, though that from the west, where the castle is located, is somewhat gentler. Only on the east would it have been possible to bring siege engines into action without having to shoot uphill, with a consequent reduction in range, and so it is likely that Stephen's machines were deployed on that side, between the castle walls and the cathedral. Bradbury argues that, having swum or forded the Witham, the rebels must have approached the city from the south-west, in which case the battle took place on the flat ground immediately below the west gate of the castle. Today this ground is partly built up and there is no monument to indicate the site, but a panoramic view of the general area can still be obtained from the castle walls. The second day of February was the Feast of the Purification of St Mary, and Stephen was in the cathedral hearing Mass when the approach of the rebels was reported. The *Gesta Stephani* tells how the king was receiving a candle from the bishop when it broke and went out, but it was quickly repaired and relit. This was seen, at any rate with hindsight, as an omen, but Stephen's counsellors did argue at the time that he should not fight, partly on account of the holiness of the day, but also more practically because he was outnumbered, and would be wise to retire and raise a larger army before returning to give battle. This he refused to do, fearing for his reputation and perhaps, as Davis suggests, still feeling the need to redeem his family honour from the disgrace of his father's flight from Antioch. As Bradbury points out, he had also spent much of the preceding two years trying without success to bring the Empress and her supporters to battle, so he may have been reluctant to miss this opportunity despite his disadvantage in numbers. John of Hexham also records that some of his knights were equally eager to fight, and insulted those who advised caution as 'unwarlike boys'. According to the *Gesta* Stephen sent a body of knights and infantry to contest the river crossing, but the rebels quickly scattered them and advanced into the plain. So the two armies faced each other and deployed for what was to be one of only a handful of pitched battles in the civil war.

Henry of Huntingdon says that Ranulf of Chester deployed the army in three lines, with his own followers in the first line, the disaffected barons in the second, and the contingent of Robert of Gloucester in the third. In an alternative interpretation, favoured for example by Bradbury, these three battles might have been drawn up side by side in a single line, with Ranulf on the right, Robert in the centre and the disinherited barons on the left. It is of course possible that the army advanced in column, with one division behind the other, and then deployed into line abreast before joining battle. We cannot be certain of the precise command arrangements; Earl Robert was senior in rank and is usually assumed to have been in overall charge, but on this occasion the chroniclers prefer to emphasize the role of Ranulf. Other men of high rank in the army included Miles of Gloucester, Brian fitz Count, and Stephen's old enemy Baldwin de Redvers, who may have commanded the 'disinherited' barons. On the rebel right, or possibly on both flanks, were bodies of Welsh soldiers whom Orderic says were led by three princes – Magog ap Maredudd of Powys, Morgan ab Owain of Glamorgan and Cadwaladr ap Gruffydd, the brother of Prince Owain of Gwynedd. They seem to have come at Ranulf's instigation, but they probably fought under their own leaders. Crouch argues that they would have included the '*teulu*' or household troops of these princes, and so at least some them might have fought on horseback, though perhaps not as effectively in a close-quarters melee as the Anglo-Norman knights. The *Gesta Stephani*, prejudiced as ever, describes the behaviour of the Welsh troops as 'intolerable', perhaps alluding to a lack of discipline or a propensity for looting, but they are unlikely to have been the rabble that the author would have us believe they were.

Stephen seems to have tried to counter the enemy's superior numbers by concentrating his force in the centre. Here he placed himself in the middle of a 'densely packed' body of dismounted knights, while the contingents commanded by the loyal earls remained mounted, probably forming two small wings on either side of the centre. William of Aumale and William of Ypres, both experienced commanders, were probably on the left wing, since we are told that they engaged the Welsh, whom Henry of Huntingdon places on the enemy right. Although not mentioned specifically in this passage, a large group of citizens from Lincoln were also present; Henry later quotes Robert of Gloucester as telling his men that the citizens were deployed very close to the city walls, and would no doubt retreat inside them as soon as they were threatened. It is therefore reasonable to suppose that they were placed on the left flank of the royal army, not far from the west gate of the castle. Possibly they were tasked with preventing a sortie from within the castle, which could have threatened the rear while Stephen's men were preoccupied with the attack from the front. Unusually, no archers are mentioned as being present on either side, though if they had been fielded they might have had only a limited role thanks to the speed with which the armies clashed hand to hand.

Henry of Huntingdon then reports the customary pre-battle speeches. These – whether genuine or not – are as ever worth examining as evidence of what educated contemporaries thought the two sides were fighting for. It is remarkable how little the rebels apparently had to say about the cause of the Empress Matilda. Ranulf of Chester began by thanking his allies for supporting him against the 'treacherous king', who had broken the truce that had been agreed. 'Since I am the cause of your peril', he added, 'it is right that I should put myself in danger first', proposing that he should lead the charge in person. But Robert of Gloucester replied that his own motive for being there was quite different. After mentioning in passing that the king had 'usurped the realm, contrary to the oaths which he swore to my sister', he went on to condemn him for taking lands from those who had the right to them in order to reward his own cronies. Robert concluded that the disinherited earls were those who had been most wronged, and so they should have the honour of attacking in the front rank. If the chronicler is to be believed, he continued by saying that the rebels had no choice but to fight, as there was no hope of saving themselves by flight because of the marshes behind them. He then proceeded to insult the commanders on the opposing side, in a passage which one imagines Henry, who was no admirer of Stephen, composing with some relish. Alan of Penthievre, Duke of the Bretons, was an 'abominable man' whose ambition was to excel all others in cruelty. Waleran of Meulan was not only wicked but a coward, 'slow to attack, quick to retreat'. Hugh Bigod, making a rare appearance on

Stephen's side, was well known to be a liar and a perjurer on account of the oath he had sworn in support of Stephen's accession, while the behaviour of William of Aumale was so disgusting that his wife had left him. Somewhat inconsistently, Robert then singled out an unnamed nobleman who was presumably William de Warenne, the Earl of Surrey, as an adulterer who had stolen William of Aumale's wife, and was furthermore a drunkard who knew nothing of the art of war. Like Waleran, Simon de Senlis of Northampton was all talk and no action. Finally Robert comes to William of Ypres, about whom he has little to say, because 'words have not yet been invented which can properly describe the extent and ramifications of his treacheries, the filth and horror of his obscenities'. In general, the earl concludes, Stephen's supporters are all 'of the same character as their king'.

On the other side the king, who was aware that he was a poor speaker, entrusted the task to Baldwin fitz Gilbert, whom we last saw leading a failed expedition to Wales. Two of the surviving manuscripts of Henry's History feature drawings of Baldwin, standing on a small hillock and leaning on a long-handled axe as he addressed the troops. He pointed out that there were three factors that should be considered before joining battle: the justice of one's cause, the number of the troops, and the relative abilities of the two sides. In all these respects the king's army had an advantage. As far as justice was concerned, they were fighting for the lawful king, to whom they had sworn allegiance. Their knights were no fewer than those of the rebels (a statement which was almost certainly untrue), and the royal infantry was more densely packed. And Stephen, a knight of 'boundless valour', was himself worth thousands of lesser men. On the other hand, among the enemy commanders, Earl Robert was a blusterer with 'the mouth of a lion and the heart of a rabbit', who threatens but does nothing, while Earl Ranulf was reckless but unreliable and quick to give up, and in his previous battles he had either run away or had to make do with a Pyrrhic victory in which he suffered more casualties than his opponents. The Welshmen lacked experience and knowledge of warfare, and the rest of the rebel army were nothing but deserters and vagabonds. You could see, Baldwin concluded, that the enemy were already thinking of how to escape, but could not do so because of the difficult terrain to their rear. Therefore they were already destined to be taken prisoner. If only there were more of them!

There is a strong impression here that Baldwin was whistling in the dark, and it was not long before he was proved to have been overly optimistic. Even as he finished speaking, the rebel army attacked. As Robert of Gloucester had suggested, the 'disinherited' were now in the lead, and they crashed violently into the royal line, at least part of which was formed of knights fighting on foot. William of Malmesbury says that some of the royalists attempted to engage in a pre-battle activity with lances 'which they call jousting' ('*quod iustam vocant*'), meaning presumably that they mounted their horses and rode out to challenge their opponents to single combat. But when they saw that the rebels were not fighting with lances but with drawn swords, and instead of seeking out individual opponents were charging en masse into the king's line, they abandoned the attempt and fled. It is possible that a few of the royalist barons still did not believe that Robert and Ranulf intended to make a serious attack on the king in person. Alternatively, Orderic suggests that some of them were secretly in communication with the enemy, and had even hedged their bets by sending men to join both armies, so it is possible that this 'jousting' was part of a prearranged plan, a sort of token resistance before they rode off and left the king to his fate. According to Henry of Huntingdon the royal centre was overthrown almost immediately by the force of the charge, with some being killed, others taken prisoner and a third group running for their lives. Nevertheless, the fact that there were casualties suggests that an actual physical clash did take place, however briefly, and this may be a rare instance from the wars of Stephen's reign of two bodies of mounted knights charging into contact with each other. Several historians have attempted to reconstruct what actually happened in such a clash, because it is obvious that two lines of cavalry advancing in close order could not ride into each other at speed; even if the horses and men could be persuaded to do something so evidently suicidal, the result would have been a pile-up with casualties on both sides far in excess of what we read about in the sources. Presumably if such a collision seemed imminent, both sides would halt or slow their horses to a walking pace before attempting to fence with their weapons, and the greater length of lances over swords might be expected to have given them an advantage in this situation. But at Lincoln the royalist knights were not in close formation, and so any of them who stayed to fight might have found themselves opposed by several of the enemy at once. In this situation the lance's length would be a liability, as the point could only be directed against one foe at a time, while the remaining opponents could avoid it and get close enough to use their swords.

Henry's statement that the royalist cavalry was 'divided into three' has been interpreted to mean that it was split into three groups by the charge, and must therefore have originally been in a single continuous line, deployed all the way across Stephen's front ahead of the dismounted men (Bradbury). But this would have been tactically very unwise, especially in view of the inferior numbers and political unreliability of the earls' contingents, and Henry may have intended only to describe the three different fates of the defeated cavalry on the two wings – as casualties, prisoners of war or fugitives. Meanwhile William of Aumale and William of Ypres attacked the Welshmen on the rebel wing, and routed them with ease. This was not surprising, as the Welsh were fighting on flat, open ground which gave all the advantages to the Norman cavalry and William of Ypres' heavily-armed Flemish infantry, and it is likely that Earl Ranulf had anticipated their defeat and kept some of his knights in hand ready to take the royalists in the flank as they pursued them. Henry of Huntingdon merely states that William of Aumale's force was in turn 'routed in a moment' by the Earl of Chester's men. Henry goes on to say diplomatically that William of Ypres, who was a very experienced soldier, was now cut off from the king and realized that it would be impossible to help him, so he rode away in order to fight another day. The *Gesta* is less charitable, accusing William of Ypres, along with Waleran of Meulan, of shamefully running away before ever getting to close quarters with the enemy. By this time Stephen and his remaining followers – including Baldwin fitz Gilbert – were on foot and surrounded by the victorious rebel cavalry, but they continued to repulse every charge, following the example of the heroic figure of the king. The latter seems to have fallen into a sort of berserk fury; in the words of Robert of Torigny 'like a lion, grinding his teeth and foaming at the mouth like a wild boar'. Stephen seems to have been the only man in the army who lived up to the claims made for him by Baldwin fitz Gilbert before the battle, leading Robert of Torigny to conclude that if they had had another hundred like him they could never have been beaten. Orderic Vitalis describes how the king's sword eventually broke, and a citizen of Lincoln who was nearby handed him a 'Norse axe' with which he continued to strike at all who came near him. This is interesting as it suggests that some at least of the men of Lincoln had not retreated inside the walls as Earl Robert had predicted. It also tells us something of how the men of the city were armed. Henry of Huntingdon has Stephen fighting first with an axe and then, when that broke, drawing his sword, but that sequence of events seems less likely; every Anglo-Norman knight would carry a sword, which would normally be the weapon of choice once the lance had broken or been discarded. The battle continued to rage until Stephen's axe also broke, whereupon someone hit him on the head with a stone – William of Malmesbury says that no one ever knew who struck the blow – and a rebel knight named William of Cahagnes seized him by the helmet and shouted 'Come here everyone, I've got the king!' Stephen was presumably still conscious, as according to Orderic he refused to surrender to an ordinary knight, but he was dragged before Robert of Gloucester and finally agreed to yield to him. Baldwin and Richard fitz Urse were captured at the same time, fighting beside the king with equal courage despite their numerous wounds, but other royalist knights continued to fight on, until at last they were all captured or killed. The people of Lincoln also suffered for their support of the king, as the victorious rebels broke into the city and set fire to it. Many of the militia who had been on the field were killed in this final phase of the battle. Orderic says that around 500 of them tried to cross the river to safety and were drowned when their overloaded boats capsized, but this story seems suspect. For one thing, the River Witham lay behind the rebel army and was by no means the easiest escape route, and furthermore the boats can hardly have been moored on the river ready for use, or the rebels would not have had to swim during their approach march. One wonders if this story does not conceal the deliberate drowning of prisoners, or some similar atrocity. William of Malmesbury adds that not only did the rebels feel no sympathy for the citizens, but the royalists also blamed them for the disaster, presumably because they had invited the king into the trap by asking for his help.

Robert of Gloucester at first treated his royal captive with respect and did not allow any of his followers even to insult him, but after Stephen had been brought to the Empress at Gloucester he was taken on to Bristol, where he was put in chains. William of Malmesbury tries to pass the blame for this humiliating treatment on to some unnamed persons who put pressure on the earl, though the *Gesta Stephani* suggests that, since it was out of the question to kill an anointed king, there was an agreement between Matilda and Robert to keep him locked away until he died. According to the *Gesta*, 'the greater part of the kingdom at once submitted' to Matilda, who lost no time in taking advantage of the situation. A handful of Stephen's supporters attempted to continue the fight, but they were isolated and were quickly mopped up by Earl Robert's army. Alan of Penthievre planned an attack on Ranulf of Chester in order to avenge the king, but was captured and tortured until he agreed to hand over his castles to Ranulf. Alan's fall also resolved the stand-off in Cornwall, where his rival Reginald now took control in the name of the Empress. Earl Hervey of Wiltshire and Hugh 'the Poor' of Bedford tried to hold out in their castles at Devizes and Bedford respectively, but were quickly evicted and sent into exile. One of the last of the great magnates to abandon Stephen's cause was Waleran of Meulan, but by September even he had sworn allegiance to Matilda. Only in Kent, where Stephen's Queen Matilda and William of Ypres had retired to regroup, was there still open resistance to the Empress' cause. Meanwhile at the beginning of March the Empress arrived in Winchester, where she welcomed her uncle David of Scotland, and received the homage of Stephen's brother Henry and many of the other bishops. Of even greater practical importance were the keys to the castle and the royal treasury, depleted though the latter had become. The week after Easter a great council was held, at which Henry of Winchester and Archbishop Theobald recommended that she should succeed to the now vacant throne, and conferred on her the title of 'Lady of England and Normandy'. According to William of Malmesbury, who was an eyewitness, Henry justified his betrayal of his brother on the grounds that he had proved to be an ineffective ruler, who had not imposed peace or enforced justice, and who above all had turned against the Church with the arrest of the bishops in 1139. In view of Henry's later actions it seems unlikely that he was being entirely sincere, and no doubt his main motive was to protect his own position. The *Gesta Stephani* portrays him as playing a waiting game, anticipating that a situation might arise which would enable him to help his brother. He may have understood early on that Matilda's character would make it difficult for her to retain the loyalty of the headstrong nobility, but he can hardly have expected the dramatic change of fortune which was to come.

William says that the delegates who travelled to Winchester from London pleaded for the release of the king, a request which was refused, but otherwise they seemed happy to recognize the Empress. Arrangements were therefore made for her to enter the city in preparation for her coronation at Westminster, due to take place on 24 June. But by now all the chroniclers agree that Matilda was beginning to alienate her supporters by her tactless and arrogant manner. It is easy to dismiss some of their comments as mere prejudice against a woman in a position of power, especially when the *Gesta* criticises her lack of 'the modest gait and bearing proper to the gentle sex'. But there is no doubt that she did upset many people who had previously been willing to support her. The *Gesta* says that when she held audiences with men like King David, Bishop Henry, and even her own brother Robert of Gloucester, she not only ignored the customary forms of politeness, but spoke to them arrogantly and openly disregarded their advice. Some scholars have charitably suggested that she was simply adhering to the more formal court manners of Germany, where she had spent her formative years, but the refusal to take advice surely points to a more significant failure to understand how heavily she was forced to rely on her leading supporters. Inevitably an embassy from Queen Matilda, asking the Empress to consider the rights of her and Stephen's son Eustace, was unceremoniously rebuffed. And when the citizens of London begged for confirmation of the rights which Stephen had granted them, and for relief from taxes on account of the losses caused by the war, they were instead met with a demand for vastly increased contributions.

The population of London is thought to have roughly doubled during the twelfth century from a starting point of around 20,000, so a figure of 30,000 seems a reasonable approximation for the 1140s (Pryor). Like Lincoln and a number of other cities, London could muster a town militia for the purpose of self-defence, but unlike those elsewhere, the London militia was sufficiently numerous and well equipped to be a significant military force even outside the bounds of the city. The true strength of this force is not known, but it may have been larger than all but the greatest feudal armies that could be raised in England. To the author of the *Gesta* the Londoners were 'a mob of citizens, great beyond expression or calculation'. Ian Heath quotes a source from the 1170s as giving a total figure for the militia of 80,000, comprising 20,000 cavalry and 60,000 infantry, though he plausibly suggests that the real numbers might have been around a tenth of that. If the population figure given above is approximately correct then the male population of military age might have numbered about 8,000, which fits well with Heath's estimate. However, these men would not all have been equipped or necessarily willing to fight, though they might have served to swell the 'mob', participate in the looting and urge on their better-armed comrades. Later, at the Battle of Winchester, the *Gesta* records the presence of 1,000 Londoners, 'magnificently equipped with helmets and mail corselets', and this is the best indication we have of the number of fully-armed fighters that might have been available. They were part-time warriors – some of them, as successful merchants, able to afford the equivalent of knightly arms and armour, but probably not able to devote themselves to regular training. Therefore, even if they were mounted, they probably lacked the skills to fight on horseback like the knights; we might imagine them as looking something like the Anglo-Saxon huscarles depicted in the Bayeux Tapestry, especially as we know that the two-handed Anglo-Danish axe, the characteristic huscarle weapon, was still in use among their contemporaries at Lincoln. Unfortunately we have no contemporary evidence for how they were commanded. The first mention of a Mayor of London comes from towards the end of the twelfth century, but it is likely that the institution existed earlier, and that despite the chroniclers' characterization of the citizens as a 'mob' (the Latin noun used in the *Gesta* is '*copia*', which is often used to signify an abundance of something), there was at least a rudimentary chain of command. Elsewhere the *Gesta* repeatedly refers to a '*communis*', which its translator suggests refers to a 'commune' in the technical sense of a town corporation.

In any case the military strength of the Londoners was such that the Empress would have been well advised to placate them, but she seems to have entirely ignored their potential. In fact she added insult to injury, informing their representatives that as they had previously conspired with Stephen against her, it was only just for them to have to suffer in their turn. And when Queen Matilda and William of Ypres appeared outside the city with an army and began to ravage the lands belonging to the citizens, the Empress did nothing to prevent them. The Londoners were in an impossible position, seeing their land and property destroyed by one faction, while the other confiscated their moveable wealth in taxes but provided no protection in return. Their response must have been well planned, but no hint of it reached the Empress. One evening in early June, not long before the date set for her coronation, she was sitting down to dinner – apparently in lodgings just outside the city walls – when the church bells began to ring. On this signal the Londoners opened the gates and charged out en masse. Matilda's army was formidable, but it was caught completely off guard, and she and her companions could do nothing but mount their horses and ride for safety. Among the eminent men who had apparently been dining with her and were thus put to flight were Robert of Gloucester, Henry of Winchester and David of Scotland. William of Malmesbury describes the retreat as being carried out without fuss and under military discipline, but the more plausible account in the *Gesta* is very different. Here we are told that the Empress' companions were so shaken that they forgot their duty to protect her, and instead abandoned her and made for their own strongholds. The panic spread, and the various barons and their retinues fled in all directions, while the 'mob' broke into their abandoned lodgings and seized huge quantities of plunder. However, although the *Gesta* scornfully describes the fugitives scattering 'as though the Londoners were hot on their heels', they were not actually pursued, which tends to support the conclusion that the citizens lacked effective cavalry. Matilda, Robert and David eventually reached sanctuary at Oxford, but their army was temporarily out of action until it could be rallied. Bishop Henry, whom the *Gesta Stephani* accuses of having been involved in the plot against the Empress from the start, returned to Winchester from where he reopened negotiations with Queen Matilda, who had quickly seized her opportunity and entered London to an enthusiastic welcome.

Chapter 10

Winchester and Oxford:
The Turning Points

The first target of the Empress' wrath, then, was Bishop Henry. Nevertheless she waited at Oxford for six weeks before acting against him, and even then Richard Oram argues that it was probably David and Robert who pushed her into action. The Scottish king was surprisingly reluctant to abandon her, despite the risks to his own safety. His main aim was probably to secure the backing of whoever was to rule England for his choice for the Bishopric of Durham, but Oram suggests that he may also have been anxious to ensure that Matilda did not give away his and his son's lands in England in her increasingly desperate quest for supporters. Finally, at the end of July, the Empress marched to Winchester and quickly occupied most of the city. The *Gesta* lists some of the eminent men who accompanied the army, which it describes as 'a wonderful concentration of forces', showing that the troops routed outside London had not only been rallied but substantially reinforced. Apart from David of Scotland and Robert of Gloucester, Ranulf of Chester, Baldwin de Redvers, Miles of Gloucester, Reginald of Cornwall and several others are named, though William of Malmesbury, intent on playing down the magnitude of the disaster which was soon to engulf them, says that Ranulf arrived late and his contribution was ineffective. But somehow this sledgehammer of an army failed to crack the nut at which it was aimed. Bishop Henry was forewarned (William of Malmesbury says that Matilda, still believing that his loyalty was subject to negotiation, had actually advised him of her coming), and escaped on a swift horse to his fortified palace at Wolvesey, on the south-eastern edge of the city. From there, despite the presence of a huge besieging army, Henry managed not only to send messages to those barons who had remained loyal to Stephen, but even to hire mercenary knights to harass the enemy from outside the town. According to the *Gesta* other supporters of Stephen also held out in a castle 'in the middle of the town', a description which might refer to the old royal palace near the cathedral. Queen Matilda promptly arrived with her forces from Kent, commanded by William of Ypres and reinforced by 1,000 heavily-armed Londoners, and the loyal barons summoned by Henry came from all directions to join her, picketing the roads to prevent supplies of food from reaching the Empress. The latter now found herself caught between two fires, still besieging the bishop's stronghold while being besieged in her turn by another hostile army. For a while both sides maintained their positions, skirmishing daily in the streets but avoiding a general engagement. Henry of Huntingdon says that, unlike the confusion of a pitched battle, here the exploits of individual knights were performed in full view of both sides, so that there was plenty of opportunity to display their prowess and enhance reputations. Both armies allegedly regarded this as an enjoyable interlude, though it must have been less pleasant for the townspeople. While throwing incendiary missiles at their attackers, the bishop's garrison managed to burn down most of their own town; it is not clear whether or not this was deliberate, but it must have made life even more difficult for the Empress' men, who were also now running short of food. By contrast William of Malmesbury describes how the roads between London and Winchester were crowded with supply convoys on their way to the queen's army – an interesting confirmation of the role of the city as a logistic base.

The timid response of the Empress' commanders seems at odds with the *Gesta*'s description of their strength and self-confidence, and the author himself appears to have no explanation for this other than God's intention to humiliate them. But they made no attempt to meet the queen in open battle. Instead they decided to build a castle at Wherwell Abbey, six miles north-west of the city near Andover, and garrison it with 300 knights. The idea was apparently to split the queen's forces and secure a supply route, but of course it also involved splitting the Empress' army, and could only have succeeded if the enemy had remained unaware of the manoeuvre. In fact it was quickly detected, and what the *Gesta* now describes as 'the king's forces', though still under the command of William of Ypres, caught the garrison while the work of fortification was still in progress. They killed or captured many of them in the first onset, and forced the survivors to take refuge in the church. Then, as the *Gesta* reports with obvious horror, they threw burning torches into the church, ignoring the cries of the nuns who had also taken shelter there. When the defenders emerged to escape the flames they were taken prisoner and dragged off, tied up with thongs. John Marshal, who may have been their commander, was one of the last to leave, and was partially blinded by molten lead dripping from the roof. The *Gesta* tells us that when Robert of Gloucester heard the news he regarded it as a 'grievous calamity' and despaired of being able to continue the siege. So it was decided to break out. On 14 September the Empress' army emerged from the gates of the town and formed a single close-order column, surrounding the baggage. According to William of Malmesbury Robert placed his sister at the front of the column under the protection of Brian fitz Count and Earl Reginald of Cornwall to give her the best chance of escaping, while he remained at the rear. The ensuing engagement is often dismissed as not so much a battle as a massacre, the 'rout of Winchester' as the *Gesta Stephani* calls it, but it was one of a very few occasions on which the opposing armies clashed in the open, and it is unfortunate that our sources provide so few details of what happened. If the loss of 300 knights at Wherwell had so fatally weakened the Empress' army it is possible that it had never been as large as the *Gesta* implies, and certainly this passage suggests that the queen and William of Ypres now commanded a much larger force, 'in numbers beyond expression', which was able to completely surround the column, cut it off from Winchester and charge it from all sides simultaneously.

Just as it had outside London, the Empress' army displayed little cohesion or discipline, and the troops seem to have dispersed in all directions with no serious attempt at resistance. The *Gesta* moves straight from the initial charge to the pursuit, which spread out over the countryside after the fugitives. Leaving the pursuit to the mounted knights, the men of London, accompanied by many of their comrades, entered the town and thoroughly looted it. Meanwhile the battlefield was scattered with abandoned shields and coats of mail, gold and silver vessels, fine cloaks and other plunder, and exhausted horses which wandered aimlessly about, having thrown their riders in the confusion. Many of the defeated were found in hiding and dragged out ignominiously, while others were caught by the local peasants and beaten. Matilda herself escaped to the sanctuary of John Marshal's castle at Ludgershall, then on to Devizes and finally to Gloucester. Florence of Worcester's story that she rode astride like a man, rather than side-saddle, is meant to imply that she travelled with undignified haste. The *Gesta Stephani* hints that a close relationship between Matilda and Brian fitz Count, later to be the subject of romantic stories, began with their shared hardships at this time. Chibnall is, however, surely right to point out that, had there been anything improper about this relationship, the author of the *Gesta*, as a member of the clergy and an opponent of Matilda, would have been quick to condemn them both. King David was allegedly caught on three occasions during his flight to Scotland, but each time bribed his captors to let him go, and returned home 'in grief and weariness', with only a handful of followers. Only Robert of Gloucester's rearguard kept its order. It retired as far as Stockbridge, about eight miles to the west where the road to Salisbury crosses the River Test, apparently in an attempt to cover the retreat of the Empress towards Devizes. Here it was finally surrounded by a contingent of Flemish mercenaries under William de Warenne. Robert was taken alive and handed over to William of Ypres, who imprisoned him in Rochester Castle.

William of Malmesbury says that, in contrast to the harsh treatment of her husband, the queen refused to allow him to be chained, but instead offered him enormous wealth and power in return for his support. Robert, however, refused all the bribes and refused to promise anything without first obtaining the consent of his sister. The same source describes the lengthy and difficult negotiations which followed between the Queen and the Empress, lasting until the beginning of November, but there can only ever have been one outcome. The leaders of both sides were prisoners of war, neither would compromise with their opponents, and the option which would perhaps have appealed to their fifteenth-century descendants – to put them to death – was in a twelfth-century context unthinkable in the case of men of such rank. So it was agreed that they would be exchanged, although the elaborate arrangements made for the process showed that neither side trusted each other. On 1 November 1141 Stephen was released from Bristol, in exchange for Queen Matilda and their son Eustace who were held as hostages. When two days later the king reached Winchester, where Robert had now been taken, the earl was set free, leaving his son William behind. As soon as Robert arrived in Bristol Queen Matilda and Eustace were released, and on their arrival at Winchester William too was free to rejoin his father. There followed, says William of Malmesbury, a rather awkward reunion between Stephen and his brother Henry of Winchester, who had not only defected to the Empress after the Battle of Lincoln, but had been conspicuously slow to campaign for Stephen's release. In fact a letter from Pope Innocent was read out at a conference at which Stephen was present – a circumstance surely unforeseen by both pope and bishop – rebuking Henry for his dilatoriness in this respect and urging him to make greater efforts to help his brother. To make things even more embarrassing for Henry an emissary from the Empress was also present, and he publicly reminded the bishop that two years previously he had written to Matilda urging her to come to England, and that subsequently he had promised not to do anything to the detriment of his mistress beyond sending a token force of no more than twenty knights to support Stephen. Henry defended himself on the grounds that he had only agreed to help Matilda under duress, and that she had in any case broken her promises to him regarding the freedom of the churches in the areas she controlled. In the end his brother accepted his excuses, recognizing the positive role which he had played in more recent events as well as his undoubted abilities.

From a military point of view the two sides ended the year 1141 more or less where they had started it. Perhaps not surprisingly, both the main protagonists were exhausted by what they had been through, and were incapable of taking the field again for several months. Stephen, in fact, became so ill that rumours spread that he was dead, but by the summer of 1142 he had fully recovered. The Empress' party were clearly demoralized by their setbacks, and at a council held at Devizes during Lent they decided to send for assistance to Matilda's husband, Geoffrey of Anjou, in the hope of breaking the deadlock. Geoffrey's reply, when it arrived, was to the effect that he would talk to Earl Robert in person, but that there was no point in sending anyone else. Robert was reluctant to leave England, as he claimed that he did not trust the other barons to protect Matilda, but eventually he agreed to make the journey, taking with him hostages to ensure the good behaviour of those left behind. He arrived at Caen after a difficult sea crossing from Wareham and met Geoffrey, who proceeded to make a series of excuses for not being able to help. Robert even joined him on campaign and assisted in the capture of ten of Stephen's castles in Normandy in the hope of changing his mind, but was eventually forced to return home empty handed. Geoffrey's only concession was to allow his and Matilda's son Henry to accompany Robert to England, in William of Malmesbury's words, 'that on seeing him the nobles might be inspired to fight for the cause of the lawful heir.' The implication that the current heir, the Empress, had failed to inspire them is inescapable.

Meanwhile Matilda had established her headquarters in Oxford, which with neighbouring Wallingford was the nearest place still in her possession to London. The *Gesta Stephani* describes the castle at Oxford as almost impregnable on account of the height and strength of the defences, and the depth of the water with which it was almost completely surrounded. Here the River Cherwell, flowing from the north, meets the Thames, and in the Middle Ages their combined waters contributed to a wide expanse of marshy and seasonally-flooded land which barred the approaches from the west and south. The site was further protected by the outlying castles which Matilda had built at Woodstock, Cirencester and other places. As soon as his health recovered

Stephen began operations against some of the more vulnerable of these locations. First he attacked Cirencester, where the garrison evacuated the castle before he arrived and abandoned the town, then Bampton, which the *Gesta* says was taken by storm, and Radcot, which surrendered. At some point he also took Wareham, the port from which Robert of Gloucester had sailed to Normandy, burnt the town and put his own garrison in the castle. Then on 29 September 1142 the king arrived on the banks of the Thames opposite Oxford. The garrison assembled on the far side, and believing themselves safe from attack they proceeded to hurl insults at the king and shoot arrows across the river. But, says the *Gesta Stephani*, someone showed Stephen the location of an old and very deep ford, and he immediately led his knights across it, presumably on horseback, 'swimming rather than wading'. Reaching the far bank, Stephen charged the enemy, who were driven back as far as the gates of the city, enabling the rest of the royal army to struggle across the river and deploy for battle. The Empress' troops opened the gates and fled inside, and in the confusion small groups of Stephen's men followed them and threw burning torches into the houses, starting a fire which destroyed much of the city. The *Gesta* describes this as a 'dreadful disaster' for Matilda's followers, some of whom were killed, others captured, and others – who presumably could not get inside the castle in time – forced to abandon Oxford and escape into the countryside.

What followed is probably the best-known episode in the history of the Anarchy. Matilda and her remaining knights retreated into the castle and held out for three months, while Stephen devoted all his efforts to capturing her. Siege engines were brought up to batter the walls, and guards were posted all around the perimeter to prevent supplies getting in to the garrison. By the end of December the defenders were starving, while the sufferings of both sides were made worse by a sharp frost and a heavy fall of snow. No doubt the watchmen outside the castle had relaxed their vigilance as they huddled round their fires, because they failed to observe the Empress as, accompanied by only three knights, she slipped out of a window, crossed the frozen river, and escaped on foot to Abingdon, where she found horses to take her on to Wallingford. Henry of Huntingdon is the source for the detail that she was dressed in white for camouflage in the snow. The author of the *Gesta* remarks that escaping unscathed from various disasters was becoming a speciality for Matilda, as this was the fourth time that she had done so: the first was at Arundel on her arrival in England, followed by the debacle in London, the 'rout of Winchester', and now Oxford.

When Stephen learned of her escape he abandoned Oxford, whose remaining garrison eventually surrendered, and marched south towards the coast. Robert of Gloucester had now returned from the Continent, recaptured Wareham and begun to muster a large army. His declared aim was to rescue his sister, though – perhaps because he shared the popular view that Oxford was impregnable, perhaps because she was less important to him than he pretended – he does not seem to have made any serious attempt to do so until it was far too late. Instead he wandered westwards along the Dorset coast, occupying the Isle of Portland and a castle at Lulworth. By the summer of 1143 Stephen had launched a successful raid on Wareham and then returned northwards to place his army at the abbey at Wilton, the old county town of Wiltshire. Wilton lies just west of Salisbury, blocking the direct route from Wareham to Wallingford, and it was there that the rival armies met. The Battle of Wilton was the third and last of the field engagements between the main opposing forces in the war, but once again the chroniclers give few details of events. We cannot even be sure exactly when it took place. The later chronicler Gervase of Canterbury gives a date at the beginning of July 1143, which is supported by the narrative of the *Gesta Stephani*, but Henry of Huntingdon places it before the siege of Oxford, in the previous summer. The *Gesta* tells us that although Stephen was supported by a contingent led by Henry of Winchester, and had summoned additional troops from all over England, the muster was still not complete when Robert of Gloucester arrived with 'all his chief confederates'. This may imply that the king was outnumbered and not yet ready to fight, but when the enemy army approached he advanced to meet them and battle was joined, presumably on the downs somewhere south-west of the abbey. Gervase says that Robert attacked at sunset and Stephen was taken by surprise as his army was standing down for the night, but the *Gesta* describes something more like a formal pitched battle. According to the latter source Robert deployed his men '*bellico more*' – 'in warlike fashion' – in three divisions, while Stephen drew up his army 'in squadrons on both flanks', so perhaps, because of lack of numbers, resorting to a formation of only two divisions. Henry of Huntingdon says that the royal knights tried to break through Robert's formation, but the latter responded with a resolute charge which drove the king's men back and finally encircled them. At some point Stephen and Bishop Henry realized that they were in danger of being captured and fled from the field, leaving the king's steward, William Martel, to fight a rearguard action. William was surrounded and captured, eventually being released in exchange for the castle of Sherborne, while Robert's men exacted the usual revenge on the town of Wilton, looting and setting fire to the houses. Some fugitives who had taken refuge in the nunnery were dragged out and tied up for later ransoming, another act which attracted the condemnation of the chroniclers as a violation of the sanctity of church property.

Stephen and Robert of Gloucester had now met twice in pitched battle, and on both occasions Robert had been victorious. Bradbury's verdict that the king 'was outshone as a battle leader' by his adversary therefore seems reasonable, despite the lack of detailed information on his deployments or method of command. Bradbury and others have also argued that the success of the Norman cavalry in this period was due not so much to their individual horsemanship or fighting prowess as to their use of the 'concerted charge' in close order (see also Gravett 1993). The battles of Lincoln and Wilton both seem to have been decided by such a close-order charge, led or at least organized by Robert of Gloucester, against royalist opponents who were less well-organized and disciplined. Perhaps that is what the chronicler is trying to tell us with the phrase '*bellico more*'. The *Gesta* describes how Robert returned triumphant to Bristol laden with loot, and he and the Empress subjugated the country 'from sea to sea', while Stephen's followers were demoralized by his humiliating defeat at Wilton. But in reality neither side was able to break the stalemate. As K.R. Potter, the editor of the *Gesta*, points out, '*a mari in latus usque ad mare*', translated as 'from sea to sea', must literally have only meant from the Bristol Channel to the English Channel, or roughly the south-western quarter of England, centred around the main strongholds of Bristol and Gloucester. In this region what is now often referred to – notwithstanding the lack of support from the Count of Anjou – as the 'Angevin' party was now more secure than ever. From there the Empress' territory extended eastwards in the direction of London in a narrow salient as far as Wallingford, but beyond that the southern half of the country was still mainly under Stephen's control. That, however, was not to last.

While Stephen was occupied with his enemies in England, the fate of his dynasty was in fact being sealed by the events which were happening across the Channel in Normandy. Between 1140 and 1144 Geoffrey of Anjou slowly and systematically captured the royal castles in the duchy and consolidated his own power there, depriving Stephen of what had once been a vital source of revenue and manpower for the Anglo-Norman kings. In this Geoffrey was greatly helped by the absence of a royal field army after 1138. David Crouch accuses the king of a lack of strategic insight in so lightly abandoning Normandy, and goes so far as to suggest that he would have been better off if he and his leading supporter in the duchy, Waleran de Beaumont, had stayed there, as Matilda and Robert of Gloucester would never have dared to leave for England if their Continental base had not been secure. But when Waleran returned to Normandy in 1141 it was to make peace with Geoffrey, and from then on the Angevin advance was unstoppable. In January 1144 Rouen fell to the combined forces of Geoffrey and Waleran, and soon afterwards Geoffrey began to style himself Duke of Normandy.

Chapter 11

Personal Ambition and Private War

The single event which has probably done most to colour the popular image of the Anarchy is the revolt of Geoffrey de Mandeville, the Earl of Essex, in 1143. Coming as it did at a time when the king seemed at last to have gained the upper hand, with a genuine prospect of peace, it has often seemed to be a deliberate attempt to wreck that peace in the cause of personal ambition. So argued the nineteenth-century scholar J.H. Round, whose *Geoffrey de Mandeville, a Study of the Anarchy*, published in 1892, established its subject as the archetypal selfish and turbulent baron. This view is based largely on the *Gesta Stephani*, which describes the events surrounding Geoffrey's revolt in some detail. The earl had long been regarded as a loyal supporter of the king, as a result of which he had been entrusted with the vital strategic stronghold of the Tower of London, and further rewarded with the Earldom of Essex in 1140. But according to the *Gesta* Stephen's barons grew to suspect that Geoffrey was beginning to appropriate the royal prerogatives in the districts under his authority, and was planning to go over to the Empress with the considerable resources which he commanded. What was more, he controlled not only the Tower but numerous other strong castles, where he 'took the king's place', and 'received more obedience when he gave orders'. Round's study of charters issued in his favour by both sides suggested that Geoffrey was a cynical double agent, obtaining concessions from both king and Empress with false promises of support, and he quoted a charter issued by Matilda and apparently dating from 1143 as evidence that the accusations of treachery were correct. But the dating of many of the charters of the period is uncertain, and R.H.C. Davis, writing in 1964, concluded that the document which Round had dated to 1143 was in fact drawn up two years earlier, after the Battle of Lincoln. Geoffrey is known to have defected to the Empress briefly at this time (as did almost all his contemporaries), but he quickly returned his allegiance to the king after the latter's release from prison.

If Davis was correct, there is no evidence for Geoffrey's planned treachery apart from the rumours reported in the *Gesta*. Henry of Huntingdon says that if Stephen had not acted against him he would have lost his kingdom, but he presents no evidence for this bold claim. It may be that Geoffrey was beginning to arouse the king's resentment by acting like an independent ruler, and it is possible that Stephen had not forgotten an incident described by William of Newburgh, when during his imprisonment the earl had imprisoned the king's daughter-in-law Constance in order to curry favour with the Empress. But the *Gesta*'s account of Geoffrey's flippant response to the accusations suggests not so much guilt, as a refusal to take such absurd claims seriously. Stephen, however, arrested the unsuspecting earl at his court at Saint Albans in September, took him to London, and ordered him to hand over the Tower and his other castles in Essex on pain of death. Geoffrey reluctantly agreed, whereupon he was released and immediately took up arms against the king. It is difficult not to blame Stephen for the misfortunes which this episode brought upon him and his kingdom. The presence of the Empress in England made it necessary for him to deal with his barons more carefully than might normally have been the case, as she provided a ready-made cause for the disaffected. To Edmund King the arrest, like that of the bishops in 1139, was symptomatic of Stephen's failure of nerve, in this case a panicked reaction to the defeat at Wilton. Even if there had been grounds for arresting Geoffrey, the tactic of imprisoning people in order to obtain their castles had by now been used too often, had never been successful in the long term, and must surely have left an impression of royal weakness rather than strength. If the king had investigated the charges against the earl and dealt with them fairly, there is no reason to believe that he need have lost his support. If not guilty, he need not have been placed humiliatingly in chains and provoked to resentment: if guilty, he should not have been released. What happened was the worst possible outcome, because Stephen had lost Geoffrey's friendship, but Geoffrey had not lost his power to make trouble. The king had in effect opened up a new front for his enemies, at a time when they were beginning to lose the initiative and might otherwise have been vulnerable to a determined offensive.

Instead Stephen was forced to move against Geoffrey, who fled to that favourite refuge of rebels, the Isle of Ely. He was accompanied by a large number of knights who owed him allegiance, as well as by what the *Gesta* calls ordinary soldiers and robbers, many of them no doubt unemployed mercenaries. He then proceeded to lay waste the surrounding country, burning houses, seizing goods and driving off livestock. This may have made sense strategically, by creating a zone of scorched earth around his base where the royal army would find it difficult to operate, but for the local inhabitants it was a disaster. The *Gesta* tells how the earl's men sacked Cambridge, broke down the church doors with axes, stole the valuable ornaments and then set the buildings on fire. At Ramsey Abbey, north of Huntingdon, they not only looted the monastery, but evicted the monks and turned it into a castle. Stephen brought up his army, but in contrast to his decisive campaign against Bishop Nigel three years before, after one failed attempt to catch Geoffrey he resorted to a blockade, building a screen of castles south-east of Ely in order to prevent the earl from returning to his old stronghold in Essex. For much of 1144 Geoffrey continued his raids on the countryside, according to the *Gesta* in alliance with his neighbour Hugh Bigod. Then in September he arrived at Burwell, near Newmarket. Here Stephen's men had levelled a platform for a new castle – ironically on land requisitioned from the long-suffering Ramsey Abbey – and had begun work on the foundations, but the castle was still unfinished. According to Robert of Torigny it was a hot day and Geoffrey, who was reconnoitring the site, had removed his helmet. A royal archer spotted this target of opportunity and shot him in the head, inflicting a wound from which he died a few days later. Geoffrey's death virtually ended the rebellion, though his son Ernulf held out at Ramsey for a while until he was captured and exiled. Henry of Huntingdon comments that people were wrong to say that God was asleep, and reports with relish on the fate of some of Geoffrey's followers as proof of the operation of divine justice. The commander of the earl's knights fell from his horse, fractured his skull and died 'with his brains pouring out'. His infantry commander, a foreign mercenary called Reimer, was returning to the Continent by ship with his wife when the vessel became becalmed. The sailors, superstitious as ever, drew lots to find out who was the cause of their misfortune, and decided on Reimer. They set him and his wife adrift in a small boat with the ill-gotten loot which they had brought from England, and the pair were never seen again.

The *Gesta* and Henry of Huntingdon describe a number of smaller campaigns over the next few years, most if not all of which seem to have had their roots in the activities of independent local magnates rather than in any strategic ambition of the main contending parties. This, perhaps, is the period which most closely resembled the stereotypical 'Anarchy'. Ranulf of Chester in the north, John Marshal in Wiltshire and William Peverel in the Thames Valley carried out constant attacks on royal garrisons as well as on those neighbours whom they suspected of royalist sympathies. In 1144 Stephen attacked Lincoln Castle, which had been reoccupied by Ranulf, but had to abandon the attempt when a siege tower collapsed, killing eighty of his men. William de Pont de l'Arche, the former treasurer and lord of Portchester in

Hampshire, had a quarrel with Henry of Winchester, but finding his own forces insufficient to intimidate the bishop he asked the Empress for help. She sent him a contingent of knights led by a mercenary called Robert fitz Hildebrand, who not only took over the castle but seduced William's wife and schemed with her to imprison her husband and defect to Stephen.

Another prominent knight who met his death in the chaotic fighting of this period was Robert Marmion, the castellan of Tamworth in Staffordshire and a loyal supporter of the king. Robert had once held extensive lands in Normandy, but had been driven out by Geoffrey of Anjou and returned to England with an understandable hatred of the Angevins. In 1144 he was holding Tamworth against Ranulf of Chester, who was consolidating his power base in the north Midlands by indiscriminate attacks on his neighbours regardless of their political allegiance. Ranulf's nearest stronghold to Tamworth was the castle at Coventry 20 miles to the south-east. As it was isolated from the earl's other castles further north, Robert Marmion obviously saw it as vulnerable. According to R.H.C. Davis' reconstruction of events, in August 1144 Robert seized the cathedral and priory at Coventry and fortified them in order to blockade the castle. But when Ranulf approached with an army, Robert seems to have ridden out to reconnoitre and fallen into a defensive ditch which he himself had ordered to be dug. Before he could extricate himself and remount, one of Ranulf's infantrymen ran up and killed him. According to Henry of Huntingdon Robert was the only man to be killed in this fiasco, even though he was surrounded by 'huge squadrons' of his own men, which perhaps hints at a precipitate retreat on the part of the Marmion forces. Despite Henry's rhetoric it is unlikely that the Marmions could have deployed an army large enough to match Ranulf's, and they were probably never expected to fight outside their defences. The chronicler naturally attributes Robert's death to God's punishment for his sacrilege in desecrating the cathedral. Despite this defeat the Marmions must have kept up the struggle, because according to Davis Ranulf soon afterwards signed a treaty with Robert's son recognizing his control of Coventry, though apparently not the castle itself, which was confiscated by Stephen from the earl two years later.

Meanwhile in the south-west, the royal garrison of Malmesbury had been carrying out raids against Robert of Gloucester's territories, so – probably early in 1144 – Robert attempted to blockade Malmesbury by building a number of castles in the vicinity. Stephen learned of this and came with an army to the relief of the town. He besieged the castle at Tetbury, five miles north-west of Malmesbury, but here, so close to the enemy's main base at Gloucester, he was dangerously exposed and at the end of long lines of communication. He carried the outer wall of the castle by assault and killed or captured a number of enemy knights, then brought up siege engines to attack the inner donjon. But Robert gathered a large army, which included once again a sizeable contingent of infantry from Wales, and advanced to within two miles of the king's army before halting to await further reinforcements. A pitched battle seemed imminent, but the *Gesta Stephani* says that Stephen's barons, alarmed not only by the numbers of their opponents but by the 'untamed savagery' of the Welsh, persuaded him to break off the siege and retire. In particular they are said to have been worried that the royalist knights, who were exhausted by their travels, would be endangered by the 'mass of cut-throats on foot' – presumably meaning the Welshmen. But in order to save face the king marched not back east but northwards, to Winchcombe north-east of Cheltenham, where he took the castle by assault before returning to East Anglia to deal with Geoffrey de Mandeville's former ally Hugh Bigod. Nevertheless, the *Gesta* makes it clear that after his experience at Wilton, Stephen was not prepared to face Robert of Gloucester again in open battle. What is surprising is the prominence given in this account to the Welsh infantry, whose performance on the last occasion they had met the king's forces in pitched battle, at Lincoln in 1141, had not been impressive. But if the knights were tired so must have been their horses, and they may have feared that without their usual advantage of mobility they would be overwhelmed by the enemy's greater numbers.

The retreat did have one unexpected advantage, because Hugh Bigod had anticipated that the king would be busy in Gloucestershire for some time, and so had dispersed his forces on raiding expeditions. Taken by surprise by the sudden appearance of the royal army, they were scattered, and Stephen ravaged Hugh's lands and built three new castles to contain further raids. Soon after this Stephen arrived at the castle of Saffron Walden in Essex, which he had confiscated from Geoffrey de Mandeville and placed under the command of a Norman named Turgis. This man, although one of the king's most trusted officers, now decided to refuse him entry, although it had always been made clear that he was not the owner of the castle, but had been appointed to guard it on behalf of the king. The author of the *Gesta* attributes this extraordinary act of defiance to Turgis' fear that his master might decide to give the castle to someone else. Stephen seems to have operated cautiously at first, and both sides kept out of each other's sight until Turgis apparently decided that the danger was past. One day he went out hunting, and while he was galloping after his hounds, no doubt out of sight of his attendants, the king suddenly appeared with a strong body of knights. They rushed him from all sides, carried him off in chains and threatened to hang him if he did not surrender the castle, which he reluctantly did.

Meanwhile, says the *Gesta*, Robert of Gloucester continued to launch raids against the royal strongholds at Oxford and Malmesbury, in the course of which he somehow managed to capture Walter de Pinkney, the commander of the garrison at Malmesbury. The unfortunate Walter was handed over to the Empress, who imprisoned him in a filthy dungeon and had him tortured in the hope of persuading him to surrender the castle. But Walter refused to do so, while Stephen reinforced the garrison with men and supplies. The *Gesta* later relates the fate of Walter, who was eventually released, gathered some followers and managed to capture the castle at Christchurch by stealth. From here he took his revenge by plundering across a wide area, but his choice of victims seems to have been particular indiscriminate. He annoyed the Church and the townspeople by extorting large sums of money, and allegedly began killing people 'from mere love of cruelty'. Eventually the people of Christchurch sent for help to Baldwin de Redvers, and a combined force of knights and citizens lay in wait for Walter when he went to church. They confronted him and asked him to reform his behaviour, and when they received the expected angry refusal one of them swung an axe at Walter's neck and killed him.

Matilda's forces then concentrated on Oxford, and the *Gesta* describes a vicious campaign between Robert of Gloucester's son Philip and the castellan at Oxford, William de Chesney. As usual both sides did a great deal of damage to the countryside but were unable to dislodge each other from their main strongholds, so Philip persuaded his father to build a castle at Faringdon, south-west of Oxford. From here a strong garrison drawn from Robert's army could restrain the royalist raiders, though it can hardly have been the close blockade that the *Gesta* implies, since Faringdon is more than 12 miles from Oxford. But William de Chesney was sufficiently worried to send urgent messages to the king, asking for help. Stephen reacted promptly, as he often did at such times of crisis. Arriving at Oxford he collected reinforcements, including, according to Henry of Huntingdon, a 'numerous army' of his old allies the Londoners. Then after only a few days he marched on to Faringdon, where he built a fortified camp to protect the besiegers while they surrounded the castle and set up siege engines. The impression from the *Gesta* is that the king put a predetermined plan into operation with considerable skill. A ring of archers 'in very dense formation' encircled the walls on all sides and annoyed the garrison with a constant hail of arrows, supplemented by javelins and stones hurled by other troops. When the engines had been erected they joined in the bombardment with heavy stones and other missiles, under cover of which the royalist troops climbed the mound on which the castle stood and attacked at close quarters. From the *Gesta*'s remark that the two sides had 'nothing but the palisade' to keep them apart we can deduce that Faringdon Castle was basically a wooden structure, which is not surprising given the haste with which it had been constructed. It nevertheless held out under this onslaught for several days, with heavy loss of life on both sides, until eventually its commanders approached the king and agreed to surrender. Both the *Gesta* and Henry of Huntingdon regarded his success as gaining Stephen a great deal of glory, and inflicting a demoralizing blow to his enemies. Philip of Gloucester was so disillusioned that he immediately transferred his allegiance to Stephen. It is not clear why Robert, who had moved so determinedly to relieve Tetbury, allowed Faringdon to fall so easily. Henry of Huntingdon describes the earl as waiting not far from the scene of operations to gather more troops; as Faringdon is much further away from the Welsh border than Tetbury, it is possible that he had again summoned his Welsh allies, but they had either failed to arrive or were still en route when the castle fell. The *Gesta* says that Stephen had expected a prolonged siege, so perhaps Robert had also been taken by surprise by the speed of the royal victory. Nothing could better illustrate the decline of the Empress' party at this stage of the war – from a serious contender for the throne to a local faction scarcely able to project its power beyond the vicinity of Somerset and Gloucestershire.

A further blow to the Empress' ambitions was the loss of manpower caused by the declaration of the Second Crusade at Whitsun 1146. The crusade was proclaimed by Pope Eugene III and King Louis VII of France in response to the fall of Edessa to the Turks, but most of the English participants did not leave until May 1147 and were diverted to Portugal, where they helped King Alfonso I to retake Lisbon. This was in fact the only successful operation of the crusade, as Louis' attack on Damascus was a fiasco. Some of the English and Norman troops who had fought at Lisbon went on to the Holy Land, others returned home, but many stayed in Iberia and took part in further campaigns against the Moors. The most prominent member of the Anglo-Norman nobility to join the crusade was Waleran de Beaumont, who was present at the siege of Damascus but, unlike many of his contemporaries, eventually returned home to Normandy. Waleran's half-brother William de Warenne, the Earl of Surrey, was less fortunate; he was killed when Louis's army marched into a Turkish trap at Mount Cadmus in Anatolia. Unfortunately, as the author of the *Gesta* remarks, even though many knights and their retinues left the country, so that 'you would have thought England was empty and drained of men', there were plenty more to take their places and carry on the fighting at home. In fact, he says, those who had only recently taken up arms were 'all the more zealous in doing evil'.

But not for the first time, just when Stephen seemed to be gaining a decisive victory, he reignited the conflict by his own actions. Some time during 1146 Earl Ranulf of Chester, who had recently maintained a sort of armed neutrality in his lands in the north of England, decided to approach the king with an offer of submission. He claimed to be suffering very badly from Welsh raids, and offered to give his support to Stephen if the king would join him on an expedition against Gwynedd. Stephen's presence, he added in a blatant attempt at flattery, would be worth many thousands of men, and their combined forces would surely win a quick and glorious victory. The *Gesta Stephani* is emphatic that the earl was planning treachery from the beginning, but this may not necessarily have been the case. The Welsh raids were genuine, even though they had apparently been provoked by Ranulf. His old allies Owain and Cadwaladr were now contending for power in Gwynedd and the latter had taken refuge at Ranulf's court, thus attracting the hostility of his brother. By this time Matilda's faction, whose influence no longer extended beyond the border with the southern Welsh kingdoms, was in no position to assist him. Ranulf proved his loyalty by leading troops to help the king in an attack on Bedford, and was also present with 300 of his knights when Stephen launched another unsuccessful assault on Wallingford. But the usual anonymous royal councillors argued against the expedition to Wales, suggesting that it would be dangerous to lead an army into such hilly and wooded country where it could easily be ambushed, and that in any case the situation in England was still too volatile for the king to risk leaving the country. They went on to suggest that the whole Welsh campaign was a trap, and that Ranulf was himself planning to ambush Stephen as soon as he entered the earl's territory. They pointed out that he had not offered up any hostages for his good behaviour, and argued that he should be ordered to do so before any move was made against the Welsh. The sources do not name these advisors, and it is difficult to know what their motives may have been; it is of course possible that the author of the *Gesta* is using the time-honoured tactic of diverting the blame for a bad decision from the king himself onto unspecified 'bad counsel'. When Ranulf arrived unsuspectingly at Stephen's court at Northampton he was presented with a demand not only for hostages, but for the restoration of unspecified royal property which he was said to have taken for his own use. The earl naturally responded angrily that he had not come to court to discuss these matters and had had no time to consider them. The anonymous counsellors then accused him to his face of treason, and as he was unable to mount an effective defence on the spot, he was arrested. Ranulf's apparent evasiveness, as reported by the *Gesta*, is hardly proof of his guilt as the author assumes, if he had been given no warning of the charges. The sequel suggests that Stephen did not take them seriously in any case, since he released Ranulf as soon as his friends provided hostages and agreed on his behalf to hand over his castles to the king. This was simply the same trick that had been played on Geoffrey de Mandeville, and with very similar consequences. But far from learning his lesson, Stephen went on to repeat the same mistake yet again with Ranulf's nephew Gilbert fitz Richard, who was one of the hostages for his uncle, and who was also forced to surrender his strongholds.

Ranulf was of course furious at this treatment, and immediately set about raising an army to retake the castles that he had lost. The most important of these was Lincoln, where Stephen spent Christmas of 1146. Soon after he left, Ranulf attacked the town, and according to the *Gesta*, despite the fact that Stephen had heavily reinforced the garrison, won a 'glorious triumph over the king's men'. Henry of Huntingdon, however, tells a very different story. Ranulf ordered an assault on the walls, but it was repulsed with heavy losses and the commander of the attacking troops was killed outside the north gate. The earl was forced to retreat, while the citizens, who had clearly not abandoned their royalist principles, celebrated the victory. The earl then marched to Coventry, another of the confiscated castles, and built a counter-castle there to blockade it. Stephen came with an army to relieve it, though according to the *Gesta* he had to fight his way out of several ambushes which Ranulf had laid at difficult points along the route. At some point the king was wounded, though he quickly recovered and 'joined battle' with his opponent. This brief notice in the *Gesta* might indicate another of the rare pitched battles of the period, but we have no details of the fighting. We are told only that, after many knights had been captured and some wounded, Ranulf fled, narrowly escaping being killed as he did so. Meanwhile Gilbert fitz Richard had also rebelled, but Stephen pursued him so closely that he had to abandon plans to defend the first of his castles and flee in disguise. He eventually took refuge at Pevensey, a site which was almost impregnable as it was built on a very high mound protected on all sides by sea and difficult ground. The king arrived and left a strong force to besiege the castle, including ships to attack from the seaward side. Unfortunately the *Gesta* does not tell us the final outcome, though as we hear of no further trouble from Pevensey it seems safe to assume that Gilbert eventually made his submission.

Chapter 12

Succession and Anarchy in the North: Svein Asleifsson and the Earls of Orkney

Naturally most attention has always been paid to the momentous events taking place in the south of England, but around the same time a curiously similar crisis of legitimacy was arising at the opposite end of the British Isles, in the Isles of Orkney off the north coast of Scotland. We are fortunate to have a detailed account of events in this region in the *Orkneyinga Saga*, and in order to follow the sequence of events it is necessary to understand something of the complex political relationships that the saga describes. The Orkney and Shetland Islands had originally been inhabited by people related to the Picts of the Scottish mainland, but in the ninth century AD they were discovered by Norwegian pirates, who used them as bases for raids further west as well as against Norway itself. In 875 the Norwegian king Harald Harfagri ('Finehair') took control of the islands, and according to the saga appointed Rognvald Eysteinsson as earl to govern them on his behalf. Rognvald gave the earldom to his brother Sigurd, but he himself went on to found an even more illustrious dynasty, as his son was Hrolf or Rollo, the founder of the Duchy of Normandy and great-great-great-grandfather of William the Conqueror. Thus through this line the earls of Orkney were related to both Stephen of England and the Empress Matilda; although geographically remote, the islands were by no means outside the mainstream of European affairs

Orkney was found to be good farming country, and large-scale Norwegian settlement followed. The extent to which the native population was displaced is controversial, but not only Orkney and Shetland but also Caithness, the north-eastern tip of mainland Scotland nearest to Orkney, rapidly became Scandinavian in speech and culture. Needless to say this did not put an end to piracy, and the evidence of the saga suggests that in the early twelfth century the region was still relatively lawless, especially in Caithness. There an ill-defined frontier divided the Norse settlers from the Gaelic-speaking clans of Sutherland, which comprised the north-western section of the mainland. In keeping with the saga tradition, the *Orkneyinga Saga* devotes much of its attention to the family trees of the leading clans of Orkney and the relations between them. It describes a turbulent era when the earldom was often disputed, and sometimes shared, between rival branches of the ruling family – a tendency which also plagued the ruling house of Norway, to which the earls still owed allegiance. In fact more often than not all the surviving sons of a deceased earl would lay claim to his title, so that there were usually two or even three 'earls' holding court in different parts of the islands or in internal exile in Caithness. Many of the battles and skirmishes which the saga relates are attributed to these domestic power struggles, but the old Viking tradition of the blood feud still persisted, even though the settlers had been converted to Christianity and a bishopric established in the mid-eleventh century. Whether the motives which the saga reports were genuine or not, the impression it gives is that the north of Scotland continued to suffer from a degree of violence far worse than the 'anarchy' of contemporary England. Not only were many families trapped in a cycle of violence and revenge, but Viking-style pirate raids against their southern and western neighbours remained a lucrative and socially acceptable activity.

The most notorious of the pirates was Svein Asleifsson, whose activities are the main focus of the sections of the saga which cover the 1130s to the 1150s. Svein was the son of Olaf Hrolfsson, a farmer on the island of Gairsay in Orkney (Asleif was his mother). Some time in the mid-1130s Olaf was murdered by a gang of fellow Orkney men led by Olvir, whose mother Frakokk was the sister of Ottar Modansson, a self-styled 'earl' whose stronghold was at Thurso, on the north coast of Caithness. If the saga is to be believed Frakokk was a devious schemer who was behind much of the trouble in the earldom; among other crimes she had previously attempted to murder Paul Haakonsson, one of the joint earls, with a poisoned shirt, but had accidentally killed his brother and co-earl Harald instead. Svein went to Earl Paul to report the killing of his father, but while he was there another Svein nicknamed 'Breast-rope', a notorious bully, repeatedly accused Svein Asleifsson of cheating at a drinking game. The saga's description of the Christmas festivities suggests that the influence of the new religion remained superficial, with the raucous feasts and drinking parties interrupted by the regular church services, only to be resumed immediately afterwards. Eventually an intoxicated Breast-rope was overheard muttering death threats against his rival, who was persuaded to strike first in

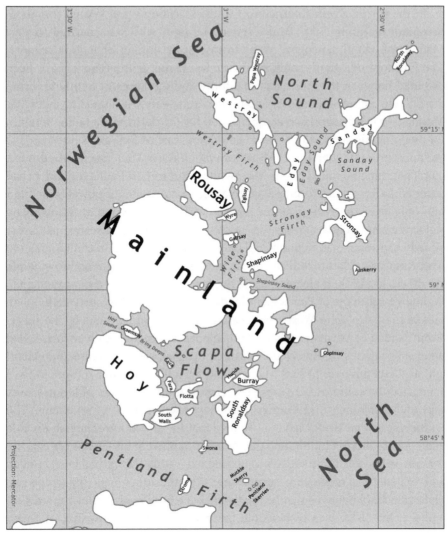

Map 2. Medieval Orkney. (Wikimedia Commons)

self-defence. Svein Asleifsson killed him with a single axe blow to the head, then fled to the island of Tiree in the Hebrides, where he took refuge with the local chief, Holdbodi Hundason. Earl Paul declared Svein an outlaw, but was unable to pursue him immediately as he was distracted by the appearance of a fleet from Norway led by one of his rivals for the earldom, his second cousin Rognvald, sometimes known by his real name of Kali Kolsson.

In the spring Svein returned to Caithness, having first visited friends in Scotland, including Earl Paul's sister Margaret who was married to Earl Maddad of Atholl, a nephew of the former Scottish king Malcolm Canmore. The Earldom of Atholl, south of Inverness, seems at the time to have been disputed between the mormaers of Moray and the kings of Scotland. From there Svein gathered a band of about thirty followers. At Thurso he met Ottar Moddansson and negotiated compensation for the death of his father in return for pledging his support to Erlend Haraldsson, one of Frakokk's protégés and yet another contender for the Earldom of Orkney. Then Svein fitted out a merchant ship and sailed home. Meanwhile, most of Earl Paul's supporters had deserted to Rognvald, forcing Paul to agree to a division of power which left him only a few outlying islands. He was with a small group of followers on Rousay when Svein's ship passed by en route to Gairsay. It seems that Svein already had some plan in mind, and may already have been in communication with Rognvald. He ordered ten of his men to remain in sight and row, while the others hid in their sleeping bags. So, taking the ship for a lightly-manned trading vessel, some of Paul's men standing on a headland shouted out to Svein to take his cargo on to Westness, where Paul was hunting otters by the shore. Svein landed at Westness where he disembarked his hidden warriors, killed nineteen of Paul's followers and captured the earl. He then returned to Atholl and handed Paul over to Earl Maddad and his wife. Margaret appears to have supported the claim of her young son Harald to the Earldom of Orkney over that of her brother, and exactly what happened to Paul is uncertain. The *Orkneyinga Saga* would have us believe that he agreed to relinquish his title and never return to Orkney, and that in order to prevent his supporters causing trouble on his behalf, he suggested putting out a story that he had been blinded and exiled to a monastery somewhere. On the other hand many people understandably believed that he really had been mutilated and later murdered, and that his sister was responsible, perhaps with the connivance of Svein Asleifsson.

But when Svein returned to Orkney in 1136 the saga story seems to have been accepted, and Rognvald, who by now had seized control of the whole of the earldom, received him amicably. In fact Rognvald realized that he owed much of his success to Svein, and he agreed to provide him with two ships manned with warriors to settle the ongoing dispute with Olvir and Frakokk, which Svein continued to regard as unfinished business despite the agreement he had made at Thurso. In this connection it would be useful to know how many men two shiploads represented, but this has long been a controversial question among historians of the period. Scandinavian warships in this period were usually described in terms of how many benches they carried for the oarsmen, with those in Orkney probably averaging between twenty and thirty benches (Heath 1989). Rognvald had a ship of thirty-five benches on his trip to the Holy Land in 1151, but this was exceptional. Counting two rowers to a bench gives a rough total of forty to sixty men per ship, but this might vary according to circumstances. Far more fighting men could be crammed onto a vessel for a short period, as must have happened in sea battles taking place close to shore, but on the other hand for long voyages, which would have taken place mainly under sail, ships could be handled by fewer than their full complement of rowers, and they may have carried reduced crews in order to preserve their supplies of food and water. As a very approximate guide, we can assume that one of the raiding vessels such as Svein took on his expeditions might have carried between fifty and eighty fighters, counting the oarsmen, their commanders, helmsmen and those with other duties on board.

The saga's description of the campaign against Frakokk gives an interesting glimpse into the conditions of warfare in the far north. Frakokk and her son were known to be based at a place called Hjalmundalr, which is referred to as being 'in the centre of Sutherland'. Palsson, the saga's translator, renders the name as Helmsdale, but it can hardly have been on the same site as the modern town of Helmsdale, which is on the east coast. No doubt the name Hjalmundalr originally referred to the whole of the valley of the Helmsdale River, now known as the Strath of Kildonan. Barbara Crawford suggests that Moddan's family was of mixed Celtic and Norse origin – their names are an unusual mixture of both languages – and controlled a large area of the border country between the two peoples, and mentions a tradition that Frakokk's farmstead was near Kinbrace on the Helmsdale River. It was evidently well inland, as Svein is described as reaching it by a roundabout route, first sailing south to Banff on the far side of the Moray Firth, then travelling inland to Atholl to get guides from Earl Maddad. From there they turned north again and marched 'by forest and mountain above all the settlements', so that they arrived undetected on a height overlooking their objective. Frakokk and Olvir were anticipating trouble, and had scouts out in all directions except the one by which Svein actually approached, presumably from the south. They were taken by surprise when the Orkney men suddenly appeared and charged down the hillside. Olvir nevertheless mustered sixty men to make a stand, but – although they may not have been decisively outnumbered by Svein's two shiploads – they soon gave way and tried to run for the shelter of a nearby forest. They were headed off and so retreated to the farmhouse, where most of them were killed. Svein's men looted the house and then set fire to it, deliberately or otherwise killing Frakokk who was still hiding inside. Olvir managed to get away across the river and eventually reached the Hebrides, where he disappeared without trace.

The following spring saw Svein back in the Hebrides, where his former host Holdbodi Hundason had been attacked by a Welsh chieftain called Robert, whom the saga describes as 'of English descent', though his name is Norman rather than English. For an Anglo-Norman nobleman to be carrying out seaborne raids against the Norse occupants of the Hebrides is a complete reversal of the roles which we would normally expect, but this may be largely a result of bias in our sources. Certainly the Vikings did not have a monopoly on piracy, even if they were more likely than most to celebrate it in their literature. In any case Robert had driven Holdbodi from his lands and stolen his treasure. Svein again asked Rognvald for the loan of two fully-manned ships and sailed west. He found that Holdbodi had retreated as far as the Isle of Man, so from there the two men launched a raid on the coast of Wales, then spent the rest of the summer at sea, 'winning a great deal of plunder' either from further raids on land or from attacks on shipping. Robert had apparently already been forced to retire from the Hebrides and had taken refuge on the Isle of Lundy in the Bristol Channel, where Svein and Holdbodi briefly besieged him before breaking off operations and returning to Man for the winter. The saga's account gives us a brief glimpse into conditions in the Irish Sea, where raiding and piracy seem to have been as routine as in the Viking heyday in the ninth and tenth centuries, but there is no indication that King Stephen or any of the Welsh princes took any action to suppress it. Over the next winter Svein married a widow named Ingirid whose husband had been killed by Robert. He began to gather forces for another expedition, presumably against the Welsh chief, but Holdbodi had by now made peace with Robert and refused to join Svein. This disagreement led to bloodshed when, according to the saga, Holdbodi treacherously attacked his former ally one winter's night, but was driven off and fled to join Robert on Lundy. The island continued to be a haunt of pirates until Henry II of England gave it to the Knights Templar in 1160. In the spring Svein returned via Lewis to Orkney a rich man, thanks to the plunder he had taken and the sale of the estates he had acquired through Ingirid.

In 1138 Rognvald was persuaded to accept as co-earl the 5-year-old son of Earl Maddad of Atholl, Harald. The *Orkneyinga Saga* claims that a deal had been made to this effect between Maddad and Svein Asleifsson, but Crawford is no doubt right to see the hand of David of Scotland in the affair. David's policy was to establish himself in a dominant relationship with the earldom, and he must have been happy to see the son of one of his vassals share power with the ruling earl. And of course, as Harald was still a child, he would be under the influence of his guardians for the foreseeable future. Why Rognvald accepted the arrangement is less clear, but as Crawford says he must have been subjected to 'very strong pressure from the highest quarters', and the visit to Orkney of a Scottish bishop around this time, mentioned by the saga, is unlikely to have been unconnected with the business. Crawford also quotes a charter issued by David to Rognvald commanding him to protect the monks at Dornoch, which suggests that although the Scottish king had no formal authority over Orkney, his influence was very strong.

Some time after this came news that Holdbodi had re-established himself in the Hebrides, so Svein once again asked Earl Rognvald for support to drive him out. This time the earl gave him five ships, one of which was commanded by a man named Thorbjorn, who was not only married to Svein's sister but was also a grandson of the deceased Frakokk. Perhaps because of this history the two men fell out, and although Holdbodi fled and there was no fighting, they argued on their return about the loot they had collected. Svein refused to give Thorbjorn more than an ordinary share, but the latter argued that they had been equal partners, and took his case to the earl. By now we are beginning to see a pattern in the saga's account of Svein Asleifsson. For some reason which is never properly explained, the leading men of Scotland and Orkney were desperate not to offend him, no matter how much trouble he caused. So Rognvald's reply is unlikely to have been a surprise to Thorbjorn: yes, he said, Svein is a bully and is being unjust, but Thorbjorn is not to bother him with demands for money in case it leads to trouble. Instead the earl will compensate him out of his own pocket. Nevertheless, Thorbjorn was not satisfied. First he divorced Svein's sister, which Svein took as the personal insult it was no doubt intended to be, and then soon afterwards seized another opportunity to damage his rival.

When Svein was in the Hebrides he had left a notorious thug named Margad Grimsson in charge of his lands in Caithness. Margad had killed a local farmer and taken refuge in a stronghold which the saga calls Lambaborg, generally identified with Bucholly Castle south of Freswick Bay. There Svein joined him and, far from bringing him to justice, collaborated in strengthening the defences and looting the surrounding countryside, stockpiling the plunder in preparation for a siege. Thorbjorn was prominent among the leading men who persuaded Earl Rognvald finally to confront

Svein. The earl's army laid siege to Lambaborg from the land, but it was difficult to attack as it stood on a small promontory almost completely surrounded by cliffs, while a stout stone wall had been built to cover the landward approach. Svein protested his loyalty to Rognvald but refused to surrender Margad, so the earl blockaded the stronghold until supplies began to run short. Eventually Svein realized that they could not hold out, so he and Margad planned their escape. They were let down into the sea on a rope under cover of darkness, then swam along the cliffs until they found a place where they could climb ashore. This was understandably celebrated as a daring exploit, and the saga quotes Rognvald as saying 'there's nobody quite like Svein . . . A trick like that shows a strong, brave heart'. On the other hand it would not have been out of character if the earl had somehow connived at the escape for fear of the consequences if Svein fell into the hands of enemies like Thorbjorn. Certainly we do not hear that Svein and Margad were seriously pursued. Thorbjorn went to the Moray Firth with forty men, but soon abandoned the hunt and went off on an adventure of his own, with which Rognvald was said to have been 'very pleased'.

The fugitives had somehow got as far as Banff, where they found a ship crewed by ten fellow Orkney men and persuaded them to take them south. According to the saga they took refuge in a monastery on the Isle of May off the coast of Fife, claiming to be emissaries sent by Rognvald to King David. After a week the monks became suspicious and sent for help, so the Orkney men stole everything they could carry from their hosts and put back to sea. Svein led them up the Firth of Forth to Edinburgh, where he met David and confessed everything. Needless to say David, far from punishing Svein, welcomed him amicably, and announced that he would compensate anyone who had been robbed by his visitor on his trip south. Then he offered to let Svein and his wife settle in Scotland, granting them whatever status they desired. When this offer was refused, the king agreed instead to negotiate a peace between Svein and Rognvald, and to grant permanent asylum to Margad. This was done, and Svein returned home to a friendly welcome from the earl, facilitated by gifts provided by David. The reader can only speculate what influence Svein had over a man like the King of Scots. Political events of this sort would surely have been public knowledge, making it unlikely that they were entirely invented. If Svein had been involved on David's behalf in the negotiations that led to Rognvald's acceptance of Harald Maddadsson as earl, it might explain why the king felt he owed him a favour. Or perhaps the fate of Earl Paul is the key to the mystery; if Svein really had been responsible for his murder, or his mutilation and imprisonment, he might have known more about the involvement of Rognvald, the Earl of Atholl, and even David, than they would have wished to be made public.

Eystein's Raid

In 1151 Rognvald decided to go on an extended pilgrimage to the Holy Land, and appointed the now 20-year-old Harald to rule as sole earl during his absence. Soon after Rogvald's departure Eystein Haraldsson, who with his two brothers was joint king of Norway, appeared unexpectedly with a fleet at Thurso. There he surprised and captured Harald, only releasing him in return for a ransom in gold and a renewed acknowledgement of Norwegian overlordship. According to Snorri Sturluson's saga history of the kings of Norway, *Heimskringla*, Eystein then sailed south along the east coast of Britain. He killed 'many people' at Aberdeen before plundering the town, then continued on to Hartlepool, which was a substantial port serving the city of Durham. *Heimskringla* quotes a series of verses by Einar Skulasson celebrating Eystein's deeds in England, according to which he put to flight a party of English horsemen at Hartlepool and stole some ships from the harbour. He then burned Whitby, which was then a small settlement of only a few dozen houses, noted only for its abbey. Einar goes on to describe battles at Skarpasker, where more English cavalry – presumably a group of local knights with their followings – were routed by an 'arrow shower', and at Pilavik. Following Norwegian victories at both places, the invaders burned Langatun, which *Heimskringla* says never recovered its former prosperity. Unfortunately none of these three places has been definitely identified. Skarpasker was presumably somewhere along the Yorkshire coast, but Pilavik and Langatun may have been in Scotland, perhaps targeted on the return journey. Eystein's motives for this raid are unclear, though the *Orkneyinga Saga* says that he claimed to be seeking revenge for the death of Harald Hardrada at English hands at the Battle of Stamford Bridge in 1066, nearly ninety years before. In any case it seems to have had little impact on England, then preoccupied with the conflict between Stephen and Henry of Anjou, where none of the contemporary chroniclers mention it.

This has sometimes been described as the last of the Viking raids as far as England was concerned, and we might not go far wrong if we imagine Eystein's soldiers as resembling earlier Vikings, or the contemporary forces of the Earldom of Orkney. Illustrations of the period show that some Norwegian nobles fought on horseback and were by now armed almost identically to Anglo-Norman knights, but this sort of equipment would not have been very suitable for a naval expedition, and no Norwegian cavalry are mentioned in the sources. The successors to the old Viking huscarles were the Hirdmen, a standing royal bodyguard equipped with sword, shield, mail armour and helmet. Traditionally the Hird comprised only 120 men, and not all of these necessarily had combat roles. In the twelfth century the bulk of Norwegian armies was provided by the '*leidang*' system, according to which all able-bodied freemen were obliged to serve for up to four months a year, though in practice only a proportion of the available manpower was ever summoned for expeditions overseas. Each man had to provide his own equipment, which included a spear, a shield, an iron helmet and a sword or axe, while groups of men had to combine together to supply a ship. A proportion of missile weapons was also often specified, varying between one per rowing bench and one per man. These might by the mid-twelfth century have been crossbows, which were later to become the characteristic weapon of Scandinavian levies, but many would probably still have been traditional bows of the type associated with earlier Norse warriors. In any case they provided a Norwegian army with formidable firepower, which to judge from the brief account of the fight at Skarpasker may have been its principal tactical strength.

Civil War in Orkney

Harald Maddadsson had survived the Norwegian intervention, but by this time he had a rival in Erlend Haraldsson, the same man to whom Svein Asleifsson had pledged his support in Thurso more than a decade earlier. Through his influential relatives Erlend persuaded the young King Malcolm of Scotland, who succeeded David in 1153, to recognize him as earl, then travelled to Norway to persuade King Eystein to back his claim. Despite his promise Svein had not so far attempted to further Erlend's cause, but while the latter was in Norway he fell out with Earl Harald. There had been some bad feeling over the outlawing of Svein's brother, who had had an illicit affair with the earl's mother, but Harald followed the example of his predecessor in attempting to conciliate Svein at all costs. Even when Svein captured a ship which the earl had sent to Shetland to collect tribute and stole the money, Harald merely remarked that he and Svein were taking it in turns to make money, and let the incident pass. But when Erlend arrived with a fleet from Norway and the news that Eystein had granted him half the earldom, Svein took his side, in spite of the fact that Erlend had been a client of his old enemy Frakokk.

At Michaelmas 1153 a battle was fought at Cairston, near Stromness on the Mainland of Orkney, as its largest island was known. Harald's ships were drawn up offshore, but when they saw the combined fleets of Erlend and

Svein approaching his men abandoned the ships and took refuge in a fort on the shore. They held out there until nightfall, and on the following day a peace deal was arranged. Harald left for Caithness, while Erlend took over the whole of Orkney on condition that he would hand over half of the earldom to Rognvald should he ever return, which neither side apparently thought likely. Nevertheless, the victors remained suspicious of Harald and stayed on board their ships until Christmas, when the worsening weather persuaded Svein to go home to Gairsay. The saga says that while he was there Svein told his men that he suspected that Harald might be trying to sneak back to Orkney, but they thought it unlikely because of the strength of the gale that was blowing. Therefore he decided not to send a warning to Erlend, who was still with his fleet off Cairston. In fact Harald did arrive over the Christmas holiday with four ships and a hundred men, landed on the east coast of the Mainland and marched overland in a snowstorm with the intention of surprising Erlend. According to the saga they lost nearly a day when they were forced to take shelter inside the great Neolithic tomb at Maes Howe. This anecdote appears to have been confirmed by archaeology, because when the tomb was excavated in the 1860s a number of runic inscriptions were found, dating from around 1150. One of the inscriptions refers to buried treasure, which might have been the incentive for Vikings to find their way into the tomb in the first place, but it was probably a well known refuge for those with the nerve to negotiate the eerie underground passages. Perhaps superstitious fears were too much for others, as we are told that two of Harald's men went mad there, which caused an additional delay. Erlend had spent the day drinking at a house on shore, but had returned to his ship by the time Harald's party appeared. With the element of surprise lost, the attack was abandoned.

The following spring Earl Harald left for Shetland in pursuit of another Erlend, known as 'the Young', who had abducted his mother, leaving Svein and Earl Erlend at least temporarily in peace. Svein proposed to take the opportunity to go raiding, and he and Erlend set off down the east coast of Scotland, plundering as they went. According to the saga they had a narrow escape after they stole a ship belonging to a wealthy merchant named Knut off Berwick-upon-Tweed. Knut offered a large reward for the ship's recovery, and fourteen vessels set off from Berwick in pursuit. The Orkney men were anchored off the coast of Northumbria, but thanks to Svein's alertness and the speed of their ships they gave the enemy the slip and returned to Scotland. The saga says that messengers were sent to Edinburgh to explain what had happened, but on the way there they met a troop of Scottish horsemen carrying bags of silver and enquiring anxiously about Svein Asleifsson. It turned out that King Malcolm had heard a rumour that Svein had been captured and was sending the money to pay his ransom. Reassured that he was safe, Malcolm nevertheless sent him gifts, and ignoring the fact that one of his own subjects had been robbed he allowed Svein and Erlend to return to Orkney. Once again Svein's strange immunity is touched on but not properly explained.

Soon afterwards Earl Rognvald returned from his pilgrimage and made a settlement with Erlend, according to which the Orkneys would be divided between them and they would unite against Earl Harald on his return. Harald, meanwhile, had made peace with Erlend the Young (who went on to marry the earl's mother, apparently with the consent of all parties), and arrived off Caithness with six ships. Despite their agreement the other two earls were caught unprepared; Erlend and Svein were in Shetland, from where their return was delayed by bad weather, while Rognvald was attending a wedding in Sutherland. Rognvald promptly double-crossed Erlend, making peace with Harald and joining him to lie in wait for Erlend off the island of South Ronaldsay. But Erlend's men spotted the enemy fleet before the trap could be sprung, and on Svein's advice he diverted his ships to Caithness. Here they rounded up and slaughtered cattle to supply the fleet, while Svein spread a rumour that they intended to seek refuge in the Hebrides. The saga suggests that Rognvald was not fooled, remarking that he expected Svein to attack Orkney at any moment, 'and all the more so when he talks about going somewhere else', but Svein's stratagem nevertheless succeeded. He and Erlend rowed westwards from Thurso, then hoisted their sails and allowed the wind to carry them back east to Orkney, where they landed under cover of a blizzard and scattered their rivals. But both Rognvald and Harald escaped, organized a counter-attack and surprised Erlend in his turn. Svein had allegedly urged Erlend to be on his guard, but the earl had ignored him, set no proper watch on his ship and was dead drunk when Harald's men attacked. Erlend disappeared overboard and was not found for some time, but two days before Christmas his body was recovered with a spear shaft still sticking through it. Rognvald and Harald offered terms to most of the late earl's followers, but Svein escaped once again to the Scottish mainland, taking to the hills with only five companions.

Of course Svein did not remain an outlaw for very long, because when Rognvald found out where he was he sent a message asking him to meet him in Orkney over Christmas, and made a peace deal according to which the fugitive was pardoned on payment of a fine to the two surviving earls which included half his estates, a mark of gold and a fine ship. Rognvald, wishing to stay on good terms with Svein, actually refused his share of the fine, but Earl Harald billeted himself in Svein's house on Gairsay and started taking the grain stored there to feed his own men. Svein complained to Rognvald but was advised to keep quiet, so he sailed over to Gairsay and was on the verge of setting fire to his own house, believing that Harald was inside, when it was pointed out to him that his own wife and daughters were also there. Harald was actually not there at the time, but when the incident was reported to him he mustered his followers and went looking for Svein. According to the saga the latter gave him the slip by beaching his ship inside a cave on the shore of a small island, then went ashore and hid in the house of one of his relatives, a man called Bard. Bard insisted that Svein and his men remain in a small side room off the main hall, and blocked the passage to it with stones. This was a wise precaution as the same night Earl Harald's steward, Jon Wing, arrived with six men and obliged Bard to light a fire for them, as it was a cold night. Jon then began holding forth on the subject of Svein and Earl Erlend, calling the former a traitor, and saying that the late earl had always been a violent man and his death was no loss. However, Svein overheard all this from his hiding place, and eventually lost his temper, pushed the stones out of the way and burst into the room fully armed. Jon received such a fright that he ran outside in just his shirt and breeches, not even stopping to put his shoes on. By the time he reached safety in another farm, he had lost several toes to frostbite. Eventually peace was made between Svein and Earl Harald, but the former's dispute with Jon Wing continued. On one occasion Svein captured two of Jon's brothers at sea, took them ashore and made a show of building a gallows before turning them loose. This prank nearly backfired when Jon heard a rumour that his brothers had actually been killed and kidnapped Svein's son Olaf in retaliation, but Earl Rognvald ordered him to release Olaf unharmed and not to risk provoking Svein any further.

The Fight at Forsie
In the late summer of 1158 both earls led an expedition to Caithness in search of Svein's former brother-in-law Thorbjorn, who had been outlawed for a murder, and was known to be visiting friends somewhere in the valley of the Forse Water near Thurso. The *Orkneyinga Saga* describes the ensuing battle in some detail, and it is worth examining not only for its momentous consequences, but as a rare glimpse of the tactics of the era. Rognvald and Harald led 120 men, of whom 20 were on horseback, and as they approached a farm near the present-day village of Forsie, north of Loch Calder, Rognvald

and four companions were riding ahead. The track to the farm was narrow and steep, and at the bottom of it the farmer, Hallvard, was stacking hay. Hallvard called out to the earl by name in a loud voice, obviously with the aim of alerting Thorbjorn, who was inside the house with fifty followers. As Thorbjorn and his men scrambled outside Rognvald approached the front door, but Thorbjorn jumped onto a stone wall which ran alongside the track and struck a blow at the earl, who tried to dismount but was hampered when his foot caught in the stirrup. One of the earl's men, who had presumably not had time to draw a weapon, lost his hand trying to parry the blow, but was not able to prevent Rognvald sustaining a wound to his chin. Then another of the outlaws ran up and fatally wounded the earl with a spear thrust, while almost simultaneously one of Rognvald's party stabbed Thorbjorn in the abdomen. Thorbjorn and his men then ran behind the house, down a slope and across a strip of swampy ground at the bottom. Earl Harald came up with the main army, but the narrow track was clogged with men crowding around the dying Rognvald, and it was some time before he could deploy his troops, by which time the outlaws were drawn up in a line behind the swamp, with a ditch along one side. Harald's men could not reach them except by throwing spears, but Thorbjorn ordered his men not to throw them back, so they were soon out of ammunition without having inflicted any serious damage. There then followed a long parley, at the end of which Harald was inclined to offer the outlaws mercy, but was talked out of it by Magnus, the leading man among his followers. Magnus then began leading men along the ditch to outflank the enemy, who started to disperse. Thorbjorn jumped the ditch, despite his wound, and tried to surrender to Harald, but the earl advised him that, although he would not kill him himself, neither would he try to prevent Magnus and the others from doing so. So the fugitive fled to another nearby building and tried to make a stand there, but by this time he had only eight men with him. Magnus then set fire to the house, and all nine were killed when they tried to break out.

The Last of the Vikings

The real significance of this skirmish, of course, was that with the death of Rognvald Harald was left as the sole ruler of Orkney, a role which he fulfilled until his death in 1206. Svein Asleifsson, we are told, continued his Viking lifestyle. He spent the winter feasting his cronies at his hall on Gairsay, then in the spring he carefully oversaw the sowing of seed before sailing off to the Hebrides and Ireland on what he called his 'spring trip'. Soon after midsummer he returned home for the harvest, then went off plundering again on his 'autumn trip'. One spring he captured five large ships while plundering in the Hebrides, the Isle of Man and Ireland. Off Dublin he took two merchant ships carrying a valuable cargo of cloth from England, as well as consignments of wine and mead – an interesting glimpse of an otherwise under-recorded trade. On their return to Orkney the crews used the expensive fabrics to make awnings for their ships, and even sewed it onto the front of their sails to advertise their success. But Earl Harald was becoming unhappy with Svein's raiding and advised him to give it up, ostensibly out of concern for Svein's safety, but no doubt also with an eye to his own relations with his southern neighbours. Svein agreed to retire, but only after one last autumn trip, which he intended to make as glorious as his previous expedition. Once again the intended target was Dublin. This time he took with him seven ships. Despite the size of this fleet, and the fact that it stopped en route to plunder elsewhere in Ireland, it apparently took the Dubliners completely by surprise, so that rather than try to resist they agreed to surrender the town and hand over a large sum of money, as well as providing hostages. Svein's habitual wiliness seems to have deserted him, for he took his men back to their ships to spend the following night, intending to return and take over the town in the morning. But during the night the people of Dublin dug deep pits at strategic points inside the city gates and between the houses, camouflaging them with branches and straw, and concealing armed men to keep a watch on them.

When the unsuspecting Orkney men passed through the gates next morning, the citizens formed crowds which funnelled them towards the pits so that they fell in, whereupon the people barred the gates behind them and killed their victims at their leisure. Svein, in true saga fashion, accepted his fate philosophically and made a speech before he died, protesting his loyalty to the memory of Earl Rognvald. The *Orkneyinga Saga* concludes this account with the verdict that 'apart from those of higher rank than himself', Svein was 'the greatest man the western world has ever seen in ancient and modern times'. But his era was now over. The saga also tells us that the summer after Svein's death his sons 'set up partitions' in his hall on Gairsay. They were farmers, and they no longer had any need to feast armies of retainers in the great drinking hall that their father had built.

Precisely when this took place is uncertain. The only historically-attested battle at Dublin in the period after the death of Rognvald was in 1171. The *Annals of Ulster* refer to a certain 'Eoan Mear a h-Innsibh Orc', or 'Mad John from the Orkney Islands', who led a party of Orkneymen in this campaign, and has sometimes been identified with Svein Asleifsson. 'John the Wode' from

Norway, who appears in another account in *The Song of Dermot and the Earl*, could also be the same man if we accept that his Irish victims might have been unaware of his real place of origin. But neither of these sources describe the death of their subject in a trap, and it is hard to see why the saga would invent such a humiliating end for its hero. Most likely the last of the northern pirates met his fate in a minor and otherwise unrecorded skirmish some time in the 1160s. From the time of Harald Maddadsson onwards the earls of Orkney gradually saw their independence wane as the Scots competed for influence with the kings in Norway, until in 1468 the islands were formally ceded to Scotland.

Chapter 13

Henry Plantagenet

Back in England, at some time in late 1146 or early 1147, Matilda appears to have appealed once again to her husband for assistance from Normandy. And again Geoffrey refused to commit himself and sent their son Henry, who still cannot have been more than 14 years old at this time. The *Gesta Stephani* says that Henry's landing caused consternation all over England, until it was realized that he had come not with an army, but merely a small group of mercenary knights. Furthermore, he had no money to pay these knights, who consequently served without enthusiasm. It is not clear where they landed, but their first objectives were the town of Cricklade, south-east of Cirencester, and the nearby castle at Purton, both of which were occupied by royalist forces. The campaign was a fiasco, because the mercenaries were driven off from both places, and after a few clashes with Stephen's men which are not described in detail they all deserted, abandoning the young Henry in a hostile kingdom. He appealed to his mother for money, but she had none to spare, and his uncle Earl Robert also refused to help. The boy was forced into the ultimate humiliation of accepting an offer from Stephen of money for his passage home. The author of the *Gesta* says that some people criticized the king for his foolish generosity, but points out that it was not only in accordance with Christian precepts but was also good psychology, because 'the more kindly and humanely a man behaves to an enemy the feebler he makes him'. About the same time, and perhaps as a deliberate ploy to emphasize the contrast between the two young men, Stephen ceremonially knighted his own son Eustace and bestowed on him the title of Count of Boulogne. Eustace was then given the task of suppressing Ranulf of Chester, who was still at large in the north-west. The *Gesta* describes Eustace's performance in glowing terms, claiming that he triumphed in several battles, although this may be an exaggeration as Ranulf remained active against the king, and would be strong enough to take part in another offensive two years later.

The *Gesta* also describes two royalist victories around this time in the south, although unfortunately their exact locations are not clear. The first was a castle called '*Castellum de Silva*', or the 'Castle in the Wood', which had been a hideout for 'the enemies of all peace and tranquillity' until the king arrived unexpectedly and took it by storm. Another castle, at 'Lidelea', had belonged to Henry of Winchester, but had been captured by trickery by one of the followers of Brian fitz Count. Potter, the translator of the *Gesta*, favours a location at 'Beddelie' near Farnham in Hampshire, though this cannot be proved. Bishop Henry reacted vigorously to the loss of the castle and laid siege to it, building two counter-castles to maintain the blockade. Robert of Gloucester apparently planned to relieve the place and mustered a large army, accompanied by three other earls (who are not named), but the bishop sent to Stephen for aid, and the sudden appearance of the royal army caused Robert's men to scatter in panic. Stephen then negotiated the surrender of Lidelea and returned it to his brother. Once again Earl Robert had failed to put up serious resistance when operating at a distance from his base. Bishop Henry, in fact, continued to fight vigorously in defence of his own possessions. When in 1148 his castle at Downton was seized by Patrick, the Empress' appointee as Earl of Salisbury, Henry first excommunicated him, and when that had no effect he hired a large force of knights who besieged the castle and starved him out.

The final blow to the Empress' ambitions came at the end of October 1147, with the unexpected death of Robert of Gloucester while he was mustering a new army at Bristol. The earl had always been the mainstay of her cause, and despite his recent lack of success he remained the only commander who had ever proved able to defeat the royal armies on the battlefield. His son and successor, William, was incapable of taking over his role; the *Gesta* describes him as no longer young (though he could only have been in his late thirties), and more fond of the bedchamber than the battlefield. Earl William did, however, win one notable victory when he led his army against Henry de Tracy, who was building a new fortification at Castle Cary in Somerset, and scattered his forces before the work could be finished. But by now Matilda knew that she had no hope of taking the crown, and early in 1148 she made her way to the south-coast port of Wareham and took a ship to Normandy to join her husband and son. She lived at Rouen for another nineteen years, and played a prominent role in the Church and the administration of the duchy, but she was never to return to England.

Matilda's ambitions now rested with her son Henry, whom her supporters now recognized as the heir to the English throne. Henry's previous efforts in England had been unimpressive, but he was not easily deterred. By 1149 he was old enough to be knighted, and although his father could have performed the ceremony, he chose instead to go to King David of Scotland, whose support, both moral and physical, could be extremely valuable to his cause. Henry again landed in England, and accompanied by Earl Roger of Hereford and a few loyal knights he managed to cross the country to Carlisle, where David was holding court. Also present was Ranulf of Chester, and after Henry had been duly knighted the three men decided to combine their forces for an attack on York. But Stephen received warning and hurried north with a large number of well equipped knights, so that as the invaders approached the city they saw the royalists, deployed according to the *Gesta* 'with resolution and skill', advancing towards them. David and his allies realized that whereas they had mustered all the forces available to them, Stephen's army was not only larger but was still being reinforced with fresh contingents. So the allies dispersed and returned to their homes – wisely, as the author of the *Gesta* was convinced that if they had not done so they would have quickly been overwhelmed. Henry and his companions escaped to Hereford by little-used paths, and then made for safety in Bristol. Stephen had sent instructions to Eustace, then in London, to intercept them, which he almost succeeded in doing near Dursley in Gloucestershire, but Henry was warned in time and finally reached Bristol. Meanwhile Ranulf had regrouped and again attacked Lincoln, but the citizens held the town against him and resisted long enough for Stephen to arrive from York to relieve them. The *Gesta* describes a protracted campaign including several pitched battles, some of which were won by Stephen and others by Ranulf, but it is hard to believe that the earl, who would not face the king at York when in the company of his allies, was now somehow strong enough to take on the royal army alone. No doubt the *Gesta*'s account preserves the memory of some hard skirmishing, but it is likely that Stephen was unsuccessful in bringing his enemy to a decisive battle, as he eventually had to resort to the usual method of building and garrisoning a new castle to keep him in check.

Despite his setbacks, Henry was not content to hide in Bristol, but launched an invasion of Devon in alliance with William of Gloucester and Roger of Hereford, capturing Bridport and forcing Henry de Tracy, the main supporter of the king in that county, to take refuge in his castles. Henry of Anjou then received news that Eustace was threatening Devizes, so he went there at once with all the troops he had, entering the town just as Eustace was arriving from the opposite direction. The garrison was at first reluctant to fight, but Henry's arrival restored their morale, and they launched an attack on the royalists and drove them out. Nevertheless, it was obvious to his supporters that it was too dangerous for Henry to remain in England, and he was persuaded to return to

Normandy to gather more support. Normandy was by now firmly under the control of his father the Count of Anjou, who conferred on him the title of duke. The winter of 1149–50 was exceptionally harsh, with snow lying until April according to Robert of Torigny, and the weather and a famine which resulted made large scale campaigning in both England and Normandy impossible for most of the following year. Henry set about raising a large army from his new possessions on the continent, with which the *Gesta* says that he was resolved to overthrow Stephen, but long before his preparations were complete events occurred which were to further strengthen his hand.

First, in September 1151, Geoffrey of Anjou died, and Henry inherited his title of count. He also inherited his father's nickname, Plantagenet (derived apparently from the Angevin field sign, a sprig of broom or '*plante geneste*' in medieval French), which was later to become the family name of the kings of England. Then in the spring of 1152 he married Eleanor of Aquitaine, whose previous marriage to Louis VII of France had been dissolved. Eleanor brought with her the rich county of Aquitaine, which was in effect added to Henry's dominions. Within a very short time the young Henry Plantagenet had been transformed from a minor nuisance into a serious threat to Stephen's crown, able to control the resources of almost the whole of what is now western France, from the English Channel to the Pyrenees. King Louis also felt threatened by this new power bloc, and attempted to neutralize Normandy by granting several castles along the border with France to Stephen's son Eustace, with the idea that he could use them as a base from which to launch attacks on Henry's lands. While Henry was kept busy in Normandy by Louis and Eustace, Stephen made a determined attempt to capture the last major strongholds in central England still holding out against him. His first target was Worcester, which still belonged to Waleran de Beaumont, who was out of England on crusade but was by now openly supporting the Angevins. In 1150 the king had burnt the town but failed to capture the castle, so in the following year he returned with a siege train. He built two large earthworks outside the castle and left troops to continue the siege while he attended to affairs elsewhere, but Waleran's brother Earl Robert of Leicester brought up an army and destroyed the siege works. Henry of Huntingdon remarks that this was yet another example of Stephen beginning things energetically but not following them up. It was also an ominous development in another respect, as Earl Robert, who had previously been a dedicated royalist, was now putting family and personal interests before his loyalty to the king.

More serious was the attempt on Wallingford, which had been holding out against the king since 1139. As well as barons 'from all over England', the

Gesta says that Stephen was assisted by the London militia, with whose help he seized the bridge that led to the entrance into the town and built two counter-castles, which the *Gesta* says required 'wondrous art and vast labour'. Earl Roger of Hereford, the son and successor of Miles of Gloucester, brought up a relieving army, but Stephen forced it to retreat after killing or capturing a number of knights. Roger then sent messengers to the king and offered to join him if he would help to retake Worcester and hand it over to William de Beauchamp, one of the earl's protégés. Stephen, who of course intended to confiscate Worcester from Waleran de Beaumont in any case, agreed to this and marched his army away from Wallingford, though the blockade continued. The chronology is confused at this point, and it is not entirely clear whether the *Gesta* is referring here to the 1151 siege of Worcester, or whether the town was attacked yet again in the following year. The latter interpretation seems most likely, as the same source goes on to state that while the king was outside Worcester, confident that Earl Roger would support him, the latter secretly sent messages to Duke Henry of Normandy, as the chroniclers now refer to him, urging him to return to England urgently before Stephen succeeded in suppressing the last of his supporters.

Henry arrived on the south coast early in January 1153 after a dangerous voyage in stormy weather, bringing with him what the *Gesta Stephani* describes as a 'vast army', though according to William of Newburgh it comprised only 140 knights and 3,000 infantrymen. That the army was in fact quite small is confirmed by Henry of Huntingdon, who tells us that the young duke's supporters were disappointed, and the king's party correspondingly relieved, when its strength became known. Nevertheless Henry quickly began to gather reinforcements from among the English barons, and immediately took the offensive by marching to Malmesbury and placing it under siege. The *Gesta* says that the 'common people' lined the walls to defend the town, but they were no match for the duke's veteran infantry, who were 'men of the greatest cruelty'. Some of the latter shot arrows to keep the defenders behind cover, while their comrades brought up ladders and scaled the wall. The townspeople fled to the church, but the attackers broke in after them, plundered the church and committed 'various abominations'. The precise nature of these crimes is not specified, but they were serious enough for Henry's English supporters to demand that the perpetrators should be sent home before their actions brought the wrath of God down on the Angevins. This, says the *Gesta*, was done at once, but God still had his revenge as their ships were caught in a storm and 500 of the mercenaries were drowned.

Having captured the town of Malmesbury, Henry went on to lay siege to the castle, but the commander of the garrison, a man named Jordan, seems to have escaped and gone to Stephen to ask for help. The king arrived with a large army, and the two rivals faced each other across the River Avon, Stephen on the north bank and Henry on the south. The royal army was undoubtedly larger, and Stephen seems to have attempted to bring about a pitched battle. Henry of Huntingdon describes the professional manner in which the king deployed his army, which looked 'terrible and beautiful' with its array of golden banners. But the river was in flood (it was still late winter), and its steep valley proved to be impassable, while a storm of rain and snow blew up from the south into the faces of the royalists. Seeing that his men were so soaked that they could hardly handle their weapons, Stephen had no choice but to negotiate with Henry. The *Gesta* also says that the king was uncertain of the allegiance of some of his barons, a concern which was soon shown to be fully justified. It must have been around this time that Robert of Leicester defected to Henry, since the *Gesta* mentions him as one of the duke's chief advisors. It appears that an agreement was made to demolish the castle, but that when Jordan was sent to supervise the work, he instead shut the gates on the king's men and handed it over intact to Henry. At about the same time Warwick Castle, which had been held for the king for many years, was also surrendered without a fight. Robert of Torigny says that the Earl of Warwick was serving with Stephen and had left the castle in the care of his wife, who handed it over to Henry's supporters in the belief that her husband was dead. According to the no doubt exaggerated report in the *Gesta* the earl, who was one of the king's most loyal supporters, died of shame when he heard the news. But it is likely that there was more than a mere misunderstanding involved in this incident, as the Countess of Warwick was the sister of Robert of Leicester, now himself in the Angevin camp.

Henry then moved north-eastwards to open communications with Ranulf of Chester, attacking Tutbury on the River Dove north of Burton on Trent, which belonged to Earl Robert of Derby, then moving south-east to Bedford and Stamford. At Bedford he had to content himself with burning the town, but the castles at the other two places eventually surrendered to him. The *Gesta* says that the garrison at Stamford held out for a long time in the hope that Stephen would relieve them, but the king was prevented from doing so by his old enemy Hugh Bigod, who was launching diversionary attacks from his base in East Anglia. The duke then turned south and attempted to break the siege of Wallingford, which Henry of Huntingdon says was by now on the verge of starvation. Henry Plantagenet began by attacking one of Stephen's counter-castles, on the other side of the Thames at Crowmarsh. Here the *Gesta* describes how the royalist commander, a man of obvious ability who unfortunately is not named, deployed most of his men in ambush positions, leaving only a small force to defend the castle, which was built on top of the usual high mound. Then when Henry's troops were fully engaged in climbing the mound and fighting the defenders on the top, the concealed troops emerged and attacked in small parties from different directions. The Angevins were put to flight, but Henry continued to reinforce his army and settled down to blockade the castle from within earthworks of his own. Robert de Torigny says that he executed sixty archers who had been captured in the fighting – the first known instance of the dislike of such troops which he was later to show as king.

Stephen reacted quickly to the threat to Crowmarsh, sending 300 knights to Oxford to harass the besiegers while he mustered his army. With him was his son Eustace, who had now returned from Normandy, as well as most of the remaining loyal barons. The *Gesta Stephani* describes how the two armies once again deployed for battle, facing each other with drawn swords, 'with only a river between them'. This is odd. Crowmarsh is on the east bank of the Thames, which in this stretch flows from Oxford in the north, southwards towards Reading. So this would mean that Stephen was approaching not from his power base in the south-east but from the west. More likely both armies were on the east side of the river, and the implication of the *Gesta* that it was this obstacle that prevented them from fighting, as had happened at Malmesbury, is wrong. Henry of Huntingdon does not mention the river, but says that the duke marched out from his defences to meet the king, who ordered his men to counter-attack. However, the nobles on both sides refused to fight, allegedly because they did not want either leader to achieve a decisive victory that might put an end to the independence which they had been enjoying. Their motives might of course have been more honourable, and the *Gesta* says that they were simply weary of war. Gervase of Canterbury records that Stephen's horse threw him three times, which if true must have left the king shaken and temporarily unfit to fight. Stephen and Henry found themselves with no choice but to agree a truce; according to Henry of Huntingdon they met along the banks of a stream, where they commiserated with each other over the unreliability of their own supporters. But they also agreed to demolish Crowmarsh Castle and disband their armies.

This was a temporary truce rather than a final peace deal, but it seems to have signified to all concerned that the fighting could no longer be sustained. Eustace was furious, as he felt that by failing to destroy Henry his father had deprived him of the chance of inheriting the throne. To add to his humiliation,

Stephen's plan to forestall his rival by having his son crowned during his own lifetime had been vetoed by Archbishop Theobald of Canterbury on instructions from the Pope. Eustace took his followers into East Anglia where he committed various depredations, apparently with the aim of provoking further conflict, but on 17 August 1153 he died unexpectedly, 'from grief' according to the *Gesta Stephani*. To the author of the Peterborough version of the *Anglo-Saxon Chronicle*, scandalized by the punitive taxes which he had imposed to fund his final campaign, Eustace was 'an evil man' whose career was brought to a premature end by Christ himself. Whatever the real cause of his death, it cannot have been unwelcome to many of those who were hoping for a peace settlement. The death of Earl Ranulf of Chester in December removed another potential obstacle; in fact this seemed too convenient to some, and it was rumoured that William Peverel had poisoned him. Henry of Huntingdon and the *Gesta* respectively credit Archbishop Theobald of Canterbury and Bishop Henry of Winchester with opening the peace negotiations, which culminated with the Treaty of Winchester in November, the provisions of which were confirmed by Stephen in a charter issued at Westminster before the end of the year. Duke Henry accompanied Stephen to London, where Henry of Huntingdon describes how both men were received with joy by the crowds. The main point of the agreement was that Henry recognized Stephen as king for his lifetime, and to that extent it was a victory for the latter. But Stephen's hopes of founding a dynasty had died with Eustace, and he had little option but to acknowledge Henry as his heir. It was further agreed that all foreign mercenaries were to be sent home, unauthorized 'adulterine' castles demolished, and customary laws enforced throughout the realm. Henry of Huntingdon says that there was some disagreement between the two parties when they met at Dunstable in 1154 because Henry suspected that Stephen was allowing his supporters to retain their castles, but neither side was anxious to resume the war and the trouble was smoothed over. The duke then 'received the king's permission' to return to Normandy – possibly, as Gervase of Canterbury reports, a precaution made necessary because of the discovery of a plot by some Flemish mercenaries to assassinate him.

The Huntingdon chronicler describes Henry as 'victorious', but this description can have seemed appropriate only with hindsight. He had been promised the throne on Stephen's death, it is true, but this event would not necessarily have seemed imminent (Stephen was then about 56 years old), and given the precariousness of life in the twelfth century it was by no means certain that Henry would outlive him. Henry's mother Matilda was of course still alive, but although the war had originally been waged in pursuit of her claim to the throne, she never attempted to revive this claim. If Stephen had gone on to rule over a peaceful kingdom and begun to restore its order and prosperity, support for the Angevins might have gradually waned. He still had a surviving son, William of Blois, who could have pressed his claim to the succession. But the final twist in the story was still to come. After nearly two decades of fighting to defend it, Stephen enjoyed his throne in peace for less than a year. For the last nineteen years he had lived a life of continual toil and stress, and it would not be surprising if this had eventually undermined his health. As the *Gesta Stephani* puts it, the endless labours of men like King Saul or Alexander the Great were proverbial, but they could scarcely be compared with what Stephen had suffered. Apart from his endless campaigning he had been wounded in battle at least twice, repeatedly thrown from his horse, and had suffered a harsh imprisonment followed by a serious illness as well as the loss of many friends, and eventually his wife – who had died in 1152 – and his eldest son. The king himself died at Dover on 25 October 1154. Gervase of Canterbury suggests some sort of abdominal problem, perhaps appendicitis, but no certain diagnosis can be made. He was buried at Faversham in Kent, alongside his wife.

Conclusion:
A Graveyard of Reputations?

Like the second decade of the twentieth century, the twelfth was an era in which defensive technology, in the form of the stone castle, had temporarily achieved the ascendancy over the means of attack. Such times seldom show to best advantage the sort of military virtues which we traditionally admire: the dazzling campaign of manoeuvre; the *coup d'oeil* which decides a great battle in a moment; the desperate charge, sword in hand, at the head of the last reserves. So it is not surprising that from a military point of view this is an era devoid of the 'Great Captains' on whom popular history generally focuses. Stephen often showed considerable energy in reacting to events, and his rapid marches frequently took his opponents by surprise and seized the initiative. For example, on two occasions, in 1136 and 1149, he foiled a Scottish invasion almost without striking a blow by the speed with which he led his army up the Great North Road to York. But although he was skilled at thwarting the moves of his enemies, he lacked a coherent vision of the 'big picture' and was too easily distracted from the real strategic issues by transient threats originating closer to home. Crouch has argued that his greatest weakness was his neglect of Wales and Normandy, as a result of which the military resources of the former were monopolized by Robert of Gloucester and Ranulf of Chester, and those of the latter fell into the hands of Henry Plantagenet. Stephen's biographer Edmund King goes so far as to say that the only time when the king's party pursued a consistent and determined course of action was during his imprisonment, when Queen Matilda and William of Ypres were in charge. The same writer also points to the role of his manipulative but able brother Henry of Winchester in propping up the crown, even if he did so in pursuit of his own ambitions; 'Without Henry, so people said at the time, Stephen would have been nothing.' It is also noteworthy that – despite his reputation as a fighter and his undoubted personal courage – Stephen's forces never won a major victory in the field while he was in command. The two great victories that saved his rule, at The Standard in 1138 and Winchester in 1141, were both achieved by others, in the latter case while the king was in prison as a direct result of his previous attempt to bring his enemies to battle. Ultimately we must concur with the view of most of the commentators on the reign from William of Malmesbury to Edmund King in our own time. Admirable as he was in many ways as a man, Stephen lacked the vision and the toughness of mind to be a great king in such difficult times. In Boulogne, which remained outside the expanding Angevin Empire, his dynasty endured for a short time. His youngest son, William, succeeded him as count and ruled until 1159, whereupon Stephen and Matilda's only surviving daughter, Marie, who had been living as a nun in England, became countess.

Of those who led the king's armies, we know too little about the command arrangements at The Standard to give the credit for that victory to any one individual. William of Ypres, despite his dubious behaviour at the Battle of Lincoln, engineered important victories at Wherwell Abbey and Winchester, and seems to have been the leading military commander of Stephen's faction until the middle of the 1140s when he disappears from view, probably due to ill health. It is likely, though, that the personality that really held the royalists together in their darkest hour was that of Queen Matilda, whose diplomatic skill was also evident in the settlement with Scotland in 1138. As King suggests, William of Ypres seems to have owed his loyalty primarily to her. Of Stephen and Matilda's son Eustace we know very little. The *Gesta Stephani* describes him as victorious in numerous actions, but we have no details of the fighting and so cannot evaluate the strength of the opposition which he faced. He may well have been the dashing cavalry commander that the *Gesta* portrays, but he never had the opportunity to demonstrate his abilities in a major battle.

Among Stephen's opponents, the Empress Matilda is portrayed as providing her supporters with decisive leadership only for a brief period after Stephen's capture at Lincoln, and then the results were disastrous. In London in the summer of 1141 she alienated many potential supporters with her arrogance and her excessive demands. After that she appears in the narrative of the English wars mainly as a figurehead, remembered more for her narrow escapes from capture and the self-sacrificing loyalty of men like Robert of Gloucester and Brian fitz Count than for the strong personality and formidable intellect which we know she possessed. How far this can be ascribed to the prejudice of our sources against a woman in power is impossible to know, but it should be emphasized that taking her life as a whole, including her career in Normandy after 1148, she was by no means a failure. She never ascended the throne, but her son did, and she was remembered in Normandy as an able administrator and a pious patron of the Church. For an in-depth and generally sympathetic account of Matilda see Chibnall, 1991.

Her principal supporter, Robert of Gloucester, is generally credited with the strategic direction of the Angevin war effort until his death in 1147, but as a military commander he can only be described as competent but erratic. Twice he defeated the king in battle, at Lincoln and Wilton, but on several other occasions he either avoided a decisive clash or failed to bring up his army until it was too late. At least after his defeat at Winchester, he seems to have been much more confident when fighting on home ground, near to his strongholds of Bristol and Gloucester and the border with his Welsh allies, than when taking the fight to his enemy. Possibly his capture and imprisonment shattered his nerve to an extent that does not seem to have happened in Stephen's case. Ranulf of Chester may also be due some of the credit for the victory at Lincoln, but in the numerous engagements which he fought in the north in the late 1140s, most of them against barons with fewer resources than he had, he did no more than hold his own. We have too little unbiased information about the Welsh leaders, like Owain and Cadwaladr ap Gruffydd, to evaluate them as soldiers. Crug Mawr in 1136 was a very significant victory over better-equipped Norman forces, but we have no details of how it was achieved. On the whole the Welsh leaders performed very effectively in their native mountains and forests, but failed in the unfamiliar environment of lowland England, as was seen at the Battle of Lincoln.

David I's reign saw Scotland achieve an unusual position of dominance in northern England, but this cannot be attributed to David's skill as a conqueror. The Scots lost at The Standard mainly because of their indiscipline and poor deployment, for which their king must be held largely responsible. Like Stephen, he 'won' his greatest victories, like Stracathro in 1130 and Clitheroe in 1138, when he was not present in person. Embarrassingly, for one of his greatest successes, the capture of Malcolm mac Alasdair, he seems to have had to rely on English help. It was his skill as an administrator, a diplomat and a patron of religion, not as a soldier, that account for his reputation as one of Scotland's greatest monarchs. To judge from his performance at the Standard, David's son Henry was, like Eustace, a dashing cavalry leader, but he never had the opportunity to test his ability as a commander-in-chief. Like Stephen's, David's last years were marked by personal loss. In 1152 Henry died unexpectedly, and although, unlike Eustace, Henry had sons to whom the throne could be handed on, the eldest of them, Malcolm, was still only 11 years old. David took energetic steps to secure the succession by appointing Earl Donnchad of Fife as the boy's guardian, and presenting Malcolm formally to his subjects as the designated heir. David also designated Henry's second son William as Earl of Northumberland, and obliged the local barons to give hostages to guarantee their loyalty to him. At the end of May 1153 David died at Carlisle at the age of about 72. By the standards of the time his had been an exceptionally long and successful reign, and in sharp contrast to Stephen he was to be remembered in Scotland for the peace and stability which he had brought, as well as for his devotion to the Church. He had extended the borders of his kingdom further than they had ever been before, or ever would be again. We can only speculate how different the histories of Scotland and England would have been if the former had been able to permanently consolidate its control over Carlisle, Durham or even York. But it was not to be. An able and experienced Scottish king had been able to achieve this expansion at the expense of an English monarch who was distracted by continual civil wars, but his young successor was to prove no match for Henry Plantagenet. In 1157 Malcolm arrived at Peveril Castle in Derbyshire to pay homage to Henry for his lands in the north of England, but was bullied into handing them over in exchange for the restoration of the Earldom of Huntingdon which his father had once held. David's gains had been reversed without a fight, and though there was a great deal of fighting still to come along the Anglo-Scottish border, the Scots were never able to make such gains again. Finally in 1237 the Treaty of York, signed between Henry III of England and the Scottish king Alexander II, formally recognized Cumberland and Northumberland as English.

As for 'the greatest man' of the north, Svein Asleifsson, he was surely an anachronism even in twelfth-century Scotland. He achieved fame as a swashbuckling pirate and an astute political fixer, but he never commanded what could be described as an army – except perhaps in his final campaign against Dublin, when he led it to a humiliating defeat. What he symbolizes, however, is in some ways one of the most interesting aspects of this period. The years of the Anarchy saw not only the last of the Vikings, but also the last occasions on which men fighting in the old Celtic or Norse military traditions took on the armoured and disciplined formations exemplified by the Normans on more or less equal terms. Lightly-equipped Welsh forces continued to fight even after Edward I overran their country in the late thirteenth century, and even sent their famous archers and spearmen to fight in England's wars, but never again would an English army, operating in the heart of its own country, retreat for fear of them as Stephen's men had done in 1144. David's wild-charging Galwegians at The Standard might have been part of the last Scottish army that a Roman would have recognized; the Scots who beat Edward II at Bannockburn a century and half later fought as conventional men-at-arms and pikemen in contemporary European style.

Henry Plantagenet was later to become one of England's most successful rulers, but this tends to obscure the fact that his performance during the war with Stephen was at best erratic. His first invasion of England was an embarrassing failure, but then he was very young and still inexperienced at the time. His march through central and eastern England in 1153 was spectacular, but achieved little and ended up with him back more or less where he had started. He was outwitted by the garrison at Crowmarsh, and both there and at Malmesbury he showed little enthusiasm for a decisive pitched battle. His greatest asset at this time seems to have been simply his youth and energy, which enabled him to survive his setbacks until a war-weary country and an exhausted king could no longer sustain the fight. When Stephen died Henry was still in Normandy, but according to the Peterborough Chronicle, in contrast to the chaos which followed the death of Henry I, he inherited a peaceful kingdom: 'no man dared do other than good because of great awe of him'. Henry was still a young man and untried as a king, so 'awe' seems rather inappropriate, but certainly there was little desire to contest his accession. England and Normandy were now reunited, only for Normandy to be irretrievably lost again in the reign of Henry's son John. By 1158 Henry II had not only recovered the north of England, but had also reversed most of the losses sustained by Stephen along the Welsh Marches, despite suffering an embarrassing defeat at the hands of Owain ap Gruffydd, who ambushed him at Ewloe Wood in July 1157. By the end of Henry's reign the whole of Wales had acknowledged his overlordship, and although the country was not formally brought under the English monarchy until 1284, the time of Stephen represented for the Welsh, just as it did for the Scots, a high point which they were never to see again.

Who Was Who in the 'Anarchy'

Adela of Blois (subsequently Saint Adela):
Daughter of William the Conqueror, wife of Count Stephen-Henry of Blois, and mother of King Stephen. After her husband's death in 1102 she ruled Blois as regent until retiring to a convent in 1120. She died in 1137.

Adeliza of Louvain (also known as Adela of Louvain):
Wife of Henry I and Queen of England, 1121 to 1135. Married William d'Aubigny, Earl of Arundel, in 1138. In 1139 she welcomed the Empress Matilda to Arundel, apparently without her husband's agreement. Later she retired to a nunnery, and died in 1151.

Ailred of Rievaulx (subsequently Saint Ailred):
As a young man Ailred had lived at the court of David I of Scotland and served as his steward before joining the monastic community at Rievaulx in Yorkshire in 1134. Abbot of Rievaulx from 1147 to 1167, and author of several valuable historical works, including *Relatio de Standardo* and *Vita Davidis Scotorum Regis*.

Alan of Penthievre:
Descended from a noble Breton family, Alan inherited the Earldom of Richmond, and about 1140 received the Earldom of Cornwall from Stephen. The *Gesta Stephani* describes him as a man of 'boundless ferocity and craft'. Fought for Stephen at the Battle of Lincoln in 1141, but was later captured and forced to relinquish his castles and his Cornish title. He returned to Brittany and died c. 1146.

Baldwin de Redvers:
Lord of Plympton in Devon and an irreconcilable opponent of Stephen. Rebelled in 1136 but after unsuccessfully defending Exeter and Carisbrooke he was forced to flee to Anjou, where he gave his support to the Empress Matilda. Baldwin led a diversionary raid in support of Matilda's landing in England in 1139, and was made Earl of Devon as a reward for his services. He died in 1155.

Baldwin fitz Gilbert:
Youngest son of Gilbert fitz Richard de Clare, and brother of Gilbert and Richard fitz Gilbert. After the death of Richard at Welsh hands in 1136, Stephen supplied Baldwin with troops to mount an expedition into Wales, but he failed to carry out his mission. Baldwin redeemed himself at the Battle of Lincoln in 1141, when he gave the pre-battle speech on behalf of Stephen and was captured fighting alongside the king. His subsequent fate is unknown.

Brian fitz Count (also known as Brian of Wallingford):
An illegitimate son of the Duke of Brittany, raised at the court of Henry I. A loyal supporter of the Empress Matilda, he held Wallingford Castle for her from 1139 until 1148, despite several attempts by Stephen to besiege it. The date of his death is unknown; it may have been before 1151, when one of his relatives was in charge at Wallingford, but later accounts suggest that he had entered a monastery or gone on crusade.

Cadwaladr ap Gruffydd:
Son of Gruffydd ap Cynan, King of Gwynedd. With his brother Owain, Cadwaladr defeated an Anglo-Norman army at Crug Mawr in 1136. He fought against Stephen at the Battle of Lincoln in 1141. Exiled twice from Wales as a result of dynastic quarrels, he was given refuge in England by Earl Ranulf of Chester in 1146 and Henry II in 1155.

David I:
Youngest son of King Malcolm III and Queen Margaret of Scotland, David succeeded his brother Alexander as King of Scots in 1124. Brought up at the court of Henry I, he enthusiastically promoted feudalism and the development of towns as well as being a patron of the church. After his victory at Stracathro in 1130 David extended his power over the Earldom of Moray in the north. He invaded England several times in the early years of Stephen's reign, and despite his defeat at The Standard he obtained an advantageous peace in 1139 which gave him control of most of northern England. He died in 1153, after which most of his gains in England were lost.

Erlend Haraldsson:
Great nephew of Frakokk Moddansdottir. Granted the joint Earldom of Orkney by King Malcolm IV of Scotland in 1153, Erlend briefly seized sole power from his fellow earls Rognvald and Harald, but was killed by his rivals in 1154.

Eustace, Count of Boulogne:
Eldest son of Stephen and Queen Matilda and heir to the English throne, born
c. 1131. He campaigned against Geoffrey of Anjou in Normandy in 1151, then
returned to England in the expectation of being formally crowned as his father's
heir. When Archbishop Theobald refused to do this, Eustace retaliated by
plundering Church lands, and died while doing so in August 1153. His death
dashed Stephen's hopes of establishing a dynasty, but opened the way to the
peaceful accession of Henry II.

Eustace fitz John:
Brother of Payn fitz John. Eustace was Lord of Bamburgh Castle and an
important magnate in Northumbria under Henry I. He supported David I of
Scotland in the war of 1138 and fought at The Standard, but survived the defeat
and regained control of his lands in the subsequent peace settlement. After 1143
he became an associate of Earl Ranulf of Chester, who rewarded him with
lands in Yorkshire and Lincolnshire. He later joined the service of Henry II,
and was killed in an ambush in 1157 while campaigning in Wales – ironically
meeting the same fate as his brother Payn had done twenty years earlier.

Eystein Haraldsson:
Son of Harald Gille, king of Norway from 1130 to 1136, Eystein was born in
Scotland c. 1125. In 1142 he became joint king of Norway with his brothers
Inge and Sigurd. He campaigned in Scotland and England during 1151, and
was defeated and killed by Inge in 1157.

Fergus of Galloway:
Lord or '*ri*' of Galloway; the date of his accession is unknown but he is first
recorded in 1136. Believed to have been married to an illegitimate daughter of
Henry I of England. Fergus fought for David of Scotland at The Standard, but
in 1160 was deposed by David's successor Malcolm IV. He died in 1161.

Frakokk Moddansdottir:
Wife of Ljot of Sutherland, aunt of Earl Harald of Orkney and great aunt of
Earl Erlend. *Orkneyinga Saga* describes her as ruthlessly manipulating the
power-struggles in Orkney from behind the scenes. Burnt to death in her house
by Svein Asleifsson in 1136.

Geoffrey II de Mandeville:
The son of William de Mandeville, whose lands in Essex had been confiscated

by Henry I, Geoffrey initially gave his support to Stephen, and was rewarded in 1140 with the restoration of his lands and the title of Earl of Essex. Arrested by Stephen on suspicion of treachery in 1143, Geoffrey was forced to surrender his castles in exchange for his freedom. He subsequently rebelled, using the Isle of Ely in the Fens as a base from which to raid the neighbouring territory. He was killed in 1144 while attacking Burwell. Reviled for his attacks on Church lands, Geoffrey has traditionally been seen as the archetypal robber-baron of the Anarchy, but modern scholarship has tended to modify this judgement.

Geoffrey Plantagenet (Geoffrey V of Anjou):
Count of Anjou from 1129, when his father Fulk of Anjou left on crusade. In 1128, at the age of fifteen, Geoffrey was married to the widowed Empress Matilda. When Matilda went to England in 1139 to pursue her claim to the throne, Geoffrey supported her by attacking the possessions of Stephen and his supporters in Normandy, at which he was so successful that by 1144 he had conquered the duchy and was proclaimed Duke of Normandy. In 1149 he granted the title to his and Matilda's son Henry, the future Henry II of England. Geoffrey died of a fever in 1151.

Gerald de Barri ('Giraldus Cambrensis', 'Gerald of Wales'):
Born c. 1146 in Pembrokeshire, Gerald entered the church and in 1184 became chaplain to Henry II. He travelled on official business in Ireland and Wales, and described both countries in his influential *Topographia Hibernica*, *Itinerarium Cambriae* and *Descriptio Cambriae*. The latter especially is a valuable source for twelfth-century Welsh history and society. He died c. 1223.

Gilbert fitz Gilbert (Gilbert de Clare):
A younger son of Gilbert fitz Richard de Clare, and brother of Richard and Baldwin, Gilbert was created Earl of Pembroke by Stephen in 1138, but defected to the Empress Matilda in 1141. Later reconciled with Stephen, he rebelled again in 1147, but died in the following year.

Gillebrigte:
A warlord of Norse-Gaelic descent, ruler of the region of western Scotland known as Argyll. Ally of Malcolm mac Alasdair and father of Somerled. The date of his death is unknown, but he had been succeeded by Somerled by 1153.

Gruffydd ap Cynan:
King of Gwynedd 1081 to 1137, a leading figure in the resistance to the Normans and regarded by many contemporaries as 'King of all Wales'. Succeeded by his son Owain.

Gruffydd ap Rhys:
King of Deheubarth from c. 1093, but much of the kingdom was occupied soon afterwards by the Anglo-Normans, and Gruffydd spent several years of his reign in exile. In 1136 he joined forces with Owain and Cadwaladr ap Gruffydd of Gwynedd, and was one of the leaders of the victorious Welsh army at Crug Mawr. Gruffydd died of unknown causes in the following year.

Harald Maddadsson:
Son of Earl Maddad of Atholl, who with the aid of Svein Asleifsson installed him as Earl of Orkney in 1139. He defeated and killed his rival earl Erlend Haraldsson in 1154, then continued to rule Orkney and Caithness as sole earl until his death in 1206.

Henry, Prince of Scots:
Son and heir of King David of Scotland, born c. 1114. Inherited the title of Earl of Huntingdon through his mother. Henry's bold charge at the Battle of the Standard in 1138 was unable to prevent defeat for the Scots, but he escaped, and from 1141 onwards held most of northern England effectively independently of Stephen. In 1139 he was also granted the Earldom of Northumberland by Stephen as part of the peace settlement with David. Henry predeceased his father, dying in 1152.

Henry of Huntingdon:
Archdeacon of Huntingdon and chronicler, who wrote his *Historia Anglorum* at the request of the Bishop of Lincoln. Little is known of his personal life, but he is presumed to have died soon after 1154, the point at which his narrative breaks off.

Henry I:
Third son of William the Conqueror, King of England 1100 to 1135. Although a strong and widely respected ruler, Henry's legacy was damaged by his failure to ensure the succession after his only legitimate son William was drowned in 1120. In 1127 he designated his daughter Matilda as his heir, but later quarrelled with her and her husband, lending credibility to rumours that he

favoured his nephew Stephen of Blois. Henry died in 1135, allegedly from food poisoning after eating too many lampreys.

Henry Plantagenet, Count of Anjou and King of England:
Son of the Empress Matilda and Geoffrey of Anjou, Henry was made Duke of Normandy at the age of 16 in 1149, and succeeded his father in Anjou in 1151. Invaded England in 1153, and in 1154 was recognized as Stephen's heir. King of England from 1154 to 1189.

Henry V:
Holy Roman Emperor 1111 to 1125. Married the Empress Matilda in 1114. Died in 1125, leaving no surviving legitimate children.

Henry of Winchester (also known as Henry of Blois):
Younger brother of King Stephen, Bishop of Winchester 1129–71. Passed over for the Archbishopric of Canterbury in 1138, he secured an appointment as Papal Legate from 1139 to 1143, a position which effectively outranked Archbishop Theobald of Canterbury. Henry played an important role in the events of his brother's reign, despite temporarily defecting to Matilda in 1141. He retired in 1154 but later returned to serve Henry II, and died in 1171.

Hugh Bigod:
Son of Roger Bigod, Sheriff of Norfolk, Hugh became Constable of Norwich Castle in 1122. He supported Stephen in 1135, claiming to have witnessed Henry I's change of heart in favour of Stephen's accession, but defected to the Empress after the Battle of Lincoln, receiving from her the title of Earl of Norfolk. He supported Geoffrey de Mandeville's revolt in 1143 and Henry II's invasion in 1153, but managed to avoid punishment by Stephen and was confirmed in the earldom by Henry. Probably died in Palestine c. 1177.

John fitz Gilbert (John the Marshal):
John inherited the title of Marshal of the Horse to Henry I c. 1130 and was at first a supporter of Stephen, but defected to the Empress Matilda in 1139 and fought for her two years later at Winchester, where he was seriously injured. In 1152 Stephen unsuccessfully besieged John in Newbury Castle. He was the father of the famous William Marshal, 1st Earl of Pembroke, who fought for Henry II and three of his successors. John died c. 1165.

John of Hexham:
Prior of Hexham and author of the *Historia XXV Annorum*, which is a useful source for events in the north of England between c. 1130 and 1153. John's dates are unknown, and his work is known only from one late twelfth-century text.

John of Worcester:
Monk and chronicler, author of the *Chronicon ex Chronicis*, a world history largely based on the work of previous authors. The chronicle ends c. 1140, which may indicate the date of John's death.

Maddad:
Mormaer of Atholl c. 1130 to c. 1160. Father of Harald Maddadsson, Earl of Orkney.

Malcolm mac Alasdair:
An illegitimate son of King Alexander I of Scotland, Malcolm fought several wars with Alexander's successor David I in an attempt to seize the throne. In 1130 he and Oengus of Moray were defeated by David at the Battle of Stracathro, but he continued to resist until 1134, when he was captured with the aid of English troops sent by Henry I to assist David. The date of Malcolm's death is unknown.

Matilda, Empress:
Daughter of Henry I of England, born 1102. Matilda was married to the Holy Roman Emperor Henry V at the age of twelve, and retained the title of Empress for the rest of her life, although after her husband's death in 1125 she returned to Normandy and was married by her father to Geoffrey, Count of Anjou. Following the death of her brother William in 1120, Matilda was recognized as his heir by King Henry, who obliged his barons to swear allegiance to her. In 1139 she invaded England in alliance with her half-brother Robert of Gloucester in an attempt to seize the throne from Stephen, but after initial successes she was defeated by Stephen's Queen Matilda at Winchester in 1141, and later nearly captured at Oxford. She escaped to her stronghold in the south-west of England, but returned to Normandy in 1148, leaving her son Henry Plantagenet to continue the struggle. On Henry's accession as Henry II in 1154, Matilda governed Normandy on his behalf. She died in 1167.

Matilda of Boulogne:
Daughter of Eustace III, Count of Boulogne, and granddaughter of King Malcolm III of Scotland and his queen Saint Margaret. She married Stephen of Blois in 1125, and became Queen of England on Stephen's accession in 1135. She played an important role in the wars of her husband's reign, especially in negotiations with Scotland and during Stephen's imprisonment in 1141. She died in 1152.

Miles of Gloucester:
Son of Walter, Sheriff of Gloucester, Miles succeeded to the title under Henry I, and became one of the semi-independent 'Marcher Lords' with responsibility for the Welsh border. At first loyal to Stephen, he defected to the Empress in 1139, and was regarded as one of her most faithful supporters. He fought against Stephen at Wallingford and Lincoln, and in 1141 was made Earl of Hereford by Matilda. He narrowly escaped from the Empress' defeat at Winchester. Excommunicated by the Bishop of Hereford in 1143 for plundering the Church, Miles was killed on Christmas Eve of that year in what was alleged to be a hunting accident.

Nigel, Bishop of Ely:
Treasurer of England under Henry I, Nigel became Bishop of Ely in 1133. He was one of the bishops arrested by Stephen in 1139, after which he fortified Ely against the king and began a revolt. He was driven out of Ely and deserted to the Empress Matilda. Although later reconciled with Stephen on payment of a fine (which the monks of Ely complained he made them pay) he did not return to high office until the accession of Henry II, who again summoned him to take charge of the Exchequer. He died in 1169.

Oengus of Moray:
The last ruler of the native dynasty of Moray, Oengus led an attempt to overthrow David I of Scotland but was killed at the Battle of Stracathro in 1130.

Orderic Vitalis:
Monk and chronicler, based at St Evroul in Normandy, who has been called 'the single most important chronicle source for contemporary warfare and chivalry in the later eleventh and first half of the twelfth century' (Strickland). His *Historia Ecclesiastica* describes events in Normandy and England up to 1142, which may indicate the approximate date of his death.

Owain ap Gruffydd:
Son of Gruffydd ap Cynan, King of Gwynedd. With his brother Cadwaladr Owain defeated an Anglo-Norman army at Crug Mawr in 1136. Succeeded to the throne of Gwynedd in 1137. Invaded Powys in 1146 and defeated its Prince Madog. Later he opposed several English invasions led by Henry II. He died in 1170.

Paul Haakonsson, Earl of Orkney:
Joint Earl of Orkney with Harald Haakonsson from 1123, deposed and probably murdered by Svein Asleifsson in 1137.

Payn fitz John:
Brother of Eustace fitz John, lord of Ludlow Castle and one of Henry I's 'Marcher Lords' with responsibility for the Welsh border. A supporter of King Stephen, he fought with him at the siege of Exeter in 1136. In 1137 he was ambushed and killed by the Welsh while leading an army to relieve Carmarthen.

Ranulf 'de Gernon', Earl of Chester:
Succeeded his father as 4th Earl of Chester in 1129. Ranulf probably became alienated from Stephen after 1136, when the king gave away his lands in the north to the Scots as part of a peace settlement. His seizure of Lincoln Castle in 1140 led to an alliance with the Empress' party against the king. On the winning side at the Battle of Lincoln in 1141, Ranulf narrowly escaped from the subsequent defeat at Winchester. He retained Lincoln Castle, but in 1145 made peace with Stephen. However, his enemies at Stephen's court accused him of plotting treason and he was arrested, only being released in exchange for his castles. On his release Ranulf again turned against the king. In 1149 he and the future King Henry II met King David of Scotland and the three men agreed on an expedition to secure the return of Ranulf's lost lands. This failed, but Ranulf remained a loyal ally of Henry. He died in 1153, possibly as a result of an alleged attempt by William Peverel to poison him.

Reginald, Earl of Cornwall:
An illegitimate son of Henry I, made Earl of Cornwall by Stephen, but later defected to the Empress Matilda. Later High Sherriff of Devon under Henry II, he died c. 1175.

Richard fitz Gilbert:
Eldest son of Gilbert fitz Richard de Clare and brother of Gilbert and Baldwin fitz Gilbert. A prominent magnate of the Welsh marches and a loyal supporter of Stephen who fought alongside him at the siege of Exeter. In April 1136 he attempted to return to his lordship in Ceredigion, but was ambushed and killed en route by men from Gwent led by Iorwerth ap Owain.

Richard of Hexham:
Prior of Hexham and chronicler. His *Historia de Gestis Regis Stephani ci de Bello Standardii* is an important source for the Scottish invasions and the Battle of the Standard.

Robert de Brus of Annandale:
A Norman magnate with lands in northern England, Robert was granted the Lordship of Annandale in the Scottish borders when David I came to the throne of Scotland in 1124. However, when David invaded England in 1138 Robert renounced his fealty to David and joined the English army at the Battle of the Standard. He died in 1142. One of his sons, also Robert, remained loyal to David and so inherited the title of Lord of Annandale on his father's death.

Robert de Beaumont:
Twin brother of Waleran de Beaumont, Robert inherited the title of Earl of Leicester from his father, also Robert. He spent the first few years of Stephen's reign in Normandy, but returned to England in 1141 after his lands on the continent were overrun by Geoffrey of Anjou. Although in general loyal to Stephen, Robert's main contribution to the king's cause was what amounted to a private war with Earl Ranulf of Chester, which lasted until 1149. In 1153 he defected to Henry Plantagenet in return for the restoration of his Norman estates, and was appointed Chief Justiciar of England on Henry's accession in 1154. Robert died in 1168.

Robert de Ferrers:
A leading magnate in Derbyshire under Henry I, Robert supported Stephen and led a contingent of troops in the campaign of The Standard in 1138. As a reward for this he was made Earl of Derby. He died in 1139. His son, also Robert de Ferrers, 2nd Earl of Derby, remained loyal to Stephen until 1153, when he surrendered to Henry Plantagenet. He died in 1162.

Robert of Gloucester:
An illegitimate son of Henry I and half-brother of the Empress Matilda, created Earl of Gloucester by Henry c. 1122. Robert declined to contend for the throne himself after his father's death, but instead gave his support to Matilda. He was victorious at the Battle of Lincoln in 1141, capturing the king, but was himself captured near Winchester later that year and exchanged for Stephen. Although he defeated the king again at Wilton in 1143, Robert was forced onto the defensive and gradually confined to his West Country stronghold. He died in 1147.

Robert Marmion:
Lord of Fontenay in Normandy from c. 1129, Robert fought for Stephen against Geoffrey of Anjou in 1140, but migrated to England after the loss of his own castle and made his headquarters at Tamworth. He fought against Earl Ranulf of Chester, and was killed at Coventry in 1144. The Marmions later claimed to hold Fontenay in return for serving as hereditary King's Champions, but we have no evidence of Robert performing this role.

Robert of Torigny:
Norman monk and chronicler, Abbot of Mont Saint-Michel from 1154. As a contributor to the *Gesta Normannorum Ducum* he is an important source for events in Normandy, though as a close associate of Henry II of England he is not always an unbiased one. He died in 1186.

Roger fitz Miles, 2nd Earl of Hereford:
Roger succeeded his father Miles of Gloucester as Earl of Hereford in 1143, and after the death of Robert of Gloucester in 1147 and the departure of the Empress Matilda in the following year he became one of the mainstays of the Angevin party in England. Roger died in 1155.

Roger of Salisbury:
Bishop of Salisbury from 1107 to 1139, and effectively chief minister of Henry I. He became a powerful secular magnate to the detriment of his reputation as a man of God (Henry had originally employed him because of the speed with which he could get through the Mass, allowing the king to get on with more important things like hunting). Roger was also famous for the great castle which he built at Devizes, and which was held by his mistress, Matilda of Ramsbury. His support for Stephen in 1135 was crucial, but he was later suspected of disloyalty, and in June 1139 the king arrested him and other

bishops, forcing them to hand over their castles in exchange for their freedom. Roger died soon after this, in December 1139.

Rognvald 'Kali Kolsson' (subsequently Saint Ronald of Orkney):
Appointed Earl of Orkney by King Sigurd I of Norway in 1129, Rognvald was forced to fight to make good his claim, which he did after the capture of his rival Paul Haakonsson by Svein Asleifsson in 1136. Ruled jointly with Harald Maddadsson from 1138, and made a famous pilgrimage to the Holy Land in 1151. He was killed in a skirmish in 1158.

Simon de Senlis:
Fourth Earl of Northampton, Simon was a loyal supporter of Stephen, and was rewarded by becoming the king's nominee for the Earldom of Huntingdon. He died in 1153.

Somerled (Gaelic 'Somairle', Norse 'Sumarlithi'):
A Norse-Gaelic nobleman, son of Gillebrigte, Somerled first appears in history as Lord of Argyll in 1153, when he supported a revolt against the new king of Scots, Malcolm IV. He then turned against his brother-in-law Godred Olafsson, who was King of the Isles, and in 1158 defeated him and seized the throne. Somerled was killed at the Battle of Renfrew in 1164, during another attack on Scotland. Many of the leading Highland clans claim descent from him.

Stephen of Blois:
Born c. 1096, son of Count Stephen-Henry of Blois and his wife Adela, through whom he was descended from William the Conqueror. Stephen spent much of his early life at the court of his uncle, Henry I. He married Matilda of Boulogne in 1125. On Henry's death in 1135 he seized the throne of England, but had to spend most of his nineteen-year reign defending it against his cousin the Empress Matilda, and later her son Henry Plantagenet. The death of his son Eustace in 1153 thwarted his ambition to found a royal dynasty, and in the following year he recognized Henry's right to succeed him. Stephen died in 1154.

Stephen-Henry, Count of Blois:
Father of King Stephen, who succeeded his father as Count of Blois in 1089. He fought in the First Crusade, but deserted during the siege of Antioch in 1098. Forced by his wife Adela to return to the Holy Land, he was killed at the Second Battle of Ramla in 1102.

Svein Asleifsson:

A central character of the *Orkneyinga Saga*, which depicts him as an archetypal Viking. Deeply involved in the rivalries among the various Earls of Orkney from c. 1134, he claimed to be a loyal supporter of Earl Rognvald, but in fact changed sides frequently. The saga hints at a strange immunity which enabled Svein to commit numerous depredations while still enjoying the favour of leading men including David I of Scotland. He led several plundering expeditions as far as south-west England, and was killed while attacking Dublin, possibly as late as 1171.

Theobald, Archbishop:

Abbot of Bec in Normandy from 1137, Theobald was elected Archbishop of Canterbury with Stephen's support in 1138. After the Battle of Lincoln in 1141 Theobald joined the Empress's forces, but continued to negotiate with Stephen and was instrumental in obtaining his release. He travelled to Rome in 1143 to meet Pope Celestine II, who instructed him not to crown any successor to Stephen as the succession was under dispute. Made Papal Legate in 1150. In 1152 Theobald refused Stephen's order to crown his son Eustace, citing the Pope's instructions. He was exiled to Flanders, but soon reinstated on orders from Rome. Theobald played a leading role in the Treaty of Wallingford between Stephen and the future Henry II, and on Stephen's death in 1154 was named as regent. Under Henry II he remained as Archbishop until his death in 1161.

Theobald of Blois:

Son of Stephen-Henry and elder brother of King Stephen, Theobald succeeded as Count of Blois in 1102. Also Count of Champagne from 1125. Seen by some as a possible successor to Henry I of England, he remained preoccupied with his continental possessions and allowed his brother to seize the initiative. In 1137 he made an agreement with Stephen by which he accepted the latter's position as King of England and Duke of Normandy. He died in 1152.

Thurstan, Archbishop:

Archbishop of York from 1114, Thurstan supported the accession of Stephen and was responsible for raising the English army that fought at the Battle of the Standard in 1138, although he may not have actively commanded it in action (he was then around 70 years of age). He died in 1140.

Waleran de Beaumont:
Count of Meulan in Normandy and twin brother of Robert de Beaumont, Waleran was a notoriously independent baron who had spent five years in prison under Henry I for rebellion. At first, however, he was a strong supporter of Stephen, on whose behalf he defeated two Angevin invasions of Normandy in 1136 and 1138. He was rewarded with a marriage to Stephen's daughter Matilda, who died soon afterwards, and with the Earldom of Worcester, which put him in the front line of the war between Stephen and Matilda when Robert of Gloucester attacked Worcester in November 1139. Waleran fought for Stephen at Lincoln in 1141, but abandoned the king when he realized the battle was lost. Later in 1141 he defected to Geoffrey of Anjou in order to save his Norman possessions, and spent the rest of his career in France and Normandy before accompanying King Louis VII of France on the Second Crusade in 1147. His French connections lost him the favour of Henry II, and in 1155 the Earldom of Worcester was taken from him. Waleran died in Normandy in 1166.

Walter Espec:
High Sherriff of Yorkshire under Henry I, justiciar of northern England, and one of the English commanders at the Battle of the Standard in 1138, at which time he was already described as 'an aged man full of days'. Also famous as the founder of many religious houses, including Rievaulx Abbey, whose chronicler Ailred gave him a prominent role in his historical accounts. He died in 1153.

William d'Aubigny:
Also known as William of Albini. He married Adeliza, the widow of Henry I, in 1138, and through this marriage gained control of Arundel castle in Sussex. A loyal supporter of King Stephen, he was rewarded with the earldoms of Lincoln and Arundel. He helped to negotiate the Treaty of Wallingford between Stephen and Henry Plantagenet in 1153, and was confirmed in his possessions by Henry when he took the throne. He died in 1176.

William fitz Duncan:
Son of King Duncan II of Scotland and Mormaer of Moray from c. 1130. Also lord of extensive territories in northern England, but his primary loyalty was to David I of Scotland. He defeated the English at the Battle of Clitheroe in 1138. William died in 1147.

William of Aumale:
Also known as William 'le Gros'. Count of Aumale from c. 1127. A supporter of Stephen, who was one of the commanders at the Battle of the Standard in 1138 and fought for the king at Lincoln in 1141. On the accession of Henry II his castle at Scarborough was confiscated, but he retained his titles until his death in 1179.

William of Blois:
The third son of Stephen and Matilda, born c. 1137. William became heir to the throne on the death of his brother Eustace, but was disinherited by Stephen's agreement with the future Henry II. The latter confirmed him as Earl of Surrey and Count of Boulogne, but in 1154 he became involved in a plot against the new king and fled to Normandy, where he died on campaign in 1159.

William of Malmesbury:
Monk and historian, whose *Historia Novella* is one of the main sources for the period 1128 to 1142. William was a supporter of Robert of Gloucester, and is generally critical of Stephen. At the conclusion of his work he promises to continue it, but apparently never did so, and may have died soon after 1142.

William of Newburgh:
Monk and chronicler, author of the *Historia rerum Anglicarum*, an important source for the period. Died c. 1198.

William Peverel 'the Younger':
Inherited the Honour of Peverel in Derbyshire from his father William Peverel 'the Elder' c. 1115. A loyal supporter of Stephen, William was captured fighting for the king at Lincoln in 1141. Accused (without conclusive evidence) of poisoning Earl Ranulf of Chester in 1153. When Henry II came to the throne he dispossessed him of his lands, and William died c. 1155.

William of Warenne:
Succeeded his father as Earl of Surrey in 1138. Half-brother of Waleran de Beaumont, he fought alongside him in Stephen's army at the Battle of Lincoln, but temporarily defected to the Empress after the king's defeat. He joined the Second Crusade in 1146, and was killed at the Battle of Mount Cadmus.

William of Ypres:

A minor member of the Flemish nobility. Exiled from Flanders in 1133, William raised a force of mercenaries and joined the service of King Stephen. He abandoned the king at the Battle of Lincoln in 1141 when he realized that defeat was imminent, but remained loyal to his cause. He led the forces of Stephen's Queen Matilda to victory at Winchester, and on the king's release was rewarded with the revenues of the county of Kent, though he seems not to have been formally styled earl. By the end of the 1140s his sight was failing and his military career was over. Banished by Henry II in 1154, he returned to Flanders where he died in 1165.

Bibliography

Main Primary Sources in Translation

Anderson, A., *Scottish Annals from English Chroniclers*, London, 1908 (includes Ailred of Rievaulx, John of Hexham and Richard of Hexham).

The Anglo-Saxon Chronicles, trans. M. Swanton, London, 2000.

Colour images from the Bury Bible can be viewed at stedmundsburychronicle.co.uk

Gerald of Wales, *The Journey Through Wales/The Description of Wales*, trans. L. Thorpe, Penguin Classics, Hardmondsworth, 1978.

Gerald of Wales, *The History and Topography of Ireland*, trans. J O'Meara, Penguin Classics, London, 1982.

Gesta Stephani, trans. K.R. Potter, Oxford, 1976.

Heimskringla: History of the Kings of Norway, trans. L. Hollander, Austin, Texas, 1964.

Henry of Huntingdon, *The History of the English People 1000–1154*, trans. D. Greenway, Oxford, 1996.

The Chronicle of John of Worcester, trans. R. Darlington, Oxford, 1995.

The History of William Marshal, trans. N. Brewer, Woodbridge, 2016.

The Ecclesiastical History of Orderic Vitalis, trans. M. Chibnall, Oxford, 1969–1980.

Orkneyinga Saga, trans. H. Palsson and P. Edwards, Penguin Classics, London, 1978.

The Song of Roland, trans. D. Sayers, Penguin Classics, London, 1937.

William of Malmesbury, *Historia Novella*, trans. K.R. Potter, Edinburgh, 1955.

Secondary Sources:

Bradbury, J., *The Medieval Archer*, Woodbridge, 1985.

——, *The Medieval Siege*, Woodbridge, 1992.

——, *Stephen and Matilda: The Civil War of 1139–53*, Stroud, 2005.

Chibnall, M., *The Empress Matilda*, Oxford, 1991.

Crawford, B., *The Northern Earldoms: Orkney and Caithness from AD 870 to 1470*, Edinburgh, 2013.

Crouch, D., *The Reign of King Stephen*, Harlow, 2000.

Cunliffe, B., *Britain Begins*, Oxford, 2012.

Davis, R.H.C., 'Geoffrey de Mandeville Reconsidered', *English Historical Review* 79, 1964.

——, *King Stephen*, London, 1990.

Embleton, G., *Medieval Military Costume Recreated in Colour Photographs*, Europa Militaria Special No. 8, Marlborough, 2000.

Gravett, C., *Norman Knight AD 950 – 1204*, Osprey Warrior Series No. 1, Oxford, 1993.

——, *Norman Stone Castles I: The British Isles 1066–1216*, Osprey Fortress Series No. 13, Oxford, 2003.

Heath, I., *Armies of Feudal Europe 1066 – 1300*, Worthing, 1989.

Hill, J. and Freiberg, J., *The Medieval Fighting Man: Costume and Equipment 800–1500*, Europa Militaria Special No. 18, Marlborough, 2015.

James, L., *The Battle of Crug Mawr 1136*, Bretwalda Battles Series No. 12, Epsom, 2014.

James, T., *The Palaces of Medieval England*, London, 1990.

King, E., *King Stephen*, New Haven and London, 2010.

Lloyd, Sir John, *A History of Wales*, London, 1939.

Loades, M., *Swords and Swordsmen*, Barnsley, 2010.

——, *The Longbow*, Osprey Weapon Series No. 30, Oxford, 2013.

Molloy, B., (ed.), T*he Cutting Edge: Studies in Ancient and Medieval Combat*, Stroud, 2007.

Nicolle, D., *Medieval Siege Weapons 1: Western Europe AD 585–1385*, Osprey New Vanguard Series No. 58, Oxford, 2002.

Norris, H., *Tamworth Castle: Its Foundation, its History, and its Lords*, Tamworth, 1899.

Oram, R., *David I, The King who made Scotland*, Stroud, 2008.

Postan, M., *The Medieval Economy and Society*, Harmondsworth, 1975.

Pryor, F., *Britain in the Middle Ages – An Archaeological History*, London, 2006.

Round, J.H., *Geoffrey de Mandeville, a Study of the Anarchy*, London, 1892.

Short, W., *Viking Weapons and Combat Techniques*, Yardley, Pennsylvania, 2014.

Slater, S., *The Illustrated Book of Heraldry*, London, 2002.

Strickland, M., *War and Chivalry: The Conduct and Perception of War in England and Normandy 1066–1217*, Cambridge, 1996.

——, and Hardy, R., *The Great Warbow*, Stroud, 2005.

Travis, H., and Travis, J., *Roman Shields*, Stroud, 2014.

Wadge, R., *Archery in Medieval England*, Stroud, 2012.

Watkins, C., *Stephen – the Reign of Anarchy*, Penguin Monarchs, London, 2015.

Index